from the collective unconscious and forged out of the persistent needs of the writer to come to terms with his own drives and desires, powerful architectural archetypes shape and galvanize literary creations.

The supply of archetypes in the collective unconscious makes a nearly infinite number of permutations available to the writer. In every case, Knapp argues, the archetype is transformed by the author's peculiar requirements into a unique artistic realization. Each metaphoric vision reveals a structural element dominant in the writer's psyche that becomes evident in his protagonists, their motivations, and the style of discourse. Knapp's exploration of the meaning of these primordial yet individual images provides an interesting new perspective on the creative process.

ARCHETYPE, ARCHITECTURE, AND THE WRITER

ARCHETYPE, ARCHITECTURE, AND THE WRITER

BETTINA L. KNAPP

Indiana University Press

Bloomington

Manufactured in the United States of America

Library of Congress Cataloging in Publication Data

Knapp, Bettina Liebowitz, 1926–
    Archetype, architecture, and the writer.

    Bibliography: p.
    Includes index.
    1. Architecture in literature. I. Title.
PN56.A73K58   1985   809'.93357   84-47790
ISBN 0-253-30857-7

    1 2 3 4 5   89 88 87 86

CONTENTS

Introduction

"I built the house in sections, always following the concrete needs of the moment. It might also be said that I built it in a kind of dream. Only afterward did I see how all the parts fitted together and that a meaningful form had resulted: a symbol of psychic wholeness."[1] So wrote C. G. Jung after he had the "Tower" house built for himself on the edge of Lake Zurich in Switzerland. It was "a kind of representation in stone of my innermost thoughts and of the knowledge I had acquired."[2]

Jung's tower, which may be considered an architectural metaphor for an inner psychic climate, was archetypal in nature: it existed as a primordial image in his collective unconscious. Jung was the chief architect (the word stemming from the Greek *architekton,* master builder) in concretizing his inner vision, in revealing relationships existing between different aspects of his psyche. Surrounded by a moat, the tower acted as both a retreat and a protection from the outer world. It could be said that Jung's emotive roots were embedded in this architectural monument: it was a sacred space where the inner riches lying buried within his collective unconscious nourished him continuously. By organizing or shaping space, Jung had articulated the mysteries existing inchoate within him in a visual language.

Architecture as a spatial creation is the outer garment of a secretive and vital system; it is a nonverbal manifestation of a preconscious condition. A completed and relatively fixed architectural structure is nevertheless a dynamic and organic entity, a system of coordinates that relates inner and outer spheres and in so doing creates a complex of new harmonies and tensions. Within its walls, columns, ceilings, chimneys, windows, turrets, or other structural elements, an edifice may be looked upon as a world in itself—a microcosm—an expression of a preexistent form that may be apprehended on a personal and temporal as well as a transpersonal and atemporal level. As such, it may be considered archetypal.

An archetype is an elusive concept that cannot really be fully defined. Jung, the creator of this seminal psychological notion, wrote:

> Archetypes are, by definition, factors and motifs that arrange the psychic elements into certain images, characterized as archetypal, but in such a way that *they can be recognized only from the effects they produce.* They exist preconsciously, and presumably they form the structural dominants of the psyche in general. . . . As *a priori* conditioning factors they represent a special psychological instance of the biological "pattern of behavior" which gives all things their specific qualities.[3]

Archetypes, perceived in the form of primordial images, are present in dreams, legends, fairy tales, myths, religious and cultural notions, and modes of behavior the world over. They are elements in perpetually mobile psychic structures, which, until manifested in events, patternings, and configurations, are nonperceptible, existing as potential energy in their dormant state in the depths of the collective unconscious. As distinguished from the personal unconscious, defined as containing "personal contents belonging to the individual himself which can and properly should be made conscious and integrated into the conscious personality or ego," the collective unconscious "is composed of transpersonal, universal contents which cannot be assimilated by the ego."[4]

Archetypal images, which arise spontaneously from the collective unconscious, are mysterious and undefinable; they are "energy centers," "magnetic fields," which not only influence but frequently dominate an individual's thoughts, feelings, and behavioral patterns. They fascinate and frequently overpower the individual if they are not—and sometimes even if they are—consciously understood and integrated into the psyche or channeled into the work of art.[5]

Arche means "beginning, origin, cause, primal source and principle." The word is also defined as "position of a leader, supreme rule and government. . . ." *Type* is interpreted as a "blow and what is produced by a blow, the imprint of a coin . . . form, image, copy, prototype, model, order, and norm," a primordial or underlying form.[6] Jung elucidates.

> The term [archetype] is not meant to denote an inherited idea, but rather an inherited mode of psychic functioning, corresponding to the inborn way in which the chick emerges from the egg, the bird builds its nest, a certain kind of wasp stings the motor ganglion of the caterpillar, and eels find their way to the Bermudas. In other words, it is a "pattern of behavior." This aspect of the archetype is the biological one. . . . But the picture changes at once when looked at from the inside, that is, from within the realm of the subjective psyche. Here the archetype presents itself as numinous, that is, it appears as an experience of fundamental importance.[7]

Archetypes may also be related to the notion of instincts. Edward Edinger writes in this regard:

> An archetype is to the psyche what an instinct is to the body. The existence of archetypes is inferred by the same process as that by which we infer the existence of instincts. Just as instincts common to a species are postulated by observing the uniformities in biological behavior, so archetypes are inferred by observing the uniformities in psychic phenomena. Just as instincts are unknown motivating dynamisms of biological behavior, archetypes are unknown motivating dynamisms of the psyche.[8]

When the words "archetype" and "architecture" are juxtaposed—as in "archetypal architecture"—the concept may be looked upon as a line, shape, or depth perception that manifests itself as an autonomous, a priori image in the collective unconscious. The effects produced by this archetypal or primordial image motivate the construction of an edifice in the workaday world—a castle, pagoda, house, temple, pyramid, ziggurat, or other type of building—and may also be looked upon as a metaphor that not only arouses the poet, novelist, and dramatist to create their verbal structures but may also dominate their ideations and sense perceptions.

Archetypal architecture is a physical representation of the psychological and functional condition of an individual, culture, class, and period. It is a composite of opposites: rhythmic yet static, subjective yet objective, timely yet eternal, affecting the senses of those who create it, live in it, and look at it in its own day, and also the generations to come, who are likewise exposed to its beauty or ugliness, to all the factors projected upon it. It is a microcosm of the macrocosm.

Archetypal architecture, then, reveals aspects of the subliminal depths of such prototypal architects as Imhotep, the master builder of the Step Pyramid of King Zoser at Sakkara in Egypt and a man who was venerated after his death as the son of the god Ptah. A cultural canon is also made evident by his works, and by the works of those who helped erect the pyramids of Khufu, Khafre, and Menkaure at Giza—not to mention the other extraordinary monuments that dot this ancient land, indicating humankind's need to relate to godly domains.

> Here in the desert the earth appears as though seen from astronomical heights: intangible, immaterial. Here there is nothing else. The two pyramids resting upon an endless plain confront only the cosmos. The heavens arch over them like the figure of the Goddess Nut. Everything earthly has fallen away and man grasps what it means to stand before eternity.[9]

Daedalus, who designed the labyrinth at Knossos, was a cunning artisan, fascinated by the complexities and intricacies of the inner world. The labyrinth was constructed to imprison the Minotaur, but Daedalus was incarcerated in his own creation for having intruded into matters not appropriate to his function as architect. Astute and imaginative, he fashioned a pair of wings that he attached to himself with wax, enabling him to fly out of the maze of halls and rooms into freedom.

The so-called eccentric Greek Sophist philosopher Hippodamus invented a system of geometrical principles that enabled him to lay out the harbor of Athens, the city of Rhodes, and other areas, guided always by his thinking function. Labeled "the chessboard plan," his vision of what a city should be allowed him to carve out open and filled spatial areas according to Aristotelian dicta, underscoring his attraction to and domination by his cerebral faculties.[10]

In ancient times sanctuaries were first built to enable mortals to reach out to their invisible gods, thereby allowing and encouraging an intimacy between the human and divine spheres: the *temenos* and the cosmos. Religious spaces—such as Stonehenge in England (1500 B.C.); the cave temples near Cahors in southern France; the Egyptian pyramids (2680 B.C.); the ziggurats, such as Aquar Quef (1400 B.C.) near Bagdad;[11] Solomon's extraordinary temple (1000 B.C.) in Jerusalem; the Parthenon (432 B.C.), with its "Divine Proportions"; Gothic cathedrals in Europe, pagodas and Buddhist temples in the Orient, or Muslim mosques in the Middle East—are all paradigms of spiritual needs. Not only is each sacred space designed to protect deity, but it also functions as a meeting ground for the community. Within these geometrically designed edifices and spaces existed, for both the architects and the people congregating there, the key to the universe. The science of numbers, which played such an important role in the construction of these houses and areas of worship, was viewed by many quantitatively, to be sure, but numbers were also mystical: active forces radiating throughout the world and the cosmos. For Pythagoras, let us recall, the space between the earth and the divine sphere was measurable in terms of numbers, each area upholding and relating to the next in a continuously mobile universal interchange. A temple for Pythagoras was not merely a house of worship or a meeting ground for people, but a "proportional link between man and the universe."[12] Plato suggests, in the *Republic*, that "geometry is the knowledge of the eternally existent" and tends "to draw the soul to truth," adding a qualitative value to a quantitative notion. In *Timaeus*, Plato goes further in describing the construction of the universe when he writes of the dodecahedron, in which space, light, line, depth, number—fundamental particles, or, as we call them, "Platonic solids"—are involved in arrangements that trigger sensation; for us this implies an emotional or psychological content.[13]

A great change in focus occurred with the separation of sacred from profane space: when humankind sought to create shelter for itself in monumental form. Not satisfied with merely erecting a house for deity, people directed attention to the existential sphere, indicating an emphasis on human dignity, the importance of life in the here-and-now. The cult of the individual took hold. Palaces such as those at Knossos, Phaistos, and Mallia were built on Crete (2000–1000 B.C.); the Arch of Constantine greeted that emperor upon his return from battle in A.D. 315; Trajan's Column (A.D. 106–13) and the Baths of Diocletian (A.D. 302) are two of many other examples. Such a dichotomy between earthly and celestial spheres cut people off from what had formerly been experienced as a *participation mystique,* or oneness with the cosmos. As a result, people began thinking of themselves in terms of their own life cycles; they still related to divinity but felt that they were, to a certain extent at least, masters of their own destinies, conscious of the space around them as separate from that of the rest of the world.

As people began playing more prominent roles in the life experience, they were thrust more and more on themselves, and thus the secular world grew in import. Physical comfort became an issue in the building of dwelling places; lighting and various spatial concepts—such as foreshortened perspectives and receding spaces, framed and unframed interiors—aroused concomitant emotional reactions, creating new orientations and needs. Colors also became important, as did their emotional equivalents; ornamentation, either abstract or concrete, introduced new modes of psychic functioning, fresh spatial dynamics, and visual centers. Styles known as "Medieval," "Renaissance," "Mannerist," "Classical," "Baroque," "Neoclassicist," and so forth, expressed a variety of inner climates, each answering the needs of the individual and the collective. Functional modern architecture designed for the masses, such as London's mid-nineteenth-century Crystal Palace, which Ruskin labeled "a cucumber frame," came into being; the novelty ushered in by Art Nouveau, or *Jugendstil,* also appealed, as did the smooth lines of the Bauhaus architects, the geometric visions of the Constructivists in Russia, the great cubes used by the "Brutalists" in West Germany, the simple, smooth lines of the Finnish school of architecture (represented by Alvaar Alto), and so many other innovative creations, all revealing both an individual and archetypal dimension.[14]

Architecture is a shape in space and shapes space. It is a manifestation of a mode of functioning in each culture; each time period expresses the evolution of consciousness—its soul—in archetypal architecture. People react in keeping with the depth of their own inner projections to a construct's height, shape, contour, and color, and to the atmosphere it creates. A building defines an area, it organizes and reveals changes in unconscious and conscious concepts, ideations, existential and spiritual valuations. As perceptions alter, eyes gazing at different verticalities and horizontalities experience inward and outer connections in a variety of ways, each making its impact felt in the inner world.

Archetypal architecture is an expression of a psychic state. In fact, the archetypal image may be at the root of created form, according to Henri Focillon.

> To assume consciousness at once is to assume form. Even at levels far below the zone of definition and clarity, forms, measures, and relationships exist. The chief characteristic of the mind is to be ceaselessly describing itself. . . . Like the artist, the mind works upon nature. This it does with the premises that are so copiously offered it by physical life, and upon these premises the mind never ceases to labor. It seeks to make them its very own, to give them mind, to give them form. . . . Form receives accent from the mind but not configuration. . . . Forms mingle with the life from whence they come; they translate into space certain movements of the mind.[15]

Paul Klee wrote in his *Diary* that "image-making must be understood as an aspect of the life force that forms itself, spontaneously." And he stated that "my hand is entirely the tool of a distant will," which suggests that he was ruled to a great extent by an archetype.[16] So, too, frequently, is the architect when creating a building, and the writer inspired by it, who then defines it in his novel, essay, poem, or dramatic work.

Just as archetypal architecture manifests itself in such varied monuments as pyramids, pagodas, the Paris Opera House, and the Empire State Building, so it exists in infinite configurations within the writer's psyche. When an architectural archetype is constellated in the unconscious in moments of creativity or deep stress, its energic charge may be so powerful as to "attract to itself the contents of consciousness—conscious ideas that render it perceptible and hence capable of conscious realization."[17] The passage from unconsciousness to consciousness may be experienced by the author as an illumination, a revelation or inspiration. Once this energic force emerges into the light of consciousness, it is apprehended by the author, who uses the riches provided by his subliminal sphere to shape his characters, mark out his story line, structure his work as he sees fit.

Under such conditions architectural imagery takes an individual from his personal and temporal world into a primordial or eternal existence. From this limited and limitless inner spatial area, he is able to reach back in time, to a mythical past, thus grounding himself in eternal predispositions, or river-beds—in a space/time continuum. What he experiences from this vantage point as a creative artist is authentic vision—not just something invented for the sake of entertainment (though it may be that as well), but a primordial experience, a burning reality that exists within his psyche and also within the culture of a people. Archetypal architecture, then, lives outside of time and is not bound to an eschatological, linear, or historical sphere. Rather, it flows in cyclical dimensions, sacred and eternal patterns.

For the writer, archetypal architecture may be looked upon as an inner space that exists amorphously in the collective unconscious until it is revealed as an image. At this point, it takes on line, dimension, and form, and may be observed as a pattern or mode of psychic functioning that determines—if powerful enough—the work in the process of being created. As such, archetypal architectural constructs have been used in both sacred and secular works since early times and are expressions of inner happenings, of emotional climates, of thoughts, credos, and religious concepts, both timely and spanning centuries.

In Aeschylus's *Agamemnon,* the archetypal palace—enclosed in a spatial area—will house a murder that represents the end of a way of life. After ten years of fighting, let us recall, Agamemnon, the leader of the Greeks at the siege of Troy, returns to his wife, Clytemnestra. Deeply angered over the loss of her daughter, Iphigenia, who was sacrificed by Agamemnon, after a period of deep inner struggle, to appease the wrath of Artemis, Clytemnestra has but one desire: to revenge herself upon her husband. In front of Agamemnon's palace at Argos, where the statues of gods stand out in all their beauty and altars burn brightly in their honor, Clytemnestra and her lover, Aegisthus, lay out the crimson-colored carpet for Agamemnon to walk upon as he enters his castle. All know that this color may be used only by the gods and never by human beings. But when Agamemnon descends from his chariot and moves toward the palace, he nevertheless steps upon the carpet.

> And stepping thus upon the sea's rich dye,
> I pray, *Let none among the gods look down*
> *With jealous eye on me*—reluctant all,
> To trample thus and mar a thing of price,
> Wasting the wealth of garments silver-worth. . . .
> Lead her within, but gently: God on high
> Looks graciously on him whom triumph's hour
> Has made not pitiless. . . .
> I will pass in on purples to my home.[18]

Thus Agamemnon yields to the hero's fatal flaw, an inflated ego, and will be murdered by his wife and her lover while in his bath in the archetypal palace, which now comes to represent the end of a certain view of the hero and his age.

Pentheus's palace in Euripides' *The Bacchantes* is the seat of an epiphany. It is within this sacred area that Dionysus becomes man: "Dionysus is in the palace! Adore him!" are the words spoken. It is he who will put an end to the repressive ways that led to the downgrading of the feminine principle by Pentheus. It is he who will encourage the birth of a new cultural and psychological orientation, with the dismantling of Pentheus's palace viewed by the audience—"the stone capitals yonder on the pillars parted asunder."[19]

A more complex situation is described in the epic poem *Orlando Furioso*, by Ludovico Ariosto (1474–1533), which is based on the feats of the famous French medieval knight Roland. Ariosto, the Renaissance diplomat, soldier, and poet, knows that what had once been considered a glorious, shimmering, and chivalric *zeitgeist* has become decadent. Though rancor, bitterness, melancholy, and resignation can be discerned throughout the poem, Rogero, one of the knights in Ariosto's work, understands that in order to experience the spiritual riches of his heritage and thus benefit from them, he must reach the castle of Logistilla, who personifies reason and wisdom. Logistilla's castle—a magnificent edifice with "arches raised" and "lonely gardens," a "lucid tower," and "battlements" she tends with "zeal and care"—represents discernment and order, and therefore perfection. It is a paradigm of the intellect and logic, imbued with Aristotelian concepts as envisaged by the Italian author. When Rogero walks toward "the lofty castle planted there," it is first delineated in concrete terms.

> Than this a stronger or more bright in show
> Was never yet before of mortal sight,
> Or after, viewed; with stones the ramparts glow
> More rich than carbuncle or diamond bright.
> We of like gems discourse not here below,
> And he who would their nature read aright
> Must thither speed: none such elsewhere, I ween,
> Except perhaps in heaven above, are seen.[20]

It is also depicted in abstract terms, thereby uniting in the castle construct the real with the ideational, the personal with the collective, the physical with the spiritual in a single arresting archetypal architectural image.

> What gives to them superiority
> O'er every other sort of gem, confessed,
> Is, man in these his very soul may see;
> His vices and his virtues see expressed.
> Hence shall he after heed no flattery.
> Nor yet by wrongful censure be depressed.
> His form he in the lucid mirror eyes,
> And by the knowledge of himself grows wise.
>
>   (LIX)

Logistilla's castle is that energic factor which catalyzes heretofore dual and disorienting forces, vestiges of a decaying and ossified medieval system that will now be assimilated to new values and components, thus creating a new blend of factors encouraging innovations of all types.

Unlike Ariosto's castle is the archetypal house in *The Faerie Queene* by Edmund Spenser (1552–99). In this epic poem the house symbolizes the body, and Alma, who inhabits it, is a paradigm of the soul. The allegorical knight, Sir Guyon (or Temperance), along with King Arthur, fights evil in every possible way. When the House of Alma is besieged by the enemies of the forces of Temperance, the battle is bloody. Finally, reason prevails over "beastial" appetites, those "vegetative" drives necessary for the continuation of life. The house as the body is said to be constructed of a substance resembling "slime," and for this reason it is perpetually under assault by the enemy: wrong human nature or raw passion. Although not evil in and of itself, the body is weak and allows itself to be dominated by extremes, which may end up controlling and destroying the positive way in life and the natural order of things. Alma, as the nourishing soul (or anima figure), leads the brave knights up to her house.

> That was so high, as foe might not it clime,
> And all so faire, and sensible withall,
> Not built of bricke, ne yet of stone and lime
> But of things like to that *Aegyptian* slime,
> Whereof king *Nine* whilome built *Babell* towre;
> But O great pitty, that no lenger time
> So goodly workemanship should not endure:
> Soone it must turne to earth; no earthly thing is sure.
>
> (Cant. IX)

In perfect proportion, architecturally speaking, each line and shape of Alma's house symbolizes a spiritual value: the two gates, the hewn stone porch, the stately halls, the kitchen with its cauldron "wide and tall," its furnace burning hot.

> The frame thereof seemed partly circulare,
> And part triangulare, O worke diuine;
> The one imperfect, mortall, foeminine;
> Th'other immortall, perfect, masculine,
> And twixt them both a quadrate was the base,
> Proportioned equally by seven and nine;
> Nine was the circle set in heavens place,
> All which compacted made a goodly diapase.
>
> (Cant. IX)

And then "Soone as the gracious *Alma* came in place," the knights entered and did homage to her, and in so doing were bathed in the light of her beauty and spiritual riches.

The elegant home situated on the magnificent country estate in Germany in *Elective Affinities* by Johann Wolfgang von Goethe (1749–1832) represents an archetypal condition of stasis. A plateau has been reached in the marriage of Goethe's middle-aged couple. Too much attention is being paid to refurbishing the house and to landscaping, and too little is focused on the inner beings.

Man and wife are forever actively engaged in looking elsewhere, outside of themselves, and do not evolve. Only after an external event intrudes in their closed sphere does transformation occur.

A hidden realm exists within the house featured in the novel *In Search of the Absolute* by Honoré de Balzac (1799–1850). Beneath the world of appearances there exists—in general for the French writer—a secret relationship between a person's character and the architectural construct within which he lives. Balzac writes: "The events in human life, either public or private, are so intimately connected with the architecture that most observers could reconstruct nations or individuals in all the verity of their habits, basing their notions on what remains of their public monuments or by examining the remains of their domestic existence."[21] The changes to which the house in Balzac's novel has been subjected parallel a transformation occurring within the protagonist: his latently demoniacal nature emerging full force.

When Samuel Taylor Coleridge (1722–1834) was reading a depiction of Kubla Khan's palatial dwelling in Purchas's *Pilgrimage,* he said he fell into an opium-induced sleep and dreamed the poem in which he situates the thirteenth-century Mongolian emperor in the summer palace at Shang-Tu, or Xanadu. This exotic and lavish dwelling place reflects the archetypal conqueror's earthly power over a kingdom that included China, Korea, Mongolia, most of Tibet, Persia, and southern Russia. The description of the palace also reveals a deep-seated need within Coleridge's own psyche.

> In Xanadu did Kubla Khan
> A stately pleasure dome decree,
> Where Alph, the sacred river, ran
> Through caverns measureless to man
>   Down to a sunless sea.
> So twice five miles of fertile ground
> With walls and towers were girdled round;
> And here were gardens bright with sinuous rills,
> Where blossomed many an incense-bearing tree;
> And here were forests ancient as the hills,
> Enfolding sunny spots of greenery.

Interestingly enough, when Coleridge awoke, he wrote down the poem he had dreamed but before its completion was interrupted by a visitor; after the gentleman's departure he could not recall its conclusion. Nor could he, by the same token, discern a way out of the archetypal architectural construct dominating his own complex inner world at the time and hence allow his own subliminal wants to emerge.

Poems, plays, essays, and novels are replete with archetypal architectural images. Suffice it to mention *The Romance of the Mummy* by Théophile Gautier (1811–72), which takes place in a pyramid in Egypt, giving the author ample opportunity for a regressive escapade; *The Fall of the House of Usher* by Edgar Allan Poe (1809–49), a paradigm for a dismemberment ritual; and *Jane Eyre* by Charlotte Brontë (1816–55), in which an insane woman is locked up in one of the towers of the house the orphan-girl protagonist calls her home. The

Gothic novels of Matthew Gregory Lewis (1775–1818), such as *The Monk*, and *The Castle of Otranto* by Horace Walpole (1717–97) are set for the most part in rambling old houses, castles, monasteries, or convents, underscoring, by the terror and suspense aroused, a need for the irrational. In contrast is the archetypal simplicity and seeming contentment of the home of Washington Irving (1783-1859) in Tarrytown, New York, which he features in some of his sketches and tales. Edith Wharton (1862–1937) built "The Mount" at the outset of her literary career, thereby fulfilling her need for harmony, proportion, good taste, and beauty. The city and country homes, the ancient cathedrals and towers in *Remembrance of Things Past* by Marcel Proust (1871–1922) reflect complex inner predispositions, each architectural construct symbolizing a network of unconscious pulsions.

An architectural archetype answers a specific need in the writer, who may be unconsciously influenced by this autonomous factor, and in the reader, who may also (and unknowingly) come under its dominion. Archetypes frequently endow writers and readers alike with vital energy, encouraging them to forge ahead by enabling them to act out what lies embedded in their subliminal sphere. In this way depression may be relieved; continuity may be added to what has heretofore been a fragmented and choppy sphere; order may replace disorder, altering in some strange way what surpasses an individual's understanding and what remains beyond his or her control.

Turning to the literary works that will be examined here, we note that the castle in Franz Kafka's novel by the same name is an architectural archetype that may be understood as an expression of the author's cultural canon, but also as a visualization of a need, a longing, even an obsession. It is the prototype of an ancient force embedded within him, which emerges dynamically and obsessively into a present reality. What is the reason for such an outward trajectory? Why should a castle have been the central and recurrent image in Kafka's novel? In Ansky's "The Tower of Rome," the locus of the action is an archetypal tower. It is in this complex of opposites that the ego of the self-made man inflates rather than evolves, and thus destroys itself, thereby paving the way for renewal in a recreated being. Ansky's tower is both real and mystical in concept, unifying temporal and atemporal visions, and in so doing, inviting the numinosum to be experienced. The archetypal edifice that lies at the heart of Henrik Ibsen's *The Master Builder* dramatizes the trauma of guilt and a man's attempt to deal with an ever-expanding inner maw by means of compulsive activity. Maurice Maeterlinck's plays *The Intruder* and *Interior* dramatize a condition of deep introversion, which rejects the very essence of life: flux, that is, the life and death process. In Henry James's short story "The Jolly Corner," the protagonist returns to the home he lived in as a youth, in an attempt to search out that "other" segment of his personality, his shadow, which he rejected thirty-three years before, when he left his family and native land to live in England. He is traumatized by the encounter. García Lorca's tragedy *The House of Bernarda Alba* uses the architectural archetype to allow a hermaphroditic matriarchate to gestate in its most absolutely perverse and sanguinary form. Jorge Luis Borges's "The Library of Babel" is a mystical meditation on the Universe/God or, transposed in psychological terms, on the Self. Or is it a homiletic engineering feat? A fusion of European and Mexican cultures is effected in Carlos Fuentes's tale "In a Flemish Garden," which depicts an unnerving parapsychological experience enacted in a baroque mansion. The thirteenth-century Chinese drama *The Romance of the Western Chamber,* by Wang Shih-fu, offers readers a mathematically conceived and ordered universe existing within the Buddhist temple complex. Following a specific blueprint designed according to minutely measured conventions, the protagonists' patterns of behavior deviate for a time from these outer visible lines and forms—making for the drama's succulence—only to return to the same structured ways. The architectural archetype in Yukio Mishima's novel *The Temple of the Golden Pavilion* is experienced by the protagonist as a destructive force: a feminine image that drives him to extremes in both his fantasy world and his behavioral patterns.

The metaphoric visions of the authors that will concern us in *Archetype, Architecture, and the Writer* reveal a structural dominant in their psyche, a biological pattern of behavior that becomes evident in their protagonists, images, moods, and dialogue, and in the other literary devices at their disposal. An exploration into the meaning of these primordial images which have gained such autonomy over the authors chosen for scrutiny will be undertaken with the hope of acquiring greater understanding of their creative works—as living and dynamic forces—and their impact on us in today's world.

ONE

Ibsen: *The Master Builder*

Emptiness, an Architectural Archetype

The Master Builder, by the Norwegian playwright Henrik Ibsen (1828–1906), dramatizes the plight of a man who seeks desperately to fill the void within. His life, his heart, his home are barren: cold, damp, hollow inner-spatial areas that lie fallow. No matter how hard he tries to stuff, satiate, replenish this untenanted sphere, like a giant maw it remains forever vacant. Emptiness, an architectural archetype, discloses an emotional condition—that of divestiture.

In part autobiographical, *The Master Builder* (1892) has a protagonist who has broken away from a rule-bound and confining family condition only to attempt to re-create it over and over again by buildings he fashions according to his own design. He rationalizes his behavior pattern by stating that an artist needs space and freedom for self-expression. During the course of time, his fame increases, but his emotionally bereft and poverty-stricken world remains stationary. The protagonist's clawing need to build a "real home," an epithet repeated frequently during the course of the drama, parallels Ibsen's own emotional destitution, haunted as he was since his earliest days by his own archetypal emptiness—a dank and insalubrious inner space that was cold and remote when he so desperately needed warmth and sunlight.

Born in Skien, Norway, into a large family, Ibsen spent his childhood and youth in such extreme poverty that he could afford neither socks nor shoes, and he frequently went out into the freezing snow wearing nothing on his feet but galoshes. His father, who was incapable of providing a home for his family, nurtured in him a sense of bitterness. An atmosphere of resentment and recrimination laid a pall upon the household. After Ibsen's confirmation, in 1843, he worked as an apothecary in Grimsted, living under even more restrictive conditions. What made matters even worse was the fact that he was cut off from family and friends. When Ibsen was nineteen he took a job with

1

another apothecary, and although his painfully depressing and humiliating years were not over, his life took a decided upward turn, economically and emotionally. It was at this juncture in his intellectual development that he became the enemy of society, of the church, and of Christianity—ideas that are voiced in so many of his plays.

Intent upon giving himself a more thorough education, Ibsen began studying Latin, and he also took an interest in the idealism pervading the revolutionary movements that swept Europe in 1848. He even wrote poetry and plays fired with the hope of a fine future for humankind. Ibsen's first play, *The Norsemen* (1850), was performed at the Christiana Theatre. Its reception was favorable and the following year he became resident writer at the National Stage in Bergen. Six years later he was appointed director of the Norwegian Theater in Oslo. In 1858 he married his beloved Suzannah. After the birth of their son, Sigurd, however, a drastic change occurred in his home life. Suzannah refused to have any more children. Henceforth the couple's relationship was seemingly Platonic, and for this reason, some scholars suggest, Ibsen went through a severe and prolonged depression. Adding to his already morbid condition were the vindictive thrashings he suffered at the hands of critics, who condemned his plays outright, for any and all reasons. Stifled by the conventional and prosaic theatrical environment prevailing in Norway, Ibsen moved to Italy, then on to Germany, and returned to his homeland only ten years later.

Two years before the completion of *The Master Builder,* in 1890, Ibsen was living in Norway at North Cape, while his wife, with whom he had quarreled, was at Valdres. That they had reached a crisis in their marriage was not surprising, since they were both highly sensitive, volatile, and fundamentally irritable people by nature. After husband and wife decided to share an apartment again, each lived in separate sections of it, and the atmosphere, according to Ibsen's mother-in-law, was like that of an armed fortress. "They are two solitary people—each one alone—absolutely alone."[1] Yet each needed and could not live without the other.

It is well known that Ibsen was attracted to young girls. His romance with Hildur Anderson, the granddaughter of good friends of his, lasted nine years. Its impact and meaning is dramatized (in veiled terms, of course) in *The Master Builder.* Ibsen first met Hildur in Norway in 1874, when she was ten years old and already most charming and accomplished as a musician. By the time she was twenty-seven and he was sixty-three (in 1891), she had become his constant companion. Intelligent, modest, and a fine pianist, she devoted much of her time to helping Ibsen furnish an apartment, discussing his plays with him

and attending his theatrical productions; and he, so deeply un-
musical, went to her concerts.

Solness, the protagonist in *The Master Builder*, is a middle-aged man
who has achieved fame in his profession. His chief employees are all
dependent upon him in one way or another: economically, emotionally, or both. They are Brovik, an architect for whom Solness
worked when he was young and who is now an old man in his employ;
Ragnar, Brovik's son, who seeks to go out on his own but needs a
letter from Solness in order to do so; Kaia, the bookkeeper, who is
engaged to Ragnar but is in love with Solness. As the play opens,
Brovik is about to die. Recalling the time when he did so much for
Solness to facilitate his career, he asks him to write the letter Ragnar
needs to build a business of his own. Solness refuses outright, heart-
lessly.

We learn that Solness, though famous and wealthy, is unhappy. He
lives with his wife, a background figure in the play, who is ill and
melancholy. She hovers about her empty home constantly and impec-
cably fulfilling her "duty" as a housewife, but her world is dark and
dismal, and she, weak and apathetic, lives in a kind of limbo. We learn
that a fire destroyed her ancestral home about twelve years prior to
the outset of the play, and though she, Solness, and their twins were
spared, she caught an infection shortly after the incident, which was
fatally passed on to her infants in her milk. This incident was the
turning point in the couple's lives. Henceforth, Mrs. Solness withdrew
from the world, growing increasingly feeble, virtually wasting away
from unhappiness, but never dying—an ever-present reminder to
Solness of his past, his egoism, his unfeeling nature.

As for Solness, the fire also marked a turning point in his career. It
ushered into his life economic and artistic success; fame and admiration were his. But he could not enjoy the fruit of his labor because of a
sense of guilt, which became increasingly corrosive with the passing of
years. He questioned his actions. Was his neglect of the old house
related to the fire? He had noticed a split in the chimney flue in the
attic. He wanted to fix it, but each time he went up there, something—
like an invisible hand—seemed to hold him back. More important
were his thoughts on the subject. He had despised that old dark home
and had wanted it burned down, but not with his wife and children in
it. He had fantasized about such a possibility and had seen the house
in flames, but his family safely away from it. In reality, the crack in the
chimney had nothing to do with the fire, which broke out in another
part of the house. Why, then, should he have felt such culpability?

Before the fire, Solness had built only churches. "I came as a boy from a pious home in the country; and so it seemed to me that this church-building was the noblest task I could set myself."[2] After the incident, however, his interests change and he devotes his talent and energy to building increasing numbers of homes. "Homes for human beings" (I), he reiterates throughout the play. No longer is he preoccupied with God and religion, those lofty heights and collective spheres that left him bereft of his sons—divested him, psychologically speaking, of the *feeling* world, the warmth and understanding that make for a real home. He has come down to earth, so he thinks, to wrestle with matter, with the things of this world. He wants to build relationships, solid and lasting, to furnish, metaphorically speaking, all those interiors he has been building for others.

The archetypal constructs he now erects, however, like the houses of worship he fashioned formerly, are also impersonal, fulfilling a collective but not a subjective need. Functional and aesthetically appealing, these residences (which his clients keep ordering and buying, and which would have satisfied most other architects) leave him bereft of contentment. They are just empty houses: more and more forms, shapes, outer garments. The pace and rhythm of his work habits keep accelerating, and understandably so. The more he works, the more he looks forward to completing yet another building, arousing sensations within him that take him outside of himself. Longingly, certainly unconsciously, he wishes to live the lives of those "other" families who will inhabit the structures he fashions. He needs the love and warmth offered by what he believes to be the well-knit household. What Solness fails to encounter is his inner world: the void, the vacant sphere—those feelings of guilt which exist within him. This powerful inner trajectory is what he seeks most continuously to escape, and does, to a certain degree, in his work and love affairs.

A house, psychologically speaking, may be considered the center of one's personal world. Its bedrooms and public rooms, corridors, the kitchen with its stove, symbolize various aspects of the personality. That the three nurseries which Solness built into his new home after the fire (to which he refers so frequently in the play) remain empty spatial areas indicates the terrible absence that, paradoxically, inhabits his world. The death of his twins symbolically indicates the impossibility of any future life for him. These infants are premonitory images. Children represent growth, a world in the process of becoming. That they have been removed from the world suggests the negative and insalubrious climate that has prevailed since the fire. What Solness is building over and over again is sound from an architectural point of view, but, psychologically speaking, he keeps erecting walls, roofs, doors, and windows without furnishing his dwelling from the inside. His archetypal constructs are, therefore, peripheral: they consist of façades, masks, ornaments, untenanted inner space. Even the outer designs are repetitive, rarely varying, revealing a lack of imagination as well as depth. They mirror the condition that exists within these buildings: a regressive atmosphere.

Important, too, is the fact that Solness associates his home, unconsciously, with pain and divestiture as well as with the feminine world. Even before the fire, it was a paradigm for overprotection, a stifling, arid condition, compelling him even in the early days of his marriage to look elsewhere, creatively and emotionally. The old homestead in which he and his wife lived had belonged to her family. Solness describes it as follows: "From the outside it looked like a great, dark, ugly, wooden box; but all the same, it was snug and comfortable enough inside" (II). Although it was not what he considered to be an ideal house, still feeling existed in this area, a certain fluidity in his relationship with his wife. Yet, it was at this very period in his life that he began to believe that if he were to grow in his profession, he needed space and freedom. He could not live boxed in, so to speak, in darkness. A master builder must be able to roam in light and airy climes.

In time Solness comes to look upon the fire as the fulfillment of an unconscious wish. It was, to all intents and purposes, since it enabled him to branch out on his own and allow his creative spirit to manifest itself. But his career has cost him a great deal: peace of mind. "That is the price which my position as an artist cost me—and others. And every single day I have to look on while the price is paid for me anew. Over again, and over again—and over again forever!" (II). His success he equates with the destruction of his family. The feelings of guilt that enslave him will virtually paralyze him in time. In some ways he is as *diseased* as his wife. At times he is aware of the imbalance existing within his psyche, since he alludes to his state as one of "madness." When speaking to his wife, he calls himself "a half-mad man" and "a crazy man" (II). From this condition, too, he seeks a way out, an escape route that will offer him some respite from the gnawing sense of blame that overwhelms him.

Fire may be looked upon as an agent of transmutation: spiritual energy that led Solness from the state of unaccomplished builder to that of master in his chosen profession. Fire is also the mediating factor that forced down a past that had hindered him in his work and paved the way for the archetypal structures Solness was to build— becoming a virtual demiurge in the process. Fire also altered his orientation: from a religious dominion, as a builder of churches, to an earthly sphere, as a home builder. "From the day I lost them [his twins], I had no heart for building churches. . . . Nothing but houses for people to live in" (II). Solness goes on to describe the work he does. "Cosy, comfortable, bright homes, where father and mother and the whole troop of children can live in safety and gladness, feeling what a happy thing it is to be alive in the world—and most of all to belong to each other—in great things and in small" (II). Fire, as an energetic factor, symbolically speaking, has redirected his flame, his powers, forcing him on *always* to build homes for others and never for himself.

Interestingly enough, Solness does not allude to himself as an architect, but rather as a builder. The reason for this, he says, is that his learning has not been conventional, nor has it been gleaned from books. "I have not been systematically enough taught for that. Most of what I know I have found out for myself" (II). He is a self-taught man and in no way may he be compared to the prototypal architect of antiquity, Daedalus, who fashioned and designed the Cretan labyrinth. He was a real master architect, an engineer and mathematician, and so thoroughly trained in the rigors of the building process that he was looked upon by those in his time and those who came later as a universal artist. Solness is more like his son, Icarus. Intuitive and idealistic, Icarus needed to fly to greater and greater heights; Solness, too, has sought to escape constriction and imprisonment. Like Icarus, Solness is an adolescent, a *puer*: though he has reached middle age, he is still unable to look within himself but has his eye cast outward on things and people—women for the most part. Also like Icarus, he is not thoroughly grounded in his métier, and thus he lacks the skill necessary to build a great monument, that is, a *living* home for himself and his wife.

Solness is aware of certain deficiencies linked to his professional life. He is cognizant of the fact that he needs Ragnar, his young assistant, because he is "exceedingly good at calculating bearing-strains and cubic contents—and all that sort of devilry" (I). For this reason he will not and cannot let him go. Furthermore, Ragnar is a thinking type; he also has imagination and knows how to deal with fundamental problems architecturally. Because Ragnar combines both thinking and imagination, he is looked upon by Solness as a future threat. The *senex* (old man), although still a *puer* (youth), refuses to yield his power and wealth to a young man. To do so would be to cease replenishing the emptiness—that architectural archetype—which inhabits his being. "I am what I am, and I cannot change my nature!" he explains (I).

So deeply immersed is Solness in his building syndrome, which consists of erecting more and more comfortable little homes for human beings, that his frenetic labor cuts him off still further from his feeling world and divests him of any time to probe inwardly. Since such a dynamic prevents emotional development, he remains the young lad who sought to build monuments to eternity. This same emotional stasis is carried over into his professional world. Here, too, he fails to mature, evolve. His designs, his building practices do not alter. A realist who is also highly intuitive, his wife understands his deeply pathetic condition. She speaks to him directly and openly, telling him that even if he builds and builds for the rest of his life, "You can never build up again a real home for me!" (II)—or for himself. Ironically, as the play opens, Solness is doing just that: building a new home right opposite the one in which he and his wife are now living. He is persuaded, at least outwardly, that things between them will be rectified once they have moved into the new home. She knows better, however, and warns him that emptiness and desolation will prevail.

What Solness has failed to understand, perhaps, is that his insatiable drive for fame and accomplishment has cut him off from his *anima*: that "autonomous psychic content in the male personality which can be described as an inner woman,"[3] the feminine principle in the psyche, represented in the play by the wife and mother figure. Solness's values have been displaced by the overpowering need to succeed; feeling has been repressed. No competition is permissible. His fantasies about a fire had indicated the enormous flame that lived within him, the constructive/destructive force that would lash at everything that might prevent him from reaching the heights he thought would bring him fulfillment. What he, as a fire principle, really devastated were his wife's talents, which were manifested in bringing babies into the world. "But her vocation has had to be stunted, and crushed, and shattered—in order that mine might force its way to—to a sort of great victory. For you must know that Aline—she, too, had a talent for building" (II). She built *real* houses, that is, "souls of little children," and these, "in perfect balance, and in noble and beautiful forms" (II). The metaphor is appropriate, for it indicates a deep-seated fear on Solness's part: not only insecurity about his profession, but a mysterious psychological ailment, to which he has alluded when calling himself mad and crazed, but which he does not really understand.

Hilda Wangel will be the anima figure who will see to Solness's salvation or destruction. It is through her, a *femme inspiratrice,* that the impasse he has reached in his métier and in his emotional life will be shattered. Hilda, an attractive and very independent, even aggressive, girl, appears early in the play. She claims to have met Solness ten years earlier, when she was only a child. He was building a tower on an old church at the time. She reminds him that he promised to build a "kingdom" for her then, and now she has come to claim her due. She describes the day he climbed the church tower at Lysanger and declared himself independent of both humankind and divinity. "Then you climbed right up the scaffolding, straight to the very top; and you had a great wreath with you; and you hung that wreath right away on the weather-vane" (I).

Hilda alludes to the incident as "wonderfully thrilling." As she stood on the ground looking up toward him—this architectural giant, this hero, this virtual deity—her admiration knew no bounds; and now she repeats her cry of joy, "Hurrah for Master Builder Solness!" (I), with the same gusto and enthusiasm she had shown as a little girl. Solness, however, informs her that he has never climbed up to such heights since that time. It makes him dizzy, he tells her. She pays no attention to what she considers his flimsy excuses and is captivated by her fantasy image. He promised her, she declares, that when she grew up she would be his princess and he would buy a kingdom for her. At the time, she also reminds him, when he reached the very top of his climb he started to sing a song, which she overheard, but which Ibsen does not reveal to the audience until the third act. Like Ozymandias of old, Solness spoke to God directly and in commanding terms. "Hear me now, thou Mighty One; From this day forward I will be a free builder—I, too, in my sphere—just as thou in thine. I will never build churches for thee—only homes for human beings" (III).

Solness grows enthusiastic as he listens to Hilda descant about his past successes. His sense of liberation has gone to his head and a condition of inflation has set in: he believes his creative powers are equal to those of God. Psychologically, his *ego*, the conscious part of his personality, is identifying with his *Self*, his total psyche. To arrogate powers to one's ego that do not properly fall within its competence is to invite imbalance—disaster. Solness, however, rationalizes his need for self-aggrandizement: he must continue to grow. But this growth factor has now expanded to such a degree that he can no longer cope with it.

His problem, he claims, is that a "troll" lives within him and forces him on and on, to pursue his work as a builder. In so doing, however, his work mirrors a sameness; the houses do not take on distinct personalities of their own. They are the products of an obsessive compulsion. He does not build from the cellar up, nor can he sound out those deepest of levels, architecturally or psychologically; the very basis for his work is wobbly. His constructs are not really the work of an artist, but rather the output of a conventional and perfunctory artisan. "It's the troll in one, you see—it is that that calls to the powers outside us. And then you must give in—whether you will or not" (II). He calls upon the mythological troll, his cultural heritage, to explain away his insatiable drive for power.

Psychologically speaking, trolls may be considered invisible forces inhabiting a subliminal realm, powers that compel people to act in specific ways. They are like "ghostly" helpers, images not yet consciously accepted and therefore still living in darkness, in caves, in the unconscious, not yet integrated into the psyche and therefore difficult to understand and nearly always impossible to deal with. That Solness should blame the troll for causing his problems indicates that there is an element within him that works in darkness and for which he refuses to take responsibility. It is an impulse toward freedom and a call for creativity—power that seeks to soar toward the sun and create brilliant and world-shaking edifices—that inhabits him uncontrollably and works its way throughout his system like a raging fire. In the process, all objectivity, all attempts at explicating and probing what is really happening to him, are obliterated.[4]

The troll within him—that hidden, secret, negative sphere—prevents him from building any real relationships with earthly or heavenly beings, with men and women alike, even as a builder. He is forever constructing edifices, but they are all vacant, empty shells, buildings for other people. Unfulfilled, he shies away from his wife, the older anima figure, unable to face the wrong he has done her, if not overtly than certainly covertly, since she was the mother and wife figure he had unconsciously wished out of the way. He also expresses boredom with Kaia, who "sinks down before him" (I) as if she were praying to a god, though moments earlier he had encouraged a relationship with her, seemingly thriving on her every word. Hilda, however, the woman of the moment, the anima figure par excellence, is the one who will guide him and drive him on to fulfill his destiny.[5]

When, therefore, Hilda again reminds him of their first meeting and of the spire he climbed and of her admiration for him during his heroic hour, she virtually demands that he fulfill his promise to her: he must build her a castle and must call her "princess" as he had once done. When Solness finally recalls the conversation he had with her ten years earlier, he tells her he was articulating his youthful dream, a fantasy: he wanted to build castles in space, he wanted to reach out into the world, to unknown heights, building innovative monuments, spectacular works of art, and making a great name for himself. The troll to which he so frequently alludes throughout the play, this earth and air spirit in Norse mythology, rumbled so powerfully within him that he yielded to its power, allowing impulse rather than thought, drive rather than creativity, to dominate him.

Solness becomes Hilda's votary. Her youthful strength, her own fiery nature, encourages him to pursue his goal. She is the "devil" referred to earlier in the play: that enticing force, that temptress, who will encourage him to climb to incredible heights and thus fulfill his promise made long ago. To build castles in the air, when life is burgeoning and virtually all options are open to an individual, is the prerogative of the *puer*. It is the articulation of a dream. To yield to such fantasies as an older man is paradigmatic of the *puer aeternus*, the youth who never grows up, who never develops into a man and remains psychologically stunted.

It is Hilda, also, who suggests that Solness write the letter for Ragnar, thus enabling the young man to forge ahead on his own. Why should Solness fear competition now that he has accomplished so much in the workaday world? He should not impede the march of youth any more than he should attempt to destroy what is creative and different in the human or artistic sphere. To do so will transform him into a modern Kronos and invite disaster. Solness, however, does not understand the real meaning of Hilda's statement; that is, he fathoms it intellectually but not emotionally. Facing his fear of being overthrown, dispossessed, would force him to face his own archetypal emptiness, the ever-expanding void that lies at the root of his being. Such a maw terrifies him. His fear of accepting the fact that he is a mediocre artist is overpowering, because such acceptance would make it impossible for him to really believe in his creative capacities, and all he has thought and accomplished would be for naught—including his corrosive guilt. Yet he has, to all intents and purposes, been foundering for years, ever since the fire, when he learned that although he built and built well and commanded respect from his clients, his potential was small. Soon he reached an impasse, and his architectural constructs were merely repetitions of what he had already brought into existence. At the outset of the play he alludes to Ragnar as a youth redolent with imagination and energy, an artist capable of creating what has never before been done. "Not the old-fashioned stuff that I am in the habit of turning out!" but seminal works, living, tenanted monuments (I).

Hilda, the anima figure, challenges Solness's condition of stasis by encouraging him to climb to the top of the tower on the house he has just completed for himself and his wife. Psychologically, she is forcing him to come to terms with his creative impulses, the "troll" that earned him success but cut him off from real life, love, friendship, relatedness. She inspires and fires him, pointing to his future greatness by asking him to make a symbolic ascent that parallels the image of his past achievements. Now the troll in him takes over, as the thinking factor recedes into the background. He is transformed into that impulsive youth, that adolescent, whose dream must be lived out in the empirical sphere. The old man vanishes and Hilda is the one who upsets his psychological balance, so tenuous to begin with.

"There exist special, chosen people who have been endowed with the power and faculty of desiring a thing, craving for a thing, willing a thing—so persistently and so—inexorably—that at last it has to happen," he tells Hilda (II). Not only has Solness reached the heights of an inflationary condition with regard to his earthly dominion, but he now identifies with that superpower within him, the troll. He intimates that he merely needs to will a thing into existence for it to happen. There are "helpers" and "servers," he states further, and he calls upon them when need be to fulfill his earthly destiny. "That is what people call having the luck on your side; but I must tell you what this sort of luck feels like! It feels like a great raw place here on my breast. And the helpers and servers keep on flaying pieces of skin off other people in order to close my sore!—But still the sore is not healed—never, never! Oh, if you knew how it can sometimes gnaw and burn" (II).

Hilda urges Solness on. She longs to see him reach those great heights: "To see you, with a wreath in your hand, high, high up upon a church-tower" (II). Solness's ardor mounts, he will yield to any whim of Hilda's. He even writes a letter on Ragnar's behalf, but it arrives only after Brovik has died and so deprives the *real* father the joy of knowing his son is on his way in his chosen career. Unconcerned by this minor tragedy, and by the suffering of others, Solness has eyes now only for Hilda and for the fulfillment of his youthful dream.

Solness climbs to the top of the tower. Hilda, who watches him from the ground, cries out, "Higher and higher! Higher and higher!" Mrs. Solness, the builder of souls, is aghast at the spectacle. "Oh, I shall die of terror. I cannot bear to see it," she says. Yet Solness stands there on those topmost planks, unflinching. "I see him great and free again," Hilda says, intensely. Ragnar stands erect in disbelief. He knows that Solness suffers from dizzy spells and has a fear of heights. "Frightfully thrilling," Hilda repeats, describing Solness as he hangs a wreath around the weather vane. She hears him sing the song he had sung ten years earlier. "Now he is waving his hat," she cries, and she urges the onlookers to respond to his gesture by waving theirs. "Hurrah for the Master Builder Solness!" Then the inevitable happens. "He is falling!" Mrs. Solness screams. Then she faints. Solness dies, but for Hilda he has earned his moment of triumph. "He mounted right to the top—my—my Master Builder!" He had fulfilled her dream: that of a father figure, an artificer, a demiurge, a would-be lover.

Solness lives out the emptiness of his architectural archetype, and although he attempts to fill the void within him by yielding to an insatiable desire to furnish it, his heart has congealed in the process. His desire for warmth and understanding is still there, but he does not know how to rectify what has gone amiss. As a *puer aeternus*, he lives in a fantasy world, his dreams take precedence, and the troll within him dominates his every move, word, feeling. It is this underground impulsive force, this unconscious content that lives in darkness and erupts so powerfully, which drives him on to work harder and never, ever allows him breathing space to think or indwell. Solness is an archetypal builder of empty homes, who repeats his constructs ad infinitum, stifled by the very fire principle that destroyed the first house in which he and his wife lived. His own murky depths smother him and he can find no way out of his constricting labyrinth. Because of the impasse he has reached both as man and as builder, he yields to the anima figure who tempts him in a marvelously Faustian image. He relives for a few minutes his youthful dream of becoming a great artist—perhaps the greatest of all time—a hero figure. Like Icarus, however, Solness did not listen to Daedalus's wise advice to his son: "I warn you, Icarus; you must remain in the middle course." Ego inflation took over and the emotions that flooded his being were so spectacular, so overwhelming, that vertigo set in—and imbalance. Solness never understood the real meaning of Daedalus's message—that of the prototypal architect, the universal artist: First build from within, solidly, soundly, invincibly, then emerge in triumph to exterior spheres. Only then will energetic fire transform the architectural archetype of emptiness into one of fullness, replete with warmth, love, and understanding.

TWO

Maeterlinck:
The Intruder and Interior
An Architectural Archetype of Introversion

The architectural archetypal image in *The Intruder* by Maurice Maeterlinck (1862–1949) is an old castle; in *Interior,* a one-family home. Each of these buildings in its own way dramatizes a pattern of behavior marked by introversion: a condition in which libido (psychic energy) flows inward, so that the individual relates with greater ease to a subjective inner domain than to an objective outer world. In such a situation, if fantasies and images alive within the unconscious are constellated and not integrated into the light of consciousness, they may fascinate and even gain autonomy over the individual or the family group.

As architectural archetypes, the old castle and the house lend both temporality and atemporality to Maeterlinck's plays. Each in its own way protects its inhabitants from the inclemencies of weather, that is, from the rigors and cruelties of life, at least on the surface; each depicts, iconographically, an emotional condition that really exists in the workaday world and also transcends this dimension, existing in a transpersonal sphere. The protagonists, in their own subjective way, understand that the shelters offered them are only provisional, that is, they are human constructs powerless to stem the tide of destiny—the inexorable march of events that spell life and death. Nevertheless, they withdraw behind the portals of these architectural archetypal images, refusing to partake of the human sphere, rejecting the life process, which is change and transformation, to welcome instead a condition of stasis, or living death.

The old castle and the house in Maeterlinck's two plays may be looked upon, psychologically, as the *ego,* the center of consciousness, the "seat of individual identity." The ego is that part of the psyche which "stands between the inner and the outer world, and its task is to adapt to both."[1] In introverted individuals of the type found in these

13

plays, the ego adjusts with greater facility to a subjective reality. It is, therefore, unable or unprepared to deal with the life experience and so fears and resists it.

Maeterlinck had always been fascinated with old castles and houses and with antique objects of all types, which he looked upon frequently as hierophanies. Such an attraction may have stemmed in part from his upbringing in Ghent, an ancient Flemish city. Somber and sunless, it housed such world-famous paintings as Jan van Eyck's *The Adoration of the Lamb,* and its city hall had a façade dating back to the fourteenth century. Such emphasis on the past may have encouraged Maeterlinck to think back to a period that was, rather than forward to a future that would be, preferring the dismal and shadowy years of a great cultural heritage to the brash and raw sunlight of an industrialized world. Maeterlinck enjoyed solitude; he valued periods of introspection and privacy and lived frequently like a recluse—far from the madding crowd.

His school years were unhappy and may have been instrumental in encouraging him to repress whatever pleasurable emotions he felt. He referred to the period he spent studying at the Jesuit College of Sainte-Barbe in Ghent as an "incarceration" and as "seven years of narrow tyranny."[2] His world at that time revolved around extreme discipline and fearful threats of eternal damnation. The dirt and ugliness of his surroundings were repugnant to him. It is no wonder that he learned from his very early days the real meaning of a lugubrious existence.

After receiving his law degree, thereby yielding to his parents' wishes, he was rewarded for having studied so well with the gift of a trip to Paris. It was there that he met Villiers de l'Isle-Adam, a symbolist writer whom he admired and called an "indefatigable magician" and an "inexhaustible visionary."[3]

It must be noted that, in keeping with his deeply introverted nature, Maeterlinck entitled his first volume of collected verse *Hothouses* (1889). Such an appellation mirrors an emotional climate, to be sure, but a realistic situation as well. Ghent was the town of horticulture and floriculture. Hothouses, however, symbolically speaking, and in view of Maeterlinck's later writings, take on broader connotations. The title reflects his profound ennui, his spleen, which weighed so heavily upon him, his lethargy, his despondency—feelings that existed within him even as a youth. He felt bound, constricted, and even at this juncture experienced the hollow and dull sensation of a walled-in personality. The dank, dismal, and suffocating air of the hothouses in his home town, as evoked in his collection of verse, discloses Maeterlinck's psychological condition. Yet this very same image also has positive elements. Because of this enclosed structure, warm temperatures may be maintained, thereby protecting the seeds within, helping them sprout, giving them the sustenance and strength necessary to burgeon. Under less protective conditions, exposed to the rigors of the outside world, these plants might perish. Within the hothouse, then, there live inchoate the forces of both destruction and construction: a *complexio oppositorum*.

A hothouse atmosphere also exists in *The Intruder* (1891), produced in Paris at Paul Fort's Théâtre d'Art. The one room in the old castle in which the action takes place houses a family that consists of a blind Grandfather, an Uncle, a Father, and three girls. They are awaiting the Mother's recovery from childbirth. A relative is expected. The Father and Uncle are convinced that the Mother is out of danger. Only the blind Grandfather senses the hopelessness of the situation. The visitor finally arrives—in the form of death.

The castle is the center of the family's world. A symbol for the maternal aspect of the feminine principle, it acts, as has already been said of hothouses, as a protecting and containing structure that may or may not stultify, may or may not nurture. The castle also represents multiple gradations within the unconscious; the unconscious contents are the characters. There is no extraneous action, nothing superfluous in the play: one room and one theme, which unfolds in only twenty-four hours. Everything onstage emerges directly from the body of the text. The set does not change. It consists of a room with three doors and a window, the window opening onto a garden. The door to the left leads to the dying woman's room; the one to the right, to the infant's room; the third, back center stage, opens onto the outside world. The doors may be looked upon as three aspects of existence: death, life, chance. Until now each outlet has been closed; the atmosphere now smolders with repressed anxiety. Hovering over this introverted, ultrastationary, and lugubrious atmosphere of doom are, as Maeterlinck wrote in this preface to the 1929 edition of his *Theatre*, "enormous invisible and fatal powers." Only when the transformatory ritual that is the play begins do the forces become mobile as the wheel of destiny begins its circular configurations.

The actors—like the building itself—are almost immobile throughout the performance; they have pared their gestures down to the barest nuances of movement, underscoring by their very restraint the mounting terror of the situation. The dialogue is sparse and consists almost exclusively of the exteriorization of inner states. Words are enunciated with objectivity but with an underlay of subjectivity and hence reverberate with infinite tonal and rhythmic variations. Sometimes the voices sound metallic; at other moments they take on the solemnity of a religious chant. An economy of gesture throughout the drama emphasizes the stilled and stayed atmosphere—libido flowing inward rather than outward, regressing instead of progressing.

The family is grouped together onstage in one room, restraining and repressing the excruciating anxiety that corrodes their lives; revealing physically the introverted architectural archetype. The glazed eyes of one, the enigmatic smile of the second, the deeply furrowed brow of the third disclose the richness of their mysterious subliminal spheres; they are also reminiscent of the canvases of certain Flemish primitives, Dirk Bouts and Roger van der Weyden, who succeeded in concretizing sensation, stifling feelings, and imposing the stamp of eternity on their works. Divested of personal elements, the characters in *The Intruder* are mythlike, mediumistic. They flay each other onstage in the subtlest of ways, compelled to do so, seemingly, by some invisible network of fatal forces.

The protagonists should be looked upon not as flesh and blood beings but rather as archetypal, primordial beings arising from the profoundest layers of the unconscious. The fact that the blind Grandfather is the only one to see his daughter's imminent death may be regarded perhaps as a theatrical cliché. However, if examined in the light of psychology, it can be termed a synchronistic or acausal happening, because the Grandfather has been exiled from the visible or outer sphere; cut off symbolically from the realm of ideas (or the rational principle in humankind), he finds solace in a world of senses and feelings. He therefore experiences life on a different level than do the Uncle, the Father, and the girls.

In order to reinforce the introverted atmosphere symbolized by the image of the ancient castle and to underscore the archetypal aspects of the protagonists, Maeterlinck omits all reference to personal names. The characters are envisaged as collective functions—the Mother, the Father, the Grandfather, and so forth—and their natures remain ambiguous and linked to that mysterious domain infused with super- or extrahuman dimensions. As such, they inhabit two worlds, the real and the unreal, the conscious and unconscious. Like phantoms, they may strut and stir, terrified and terrifying in a strangely *inhuman* yet deeply moving *human* way.

The Grandfather is a prime example of the introverted archetypal being inhabiting the old castle. His intuitions and premonitory statements throughout the play rest on an inner illumination; they come from a subjective realm where the limited linear time and space dimensions of rational humanity have been transcended. The Grandfather exists in a dimensionless universe, and for this reason some of his statements may at first appear contradictory. A blind man would not say about his daughter, when evidence points to the contrary, "I believe she is not very well . . . something has happened. . . . I am certain my daughter is worse! . . . But you people don't see clearly. . . ." Like a plant that draws sustenance from the darkness of the earth, the Grandfather gains his powers from the mysterious realm of sightlessness. Only he understands the meaning of the fourth dimension; he alone has the ability to live beyond physical space and time. Because the Grandfather lives almost exclusively in his inner world (his unconscious), he no longer responds exclusively to the temporal divisions imposed upon rational human beings in their attempt to order their existential habits. Although the Grand-father's conversation sometimes seems to relate directly to the di-alogue of the other protagonists, its import actually reaches far beyond their superficial vision. He senses the tremendous weight of doom and the presence of the Intruder because it is already there. Its spirit merely imposes itself more acutely upon him as the drama un-folds.

Ever since Newton established his theory of causality, humanity has been led to believe that everything within the universe has a causal explanation. If Newton's notions were valid, then it might be postu-lated that chance itself is the result of a causality that has not yet come into view. How is such a concept possible? How can certain telepathic, synchronistic, or acausal experiences occur in a causal universe? Swe-denborg, for example, when living in London, had a vision of his native city, Stockholm, in flames at the very moment the fire was rag-ing. The thought and the event occurred simultaneously, regardless of spatial distances. Acausal events are difficult to comprehend, yet they actually do exist. Today's physicists have not yet determined the reasons for such events but are studying them.[4]

How do acausal sensations become manifest to the Grandfather? By means of what C. G. Jung calls "archetypal patterns," which he defines as those contents or forces that exist in the deepest strata of a person's being. Under certain circumstances, archetypes emerge from the un-conscious in the form of images that, when interpreted, may be help-ful in determining the situation at hand. As archetypes flow into con-sciousness, they are accompanied by certain affects (feelings, moods, sensations) that may not always be explicated along rational lines.[5] The Grandfather in *The Intruder* experiences these affects in terms of impulses, intuitions, and perceptions. As these unconscious contents emerge, they frequently have no rational or causal relationship with the objective situation as far as the other protagonists in the play are concerned. The Grandfather therefore is at times, ironically enough, the subject of mockery. He is a being, however, who lives on the edge of two worlds and for this reason understands the meaning of the messages emanating from his spaceless and timeless universe.

To reinforce the dichotomy between the Grandfather's approach to life and the relatively superficial attitudes revealed by the rest of the family's conversation, Maeterlinck has recourse to certain theatrical vehicles based on sound, sensation, and images. These were designed to intrude upon the restrained and static atmosphere of the drama. The varying reactions of the protagonists to these devices serve to heighten the sense of growing terror and mystery. Because the dialogue is so Spartan, the action so bone-hard, and the house so claustrophobic, any change of pace or imagery is certain to arouse visceral reactions on the part of the spectators, shaking them frequently into a new frame of awareness—alienating them, in the Brechtian sense, only to reach them more deeply seconds later.

The antique Flemish standing clock in a corner of the stage may be considered a vehicle intended to jar the deeply introverted atmosphere every now and then. The clock, representing a linear frame of reference, rings out the hour and the half hour during the play—from eleven o'clock until midnight—up to the advent of death. It underscores the irreversible and destructive nature of time, humanity's victimization by this force, the fragility and ephemeral nature of life. The finality of the rings, which fall like hatchet blows, and the protracted silences between them are reminiscent of certain medieval French chants depicting the march of the hours during Christ's agony on the cross. For the Grandfather, who already knows his daughter's death is imminent, the striking of the hours merely confirms his feelings, and so his reactions to the noises are disconnected. "Am I turned toward the glass door?" he questions after hearing the sound. He awaits the fulfillment of destiny. The others in the room, because they live in a linear dimension, concentrate increasingly on the passage of time.

The sounds of birds and the wind rustling in the trees in the garden may be considered another kind of audible invasion from the existential world. The Father has asked one of his daughters to look out of the window to see if the relative they are expecting is coming down the garden path. The girl sees no one. Instead she hears the nightingales singing and the wind blowing. Suddenly, and for no apparent reason, there is silence.

Ancient Egyptians worshipped a bird deity with a human head. In their hieroglyphics, this theriomorphic god represented the *ba*, the soul, implying that the bird, being a volatile and active force, was the bearer of the soul to astral planes. In *The Intruder*, the fact that the singing birds stop abruptly would indicate the gravity of the occasion, the hushed silence at the soul's passing. According to Buddhist doctrine, wind has been associated with Buddha's breath; Hebrew tradition (*ruh* means both "breath" and "spirit") likens it to the "creative breath" as exemplified in Genesis when God "breathed in [Adam's] nostrils the breath of life, and man became a living soul" (2:7). When wind or breath ceases, life has been withdrawn.

Other intrusions serve to jar the condition of stasis on stage. The gardener, for example, who is sharpening his scythe outside, causes the Grandfather to shudder. The other protagonists react to this noise in a quasi-normal manner, as part of a natural occurrence. The scythe, associated with Saturn, the god of time (irreversible and destructive), may be considered a symbol of death. Because the scythe is curved, it takes on lunar (passive, nocturnal) characteristics, or female attributes, and may therefore be linked to the fate of the dying mother in the play. Since the Grandfather alone knows the significance of this noise, he reacts dramatically to the grating sound. He becomes tense, for he believes the sharpening of the scythe is taking place within the house and not outside, as the others claim. He lives the incident inwardly—as a psychological experience.

The sound of footsteps also intensifies the atmosphere of foreboding. The Grandfather hears not one but two sets of footsteps downstairs: those of the servant and those of the visitor. The other protagonists are uncertain but tend to believe that only the servant's are audible. A door is heard to shut downstairs. The tension mounts by degrees as the footsteps grow louder. The anxiety becomes almost unbearable as the door opens and the servant enters. The Grandfather is convinced that the visitor is accompanying the servant. "Is she crying?" he asks. "Of course not," the Uncle replies, wondering why the Grandfather should ask such a question. The servant is interrogated. Has anyone entered the house? No one, she assures them. Why, then, did she shut the door downstairs? Because it was open. "But who opened it?" the Father questions. No one knows the reply. "You brought someone into the room," the Grandfather asserts, almost accusing the others of deceit.

As the play draws to a finale, the clock tolls midnight. The anguished wail of the infant in the room to the right is heard. "The wail continues with gradations of terror." Hurried footsteps are heard from the room to the left, then silence. The protagonists listen in mute horror. The door to the left opens. The Sister of Charity appears on the threshold. She makes the sign of the cross and announces the Mother's death. The Intruder—death—has indeed arrived, as the Grandfather had predicted.

Sensations are also used as a device to render all the more acute the fright conveyed in *The Intruder*. The Grandfather complains of a growing malaise, a sense of claustrophobia. He asks for the window to be opened. Moments later, however, he requests that the window be shut. "It seems that the cold has entered the room," he says. According to the Pythagoreans, cold is synonymous with death. Fire or bodily heat is associated with the flame of life or health. Heraclitus believed that fire (heat) was an agent of transmutation, since everything is born from fire and returns to it, like the phoenix that is destroyed and is regenerated from its own ashes. The Grandfather is experiencing the chill of death vicariously. He feels life ebbing from his daughter's body.

The sensations of heat and fire are also conveyed, through the interplay of light and darkness inside and outside the room. Onstage a candle burns brightly, and because of the shadows it casts, so reminiscent of the paintings of Georges de La Tour, the life-and-death drama becomes increasingly palpable. Despite the light, however, the Grandfather declares, "It seems to me that there isn't much light here," indicating a lack of comprehension, an illusory optimism on the part of the other family members. As the play progresses, the Father notices a dimming of the light. "The lamp is not burning well tonight." The Grandfather then asks if the lamp has been extinguished because he no longer feels the light and believes himself to be more cut off from the others than ever. "I am here, all alone, in endless darkness!" Ironically, he comments on the "pallor" of the girls: "I feel that you are all paler than the dead!" The lamp is then personified: it "palpitates," it acts "concerned," the "cold wind is tormenting it." When the lamp finally goes out and the family sits in darkness, each person taking on the appearance of the shadow of death, one realizes that the various gradations of the flame were a material manifestation of an inner happening.

The moonlight in the garden also mirrors the course of the Intruder's march. The daughter looking out the window has seen an avenue of cypress trees in the light of the moon. The moon, always associated with woman because of its periodic phases and curved contours, indicates in this instance the Mother's fate. As the moon pales, hiding behind clouds and finally fading out of sight—in rhythm with the flickering candle—it becomes a sign that death and the Mother are united.

The color green, visible through the window, represents worldly productivity and fertility. The dark, drab, brownish tinctures predominating within the room spell death and decay. Both worlds are visible from the orchestra—implying that life and death are merely aspects of a totality. The Grandfather represents such a totality, for he experiences both simultaneously.

The Intruder is a play of cosmic dimension, a work that dramatizes a supreme interchange: the Mother, stage left, who is about to exit from life, and the infant, stage right, who is entering the earthly domain. It is a scenic depiction of life's cyclical orbit, but lived in an inner sphere: in myths and religions it would be called a rite of passage.

Like the old castle in *The Intruder*, the house in *Interior* takes on mythic proportions. It fuses the supernatural and the natural world, divine and mortal spheres, empirical and mystical realms. This architectural archetypal house is the seat of a series of vague or strange encounters, confrontations with occult forces over which no one has control. Let us recall that Maeterlinck was deeply influenced by the symbolist poets—Baudelaire, for example—whose inner trajectories led him to experience subliminal spheres in terms of architectural constructs: rooms, houses, edifices of all sorts. Mallarmé's poetic vision also made inroads on Maeterlinck's psyche: his creation, Igitur, was a prototypal man who walked down the circular stairway of his Intellect/Home. Villiers de l'Isle-Adam's religious drama, *Axel*, featured protagonists who made their homes in dismal cellars and halls in medieval German fortresses. The symbolists, and Maeterlinck following in their path, rebelled most forcefully against positivism, the ultrascientific and experimental spirit of the age. As envisaged by Auguste Comte and Hippolyte Taine, the same system of observation used for scientific purposes should be applied to philosophy and religion. Maeterlinck sought to divest art of the crude and obvious realities that were, he felt, so blatantly included in the writings of the scientifically oriented naturalist novelists and dramatists. Hence he refused to follow the vicissitudes of the lives of alcoholics, prostitutes, and impoverished suffering human beings in his dramas. Instead he chose an inner course, a mystical clime to which his own meditative personality responded more powerfully.

Interior, performed successfully at the Théâtre de l'Oeuvre in 1895, is even more esoteric than *The Intruder*. The word "esoteric" comes from the Greek *eisôtheô*: "I make enter"; that is, the dramatist opens the door of the outside world so that viewers may penetrate within, symbolically speaking to the world of the occult, where the hidden message, the secret doctrine, lies buried. Such riches, however, cannot be revealed through explication; they must be experienced—and they are in Maeterlinck's architectural archetype of introversion. Not a room, this time, but the façade of a house is visible onstage; its three windows disclose the fearful mystery being enacted within. *Interior* is a modern version of those ancient Greek mysteries which Plutarch believed featured "the soul, at the time of death." It tells of the slow eclipsing of existence as it sinks back into darkness. The setting of *Interior* is described as follows:

> An old garden planted with willows. At the back, a house, with three of the ground-floor windows lighted up. Through them a family is pretty distinctly visible, gathered for the evening around the lamp. THE FATHER is seated at the chimney corner. THE MOTHER, resting one elbow on the table, is gazing into vacancy. Two young girls, dressed in white, sit at their chair embroidering, dreaming and smiling in the tranquility of the room. A CHILD is asleep, his head resting on his mother's left arm. When one of them rises, walks, or makes a gesture, the movements appear grave, slow, apart, and as though spiritualized by the distance, the light, and the transparent film of the windowpanes.[6]

The action of the play unfolds both inside the house, as seen through the ground-floor windows, and in a garden in front of the mansion. The family members do not speak; they merely rise, walk, and gesticulate in serious, slow, and sparing ways. In the garden are an Old Man, his two daughters, and a Stranger. They try to determine the best way of breaking some terrible news to the seemingly peaceful family within: the death by drowning of a daughter.

The tension consists in the interplay between what is heard outside the house and the intensity of the emotions experienced by the characters within the architectural archetypal home. The three windows visible onstage, lighted from within the room, take on an increasing dimension during the course of the play, becoming in time as powerful as the archetypal protagonists whose forms move about silently and ineluctably. Windows represent an opening onto light, air, and life; they stand for a receptive state and have been identified frequently with the human eye and the taking in of the exterior world, the increasing awareness of life's dualities. Since windows are usually square rather than round, they stand, according to Pythagoras, for earth forces and existential or empirical conditions. The three lighted windows for the mystic correspond to the directional points: the Orient, the South, and the Occident—areas where the sun passes. Interestingly, the North is purposefully omitted in *Interior,* as it stands for the realm of darkness, which, paradoxically, envelops the entire house.

Great emphasis in *Interior* is placed on mimetic art, thereby enhancing the uniqueness of the drama and the introversion it expresses.

The dialogue in the garden revolves almost exclusively around the family in the house. Since no words emanate from within the building and actions alone are visible, a very close rapport exists between the emotions expressed by the Old Man and the Stranger and the bodily movements of the people within. To a certain extent, the dissociation of speech and action breaks the empathy that conventionally exists between actor and audience. Although distance separates the two groups, the emotions and thoughts articulated by the old Man and the Stranger are in an unusual way a kind of "active silence," sometimes sensed by those in the house and mirrored by their pantomime.[7] When, for example, the Old Man and the Stranger speak of the corpse that was found in the lake, the two sisters in the house turn their heads toward the window as though echoing some mysterious feeling, some excruciating presentiment.

A sense of secrecy and uneasiness—incommunicability—pervades the atmosphere as if one world were unable to hear or see the other: the inside is hidden from the outside, the supernatural from the natural, life from death. Only intermittent glimpses of the happenings inside disclose what is going on within the archetypal creatures who live there. Cloistered from the realities of life, those who remain enclosed in the house, protected, incarcerated in a psychologically hidden sphere of being, exist in a condition of virtual stasis.

The drowned girl alone—whom we may look upon, psychologically, as a burgeoning ego, a beautiful young ego—ventured forth outside the family unit to experience the empirical domain, to seek fulfillment and individuality. Unprepared for the exigencies of the outer world, for life with its conflicts and its searing pain, she succumbed to the turmoil and died. Her death is itself a mystery—not only to the family, which is still unaware of the situation, but also to those inhabiting the temporal domain. Had she wanted to die? question the Stranger and the Old Man. It was the Stranger who found the body—by chance—in the street in darkness. The peasants, he said, had told him they had seen a girl wandering by the river. They thought she was looking for a certain flower. Or was she? The Old Man insinuates the possibility of suicide: "She was perhaps one of those who wishes to say nothing . . . who has more than one reason for not living. . . . For years one may live next to someone who is no longer of this world." But then, no one knows the real facts. "You cannot see into the soul as you see into that room," the Old Man states.

Every now and then the Old Man and the Stranger look up at the windows while they talk, and when they do, the two young girls turn their heads toward the apertures only to resume their former positions a few moments later, as if they sensed the traumatic events taking place outside the house. A mysterious inner thread, some sensitive energic wave, is at work in *Interior*—linking outer and inner spheres to the universal All, the introverted to the extroverted domain, enveloping, in so doing, the spectator in its grasp.

The Stranger and the Old Man describe the activity inside: "They sit motionless and smiling. But see, the father puts his finger to his lips. . . . He points to the child asleep on its mother's breast. . . ." Then the adults look at the child, not realizing that those outside are observing them and that perhaps an even greater force encapsulates the entire scene—all living matter. The Old Man states: "They think themselves beyond the reach of danger. They have closed the doors, and the windows are barred with iron. They have strengthened the walls of the old house; they have shot the bolts of the three oaken doors. They have foreseen everything that can be foreseen. . . ."

Fixity reigns in *Interior* as it does in *The Intruder*. A flowing factor seems to come into existence only when the Old Man's granddaughter runs up to him and informs him that the entire town is following a bier and is walking toward the family's house. As the inexorable march of destiny pursues its course, the calmness that prevails within the house, the feelings of beatitude and inner joy, become intermingled with anguish. The two sisters now walk toward the first and third windows, resting their hands against the panes and gazing deeply into the blackness before them. The center window—that of the third sister, the middle and centering force in this conflicting play of opposites—lies empty: it belonged to the departed one. As if the two girls are communicating in some mysterious way with the forces outside the house, they leave the windows in a trancelike condition— to return to their mother. They kiss her, comforting her unconsciously, then they stroke the child's curls "without awakening it." Silence. As the Father observes the hands on the giant clock in the corner moving slowly around, he does not budge. The waiting continues.

Some of the people bearing the bier enter the garden. The Stranger forbids them to approach the windows. Let the news be given to the family some other day, tomorrow. Meanwhile, in the house, the two sisters walk toward the door and those outside believe the door is being opened, when, in fact, it is being closed. They wonder whether the family knows something, senses something. The Father walks toward the door and opens it ever so slightly, just enough to see part of the lawn and the fountain. Then he closes it. Meanwhile, the crowd approaches, unrelentingly. Nothing can stay their course. The Old Man enters the house. The sisters and Mother walk toward him, slowly, ceremoniously. The Mother holds out her hand to him, then draws it back. The Old Man starts to speak, the Father interrupts. The Mother hides her face in her hands. The crowd murmurs while drawing closer to the room so that they may peer into it. The Mother knows now. The family makes their way out of the house despite the attempts of the Old Man to prevent them from leaving it. The confusion and activity in the garden in this last image are sharply contrasted to the vision of the child who sleeps in unknowing serenity within the house: the cloistered and paradisiac realm, the warm and protective womblike structure.

Interior flays. Like the Greek dramas of old, it reveals the inevitability of death in such powerful terms as to become virtually unbearable. As in classical theater, all unessential material has been eradicated. The play's theme takes on greater power and dimension as the ineluctable news of the daughter's death reaches the family, as the outside realm forces itself into the inner sphere and the Self encroaches upon the undeveloped ego, still bathing in an Edenlike atmosphere, a childlike realm where conflict has been banished and harmony alone exists. The architectural archetype of the house is the image of introversion: a life of isolated comfort in an untroubled, loving relationship, a prolongation of an infantile psychological condition. Awareness is unknown to those who live exclusively in the house; nor are they exposed to the dichotomies of the empirical world—where choices and fissures require the individual to act, to force out the ego and thus strengthen it so it may fight its way into freedom, divesting itself of those forces that would incarcerate it, and earning psychological independence.

The Intruder and *Interior* demonstrate humankind's weakness when confronted with the forces of destiny. They confirm Schopenhauer's formulations in *The World as Will and Idea* (1818), a volume Maeterlinck read over and over again. Schopenhauer claimed that the individual's will, over which he has virtually no control, is the source of his unhappiness. It is will that forces him to strive and to wish the impossible. Dissatisfaction, frustration, and anguish always ensue. Only by suppressing or controlling the will through the intellect—that is, by diminishing or overcoming desires—can terrestrial needs be transcended, thus making possible the achievement of a peaceful and painless state of pure contemplation.

In such a state Maeterlinck's characters remain incarcerated within their houses, their rooms, staving off the outer world, cutting off the progress of time, the erosion of flesh and psyche. At the outset of each play an architectural structure—an old castle, a home—constitutes a sacred area, a protected subliminal realm. Although the inhabitants of this inner sanctum seek to separate themselves from the unknown and feared empirical domain, such a feat cannot be accomplished permanently, since something within the home is askew: In *The Intruder,* the mother must give way to the infant, death to life; in *Interior,* the youthful ego, in the form of a young girl, leaves a womblike condition in an effort to determine its own existence. Those within, however, seek to close the doors, to seal the glass panes; but these apertures, windows of the soul, look out longingly, ineluctably, onto the vastness and excitement of the empirical world—viewed, psychologically, as consciousness, awareness, knowledge.

Calling to mind Plato's "Allegory of the Cave," Maeterlinck's human souls are enchained in the closed world of their psyches, living out their mechanical existence in paradoxically visible, yet subterranean and vaulted, areas. The architectural archetypes they inhabit, like the human heart, function on various levels; there are gradations of vision. As in initiation mysteries (*initium* meaning "beginning" in Latin, and by extension, "to enter"), audiences may peer within these archetypes, into their various levels of introverted existence or multiple states of consciousness. The secrets learned during this period of discovery—as *The Intruder* and *Interior* unfold—are inexpressible, as were the mysteries of old, which, according to Aristotle, may not be learned but must be experienced. Maeterlinck's characters do not teach secret doctrines, but experience feelings, and during the course of the plays latent possibilities are realized and become acts. Knowledge is progressive and the tests undertaken in initiation rituals are laborious and painful, as they are in *The Intruder* and *Interior.* Only when new stages or new degrees have been reached in the inner organization of the psyche—or house—paving the way for a reorientation of the introverted architectural archetype, can consciousness be expanded.

THREE

James: "The Jolly Corner"

The Entrapped Shadow in the
Archetypal House

"The Jolly Corner" (1908), a short story by Henry James (1843–1916), fleshes out the thoughts, feelings, and psychological evolution of Spencer Brydon, an American expatriate, who at the age of fifty-six returns to his boyhood home in New York City. There he searches out that "other" segment of his personality, the youthful self he rejected when, thirty years earlier, he left his family and native land. Finally successful in his quest, he faces the lost aspects of himself in the archetypal construct of the house and is traumatized by the encounter.

From the psychological point of view, James's tale may be considered as a confrontation between *ego* and *shadow*. The ego, which is defined as the individual's ruling consciousness, attempts to cope with the shadow—that is, those factors within the psyche that the ego all too often fears and therefore fails to acknowledge. In Brydon's case, the shadow is identified with the feeling and instinctual domains, those areas which the overvalued thinking archetype that rules his consciousness is unable to control. The ego is understandably apprehensive—forever aware of the possibility of being sullied and perhaps even overwhelmed by what it considers to be a conglomerate of disorderly, disruptive forces within the personality. An individual divested of his shadow or one who is unable to accept it, as is true in Brydon's case, is not, however, really in possession of himself; his being is incomplete. Nor can his search for wholeness be effected without the help of a third force: an anima figure, that "unconscious feminine side of a man's personality."[1] It is the anima, personified in Alice Staverton, whom Brydon first knew when they were both young in New York, who will help him to forge the link between his ego and his shadow.

The "Jolly Corner" is Brydon's now-empty old home: the locus of the *agon*—the struggle. Each of the three sections into which James divides his story—all of which take place within the house—may be viewed as a stage in an initiation ritual, not unlike those practiced in the inner chambers of the pyramids, the seat of the ancient Egyptians' mystery schools. In fact, the protagonist himself suggests such an analogy in the simile he uses to describe his emergence as he steps out of his ancestral home, like a "traveller emerging from an Egyptian tomb."[2]

James, with his usual technical skill, leads the reader gradually and circuitously to the heart of the mystery, through the intricacy of the many large and small, close and remote chambers, rooms, halls, and passageways of Brydon's old home. Speaking through his protagonist, who is the central consciousness or suprapersonal authority relating the events in question, James proceeds methodically, always analogically. Brydon's eyes pierce wooden frames and lintels, doors and unlit chambers. An extension of the mind, his sight apprehends signs, veiled and mysterious abstractions, clusters of intellectualizations, ideograms, portents, floating correspondences. It is his optic nerves that transmit external stimuli to his cerebral system, translating them so as to arouse sensation and memory, which are then integrated into the narrative. James singles out feelings, thoughts, moods, circling each pertinently, conclusively, conveying multiple impressions and recording these sequences while at the same time seeking further clues that might reveal the secrets enclosed within the walls, ceilings, and floors of the empty old house. It is through Brydon's understanding, his sense of things and people, that visions are disclosed, framed, and projected into the story at the appropriate moment, determining its complex settings, scenes, and ramifications.

Oblique lighting is shed on the specific events singled out for scrutiny, thus revealing elusive, ever-altering points of view—fragments, glimpses, sparkles of light—each modulation imbricated into the next, thereby heightening ambiguities and fostering an uneasy climate of malaise, dread, even terror. Brydon's consciousness—his ego, in psychological terms—probes, penetrates, pierces the darkness in its attempt to immerse itself in the waters of the collective unconscious: that limitless transpersonal realm within which the individual may discover the treasures to nurture and heal an ailing, fragmented psyche.

Other famous authors—namely Oscar Wilde in *The Picture of Dorian Gray*, Edgar Allan Poe in *William Wilson*, Dostoevski in *The Double*, Samuel Beckett in *Krapp's Last Tape*, and Jean Vauthier in *The Character against Himself*, to mention but a few—have written of inner descents into the personal and collective past, and thereby projected inner onto outer space. The encounter dramatized in "The Jolly Corner" is different, however, in that its circlings are perhaps more constrained and its goal more obscure. James calls upon his protagonist to sort out and then become *aware* of his experiences by *feeling* into them. "The Jolly Corner" is a remembrance of abstractions and concretions, an "optical search" (p. 621) back into a banished world that stills but never immobilizes the passing of time, controls but never halts motion—a reach that bears down ever more powerfully on vanished youthful thoughts and sensations, personifying them and thereby increasing their dimensionality and power.

"The Jolly Corner" is an instance of the autobiographical transmuted into art. Born in New York City, James himself spent much of his youth in Europe, traveling with his parents, brothers, and sister. There he haunted museums and art galleries in England, Italy, and France, and was mesmerized by the civilization and culture he discovered: the style, beauty, and historicity of European and British art and architecture, the ancient churches, castles, estates, and gardens. Such man-made structures permitted James to relate to a variety of periods in time; they stood for continuity and permanence, a way of fixing perceptions, recording sensations, revealing a network of linked incidents.

It is interesting in this connection to note that at the outbreak of the Civil War, James suffered "an obscure hurt." The exact nature of the injury to his back is not known, but he was unable to fight in the Union Army, like his younger brothers, and the accident may have caused him to feel cut off from his compatriots. Remarkably enough, his father, Henry James, Sr., also suffered a severe accident in his youth, which resulted in the amputation of one of his legs, and even more incredible, both injuries occurred while fighting fires. In 1869 James returned to Europe, and in 1875 he decided to live there permanently. He visited America three times—the last time in 1904–1905, to "repair an injury and complete the unfinished experience of youth."

THE VOID: "WITHIN THE GREAT GAUNT SHELL"

The house on the jolly corner, as Brydon fondly alludes to it, is the *temenos,* the sacred ground on which the confrontation between ego and shadow takes place. Autumn is the period of the year when these events are enacted.

Described by Brydon himself as "the great gaunt shell," the empty house that he more and more obsessively visits after having lived for so many years abroad is comparable, psychologically speaking, to the inner void existing within his unconscious—that gaping maw into which he thrust his shadow when he departed from his native land. A fluid interplay is thus initiated between the house (the unconscious), Brydon's former self (the shadow), and his present self, the returning visitor (the ego). Brydon's compulsive visits to his old home are anal-agous to attempts to probe the timeless, spaceless region of the sub-liminal sphere. Each visit he makes to the house brings him closer to both the past and his shadow personality. Brydon had sought to smother within his psyche the memory of the very American individ-ual he once was: crass, aggressive, impulsive, instinctively acquisitive, uncultivated. It is this personality from which he chose to flee so many years before. Yet the shadow is in fact an intrinsic part of him. Like an unfed dog that grows angry, vicious, even murderous, when neglected and starved by its master, the shadow, when repressed and rejected, often becomes transformed into a ferocious, ravenous force. After denigrating and smothering what in his youth he considered to be negative, unworthy aspects of himself, Brydon devoted all his efforts to creating the image of the person he longed to be. While he was opting for restraint, for a cosmopolitan, poised, rational demeanor that would assure entry into sophisticated intellectual circles, that "other," the neglected shadow side of his personality, unbeknownst to him was increasing its demands—even becoming "monstrous," to use Brydon's own description of what his ego despises as unacceptable American traits. The new European Brydon is, however, top-heavy: he is overly intellectualized and cerebral; he has become dry and arid. Thus it is that his unconscious emerges, urging him in veiled terms to return again and again to his old home, to *re-collect* his childhood ex-periences, to renew the ties with his origins and to probe that ne-glected unknown void. For only by facing the abyss within can one penetrate to the very heart of being.

To the mystic, the word "void" connotes future potential. The void indeed contains all that existed prior to creation, when the cosmos "was without form, and void" (Gen. 1:2). For the Hebrew Kabbalist, therefore, this state of formlessness or void paradoxically implies plenitude. It is replete with *prima materia,* that is, invisible primal mat-ter made up of wave upon wave of what we would today term "sub-atomic" or "supergalactic" particles. To prove the veracity of their intuitions, the Kabbalists customarily had recourse to language: the Hebrew word for "nothingness" is *ain,* and for "I" (or "something"), *ani.*[3] By simply transposing a single consonant, the word "nothing" becomes "something." The same may be said to be true of Brydon. To him the vast vacant house becomes increasingly alive with amorphous matter, replete with invisible phantoms, feelings, and sensations. Gradually, however, the unformed matter takes on concretion, and in time it bristles with activity, transforming his old home into a sacred space capable of resurrecting a lost youth in highly charged sequential visions.

It is this very void, existent still in the "great gaunt shell," that Brydon has to face, the unknown collective unconscious so charged with potential life, a whole world existing before the *lux fiat*—prior to that concocted personality that Brydon superimposed on his earlier self when he went to Europe. The persona, or mask, that he manufactured for himself must have weighed heavily upon him for many a year before his return to his native land to experience the ritual of death and rebirth, to undergo a confrontation that would perhaps bring him expanded consciousness and the possibility of living out the rest of his days in a far more harmonious way.

For Brydon to experience his unembellished self, as the death/rebirth initiatory ritual prefigures, he must open the doors leading to the secret insalubrious realms in his collective unconscious. He must confront what his ego has hitherto condemned as detestable and reprehensible. Only thus can he gain understanding of his whole being and begin to evaluate the traits that lie submerged in his shadow. To sink into the deepest layers of the unconscious is not only difficult but dangerous, leading frequently to an eclipse of the ego—to a drowning of consciousness in subliminal waters that reduces the individual to insanity.

That autumn is the season of the year chosen by James for Brydon to begin his inner quest is not surprising. Brydon himself is in the autumn of life. Autumn is also the period when nature goes underground, seeking interior warmth and bequeathing bareness and emptiness to the exterior world. Brydon himself comments on the leafless trees outside his old home, their branches bare against the bleak sky like so many lonely skeletons.

Fear and trepidation, as well as expectation and elation, mark Brydon's visits to the house. He comments antithetically and by analogy about his experiences. He alludes to the visions of past time that erupt into his conscious existence as "traps for displeasure," particularly when focusing on his "overschooled boyhood" and his "chilled adolescence" (p. 604). The juxtaposition of such value judgments instills waves of affective response throughout his entire being.

Alice Staverton, his old friend, accompanies him on one of his early visits to the house. "As exquisite for him as some pale flower," she represents as anima figure the world Brydon abandoned by leaving America and acquiring his present persona (p. 606). In that she is an aspect of Brydon, she possesses some of his characteristics: she is discriminating, sensitive, and understanding. But in addition to these qualities, she sees beyond the world of appearances into the essence of things. Unlike Brydon, she is able to relate to the outside world, to other people, gently and lovingly. Always supportive, she involves herself in their lives when the need arises, withdraws when her presence is no longer needed. It is she who exudes not only warmth for Brydon but "pity." She knows what is "missing" in his life, what has been wounded and still bleeds.

As Brydon on his visits penetrates more and more deeply into his house, he seems to hear the very walls speak; he observes "the great blank rooms" where "absolute vacancy reigned," and a whole fantasy world is brought into existence. The uninhabited space becomes filled with roaming and pulsating spirits, palpable forces, "muffled vibrations." A "strange figure" appears to him as if from nowhere, "at a turn of one of the dim passages." It walks about, then suddenly vanishes from view. Brydon opens and shuts doors, one after another, removing barriers that prevent him from experiencing the fateful room, "shuttered and void" (p. 607–608), that he will ultimately discover.

The "great gaunt shell," the central image in Brydon's search, is filled with pulsating forces that are no more visible to the naked eye that Democritus's atoms as they move about, combining and recombining in constant progressions of changing configurations. Brydon's exploration of this void is filled with memories and figures, each of which draws him ever more deeply into the arcane world of his past existence. The shell imagery is particularly significant because of its connotations of protectiveness and containment. Shielding the living creature within it, a shell allows gestation to progress; it nurtures and cares for the entity it encloses. Aphrodite, let us recall, emerged from a shell thrust ashore by primal waters, and when she stepped onto land she brought love and beauty into the world. Once the shell no longer holds an occupant, however, it is no longer useful; it represents an old, outmoded way. Nevertheless, though seemingly without function, the empty shell is still able to *shelter* and contain. For Brydon, the shell of the house on the jolly corner holds all his youthful memories; it encloses the promise that his whole lost past will come forth anew and introduce him to those segments of his psyche—the American side of his personality—that until this juncture he has considered dormant and virtually useless.

After lying unused, untended, for so long, the house can only reflect the past; but it is the catalyst, the outside element, required to cause what has for all these years been hidden to act and react, thereby encouraging Brydon to pursue his quest. It is, however, not just an alteration in attitude but a specific type of effort that must come into being—the creation of a climate that will encourage the confrontation of ego and shadow. Only by re-collecting—in the Platonic sense, that is, perceiving anterior experiences and making them his own—can Brydon undertake the reshaping of his approach to life, to himself, and to the people around him. Only then can the overdeveloped cerebral side of his personality be reduced to its proper proportion.

Although the house is a preserver of past wisdom, memories, and traditions, it can only be experienced by Brydon in terms of a space/time continuum. It is also a *temenos,* an archetypal image in the true sense of the word. Each chamber or room circumscribes the scope of Brydon's vision, reduces its periphery, concentrates his focus on specific events and incidents in his early life. The atmosphere becomes steadily more dense, increasing in intensity during his twilight and midnight visits.

In darkness, the barriers erected by the rational world, their logical cause-and-effect dynamic, slowly diminish, allowing the unconscious to encroach. Emptiness and silence rule each of the rooms of the four-storied house, compelling the exterior world to yield its powers and recede. As evening by evening, night by night, Brydon penetrates this inner sanctum and hears only the sound of his own footfalls, the rhythm of his own breathing, his interest grows keener. Faintly at first, his inner world seems to become more palpable as he methodically listens to the reverberations of his own steps, hearing them echo for him alone in his brain, in keeping with the beat of the frenzied energy waves circulating throughout the secret spaces of his being. At certain moments Brydon feels he is participating in both past and present. Mysterious *eidola* seem to force him on. These atoms constantly in motion—considered by the pre-Socratic philosophers Democritus and Leucippus to be the foundation of all things—aggregate and congregate, forming images that Brydon senses and interprets according to his subjective needs. As each emerges into form, the associations it provokes trigger more and more recollections from the past; confusion takes over, beclouding the atmosphere and the sharpness of Brydon's thought processes.

Alone and in silence, he concentrates on the "odd echo," that "conscious human resonance" within his mind of which he becomes more and more aware; still-living forces seem to articulate their longings within the very beams and woodwork of the house and reverberate in his own heart. The words "echo" and "divination" used by James are particularly apt here (p. 609). Both lend an archetypal quality to the narrative, which is focused no longer on specific incidents and actual events, but upon transpersonal happenings.

As the echoes that Brydon hears set off energy patterns that vibrate throughout his being, as the reality of the past intrudes upon the present, sequences of associations activate the atmosphere; doors heretofore closed are opened—doors leading from the conscious to the unconscious realms. The floors, the stairs, upon which he treads become virtually consecrated ground; his footsteps are increasingly calculated to steer him closer to his goal, to the room where the final confrontation will take place. Increasingly a sense of urgency accompanies him during his progress through the house. Memories dormant for more than three decades are stirred, feelings aroused; incidents from his past emerge and acquire shape, form, scale, as if the lid from one in a series of boxes had been raised, permitting him glimpses of that "other" being he has sought to abandon.

The very ceiling, walls, floors, doors—an entire sensate world—take on contour, sound, and life. The feel in his hand of the old silver-plated knobs on the mahogany doors suggests "the pressure of the palms of the dead" and holds him in their thrall. Nearly three generations of his family had inhabited the house, and each "dead" object resurrected in his mind's eye contains for him worlds of past life. Brydon's thoughts and feelings pass from death to life, causing the cumulative power of the revitalized image to reach climactic force. As Brydon rakes up the "ashes" of his long-extinguished youth, he opens the shutters of the house, allowing light to penetrate and activate the surroundings, and the emotions that emerge each time he does so cause a blending of polarities. Abstractions take on solidity and weight; concrete energies pull and tug at Brydon, pursuing him like the inner furies that indeed they are.

Qualitative factors emerge as part of Brydon's probing search; his explications and rationalizations of the reasons for his departure from America seem interwoven with feelings of guilt and regret. Deeply haunted by the "ghost of perversity," the "other" within him, he seems more and more to require some potent force to allay his fears, to put to rest the haunting, gnawing scrapings that leave him so perturbed.

Nevertheless, Brydon inexorably pursues his quest; each night he steps carefully, fearfully, through the forest of correspondences and analogies provoked by what he recalls in each of the rooms he traverses. Remembrances of things past—of rugs, furniture, tapestries, receptacles—elicit specific emotions, moods, feelings in him. The very shapes of the chambers and rooms take on increasing meaning as memory transforms the inanimate past into the animate present, and the irrational takes precedence over the rational, the divine over the empirical, as "ineffaceable life" enclosed within the walls of Brydon's old home imprints its realities on his being. What are nonexistent objects to others—vase, carpet, chair, wallpaper—are visible to him as if produced by a magic wand. "For me it *is* lived in," he explains to Alice Staverton. "For me it *is* furnished" (p. 612).

The more contained Brydon's outer composure is, the greater are the inner gusts that agitate his subliminal world. His present existence is "absurd," the rational Brydon suggests. He can no longer negate or look at the irrational stirrings within him, those proddings that are tearing and tugging at some secret universe deep inside. That world of potential imponderables that Brydon set aside when developing his conscious, logical side is slowly being freed. Complacency and passivity no longer characterize him. As his inner climate alters, his vocabulary takes on greater fluidity and warmth, thereby plunging him into a whole new frame of reference. When visiting Alice Staverton and talking to her in front of her open hearth, his articulations are studded with restlessness, with fire, and he turns "to and fro between the intensity of his idea and a fitful and unseeing inspection" (p. 613).

Deep aggression flows into some of his statements: "*Not* to have followed my perverse young course—and almost in the teeth of my father's curse . . ." (p. 613). Implied here is a negation of all those values that he superimposed upon himself in his desire to become part of cultivated European society, and a need now to look within his own being and discover his discarded youthful individuality. Brydon has acquired a definite persona, a mask, an expression of cultured civility, of relatively prosperous serenity. What lurks stifled within him has remained there cleverly, concealed, unstirred, unruffled during all the time he was abroad. Now, however, having returned, his own feelings and emotions seem to have caught fire. He is aware of this and begins to translate the "fiery" feelings into flaming images; they ignite, engendering clusters of emotions intent upon liberation. More "heating," however, is apparently still needed to sear the barriers leading to what Brydon's ego considers an abyss, a fungal realm.

The very notion of mystery exerts its pull on Brydon. He pauses in his quest and ponders. What would he have been like, he wonders, had he remained in America? How would that youthful self have "turned out"? What would he have been like had he not "given up" his heritage and tried to conform to a cultured society? That self which he abandoned thirty-three years ago when he was teaching himself to censor words, acts, gestures, inner pulsations, to hinder or block their fluidity, had to be searched out and rediscovered. Brydon's persona weighs increasingly upon him, for he realizes, perhaps for the first time, that he has altered not only his life course but his very being to fit a construct fashioned by his intellect alone—an appealing yet appalling architectural edifice. To each facet of his personality he apportioned its proper place, relegating those characteristics that he regarded as unpleasant, sullied, fearsome, to some back room, where they were left unaired and forgotten. Now, however, Brydon feels impelled to seek them out, to dust them off, to let in waves of fresh air. He has hired Mrs. Muldoon to fulfill this function, to come in to clean the house and open the windows. What she is accomplishing outwardly, he will carry out in an inner way.

Brydon's destiny—his past, present, and future—seems to rest imprisoned within his old home, that archetypal empty dwelling. He uses a metaphor to concretize his thought when he speaks to Alice Staverton of his "strange *alter ego*," comparing it to a "full-blown flower" still living "in the small tight bud" (p. 614). His entire life course, then, seems still to exist in embryonic form within the house.

Alice Staverton is quick to seize hold of Brydon's image. As anima figure, she feels and senses what Brydon, a thinking type, only glimpses too lightly. A flower—say, for example, a rose—representing a feminine and ephemeral force, attracts others through its beauty and aroma; this same flower, however, may also repel by the thorns that lacerate any unsuspecting person who grasps them. Alice Staverton accepts both the positive and negative implications of Brydon's remark. The flower, she says, "would have been quite splendid, quite huge and monstrous" (p. 614). Being Brydon's anima figure—a protective, gentle, maternal image par excellence—she receives him in his entirety, as she does his image of the flower. Brydon, on the other hand, sees only the flower's "monstrous . . . hideous and offensive" sides (p. 614).

Alice Staverton's all-embracing vision, which is able to encompass both malevolent and beneficent qualities, reveals her archetypal nature. She emanates from a world beyond the qualitative and functional, the peripheral and differentiated. Neither personal nor impersonal, but rather transpersonal, she is the personification of that force which lives autonomously within the male unconscious, detached and distant when her presence is not requisite, but attentive and responsive when called upon and needed.

As Brydon reiterates his remorse for the "selfish, frivolous scandalous life" he now believes he had led, he obviously fears further encroachment from the characteristics his ego considers undesirable and destructive. "*He* isn't myself. He's the just so totally other person. But I do want to see him. . . . And I can. And I shall" (p. 615). Determined to forge ahead, his will is to be his guide, outwitting and outplaying any other characteristic that might impede him from experiencing his ordeal—that initiatory journey which is, in fact, to usher in a whole hidden dimension of anguish.

As Alice Staverton listens to Brydon's fears, she continues to play out her role as mediatrix—a supportive, warm, consoling anima figure. "You were born to be what you are," he tells her, underscoring her belief in the fulfillment of individual destinies, in "divine" needs

(p. 615). Like the echo he first encountered when he entered his old home, she will never impose her ideas on Brydon. She will bide her time, drawing him out as she replicates his soundings, hoping to distill and decant them all into his consciousness, and in so doing, to compel an inner dynamism to take hold, to gather momentum, to activate perception. "Their eyes met," James tells us, and as this new point of contact takes hold, it arouses in Brydon the feeling world and thus allows the anima to float about in his unconscious. Like a dream it issues forth its forebodings and terrors in emphatic vibrations, awakening hidden realms—subterraneanly buried prior to this moment—that are now ready to chant their litanies of progressively painful dirges.

THE AGON: THE STRUGGLE OF EGO AND SHADOW

The second phase of Brydon's death/rebirth encounter takes him ever more deeply into the exploration of his vacant, abandoned old home: it is there that he "incubates" his obsession. He is alone now, like the *mystai* of old, who sought to foster their occult awareness by withdrawing from the world into interior darkness. As the initiatory dictum states: "Visit the interior of the earth and through rectification you will find the hidden stone." That hidden secret sphere in ancient religious disciplines was found beneath the ground, within the pyramid itself; it is the very same domain that Brydon must discover, discern, and confront.

The true mystery of being can only be received and nourished in solitude and silence. To speak or to be accompanied by another person often diffuses and weakens those vital forces needed to grasp the ineffable, to realize the latent, to transform the manifest into action. The "short autumn twilight" of the "gathering dusk" seems to Brydon a particularly appropriate time for him to visit the house, perhaps because, unrecognized by him, it is the "lampless hour," when the thinking function recedes and dims and he can feel himself increasingly cut off from the hustle and bustle of the exterior world. His libido, thus channeled more deeply inward, is able to linger on the distant past in remote climes, listening and feeling the reverberations of a beating heart within the "great vague place" (p. 617).

The "glimmering light" that seeks to prolong the day casts a "deep crepuscular spell" upon Brydon, who becomes less and less consciously aware of his thoughts and actions. Submerged in the waning light, Brydon pursues his exploration in the rooms and passages of his mind; they inspire dread and chaos, those feelings imposed by the ancient Greek goddess of night, Nyx, the daughter of Chaos, who reigns during the nocturnal hours, covering the exterior world with blackness. It is in this lightless world that the burgeoning seed gestates, that dreams flourish—in all their pleasurable or nightmarish detail. The black nocturnal world invites chaos but also fosters "revelation," which mystics and psychologists alike look upon as a reconstitution of being and psyche, a repairing of those original injuries dealt in youth.

Shortly before midnight marks the time and setting of the next stage of the initiatory process: that halfway pause between one mode of existence and another, bringing new "vistas" to Brydon, fresh "reaches of communication between rooms and by-passages" (p. 617). That twelve o'clock should be selected as the starting point of Brydon's descent into his subliminal realm—his personal and collective past—is significant. Numbers are archetypal. They are not invented by the conscious mind but emerge from the unconscious, spontaneously, as does an archetypal image, when the need arises. Numbers arouse energy, foment a dynamic process; they are "idea forces," that is, concretizations or developments of virtualities—inner possibilities. They lie latent in the unconscious until consciousness experiences them in the form of images, thoughts, and typical emotional modes of behavior. In that numbers lend order to what might otherwise be considered chaotic, they endow an individual with a sense of security and in this manner may be considered as "archetypal foundations of the psyche."[4]

Duality comes into being. The sinuosities of Brydon's thinking function are not yet sufficient in themselves to afford him a rite of passage from the past. His remembrances must be linked, and powerfully so, to the long-buried feeling world if those authentic and natural responses within his psyche are to emerge from their smothered hiding place. When Brydon hears the click of his cane on the black-and-white squares of the marble floor in the entrance hall, it increasingly seems to him as if living forces are concretizing the polarities of the past and their ramifications—those forces of thinking and feeling, light and shadow, good and evil, cohabiting in his inner world. While he stands there he seems again and again to hear the "dim reverberating tinkle" that his cane recalls upon the black-and-white tiles of the marble floor; his "other life" beckons him like "some rich music." The whole domain of feeling is ushered in with this introduction of music: emotions touch him, memories move him, caught in those neatly designed and methodically engineered black-and-white marble squares. Other sonorities associated with the tinkle of bells as they resound "in the depths of the house" (p. 618) also call into existence a whole spiritual domain, that "mystical other world" that nourished Brydon and might have continued to do so had he not divested himself of his native scene and exiled himself from his land.

Brydon, placing his cane noiselessly away in a corner, feels the whole house to be like "some great glass bowl, all precious concave crystal, set delicately humming by the play of a moist finger round its edge" (p. 618)—a metaphor that includes the visible and invisible spheres and hence unites what had been disparate just moments earlier in the white-and-black tiles of the marble floor. The synesthetic experience of touch, hearing, and sight united in form and texture ushers Brydon into the center of his being. The crystal bowl takes on the iridescence and power of *scintillae*, sparks of light and fire, which represent libido, psychologically speaking, and now disclose a volatile condition. Light sparkles in its opacities, reflecting memories, secreting an entire "ghostly world." In so doing, this organic form acts as a catalyst, awakening those forces in Brydon's rational mind that heretofore he could not accept. The concave crystal bowl may be seen as a feminine image, an anima symbol, a containing entity, repository of all the lost love Brydon longed for and yet dreaded to find, expressive of those protecting, conserving elements he had sought to erase from his world along with all vestiges of the person he might have been.

In the same way that the plangent tone from the crystal bowl spreads its sound into seemingly uninhabited corners, plumbing hidden recesses within his understanding, clarifying role and function, the defense system he has erected within him to protect a weakly structured persona begins to topple. Brydon feels catalyzed by the sound from the crystal bowl; the combustible material in psyche and object merge. Like the silver doorknobs on the first floor, every similar detail sets off energic charges within him: mana, ushering in a whole sacred dimension. Indeed each room is now a sanctuary where souls from the past regain life, reshaping and blending emotions as they make their presences known. Introversion and meditation on Brydon's part—which the mystic practices in silence and darkness, as has already been indicated—encourage him, still in the thrall of his conscious self, to descend further into the transpersonal sphere, thereby enabling him to experience the empirical world from a more profound vantage point.

Energized by the images that have emerged before him, Brydon has recourse to the simile of a hunter "stalking" some "formidable beast in the forest" (p. 619). The image rings true; Brydon does indeed feel himself a hunter seeking out confrontations with his shadow or his "alter ego," poised and ready to entrap and kill it should the need arise. Brydon, the hunter, thus envisages himself in the jungle of his deepest inner realm—the untamed domain of the Great Earth

Mother. No longer part of the ordered, manicured world where logic and rationality prevail, he seeks to enter that disorderly vegetative region, that uncharted domain of dark, dangerous, uninhibited impulses. It is here that Brydon seeks to search out and hunt down his own past, using the "tremendous force of analogy" to approach his goal.

> He found himself at moments—once he had placed his single light on some mantel-shelf or in some recess—stepping back into shelter or shade, effacing himself behind a door or in an embrasure, as he had sought of old the vantage of rock and tree; he found himself holding his breath and living in the joy of the instant, the supreme suspense created by big game alone. (P. 619)

Brydon, seeking his prey, is excited at the thought of facing his "big game," the "Bengal tiger" as he calls it, but the attraction of the pursuit is mingled with dread. He adopts a vigilant course and inquires into as well as feels the whole gamut of sensations evoked by the "apparitional" forms confronting him—those shadowy presences which apparently once lived in the world of contingencies and now, like echoes, replicate their wants and needs in the clouded gloom of the unconscious.

There are periods during any mystical initiation process when the acolyte cannot pursue the ritual in a continuous and methodical manner: the strain is too great; the concentration needed too powerful. Similarly Brydon realizes that he must desist for a period if he is to survive the ordeal. Soma and psyche must have time to integrate the insights gained and the emotions experienced. He urgently needs the diurnal, or rational, sphere to help him clarify his perceptions. He shudders at the thought of going on into more esoteric realms, requiring, as it does, the opening of more and more doors. Yet he senses the meaning, in the true sense, of the word *esoteric* (we recall that it comes from the Greek verb *eisôtheô*, which means, "I make enter"). He will have to "make himself enter" into that world which for him sets off fear and trembling. Brydon has not yet achieved the degree of wisdom that comes from the expansion of consciousness, nor is he prepared for what must occur if he is to emerge whole and free, his fragmented psyche healed of its gaping division.

After an absence of three nights, Brydon again opens the closed shutters of the house. Light from the street lamps shatters the obscurity, dims the scintillae-charged memories, as Brydon gradually makes his way up the stairs to the top floors of the building. These may be likened to the intellect, the thinking function, which envelops him once again in the permanence of a secure world. "Above all in the upper rooms!—the sense of the hard silver of the autumn stars through the window-panes, and scarcely less the flare of the street-lamps below, the white electric lustre," endow him with courage to pursue his itinerary (p. 621).

James's imagery is particularly effective in replicating psychic happenings in those scenes where perspective becomes a vital factor. Objectivity, or at least a certain amount of it, now enters Brydon's inner world, enabling him to "dislocalise" the hitherto undervalued and hence feared and repressed instinctual realm. Prior to his ascent of the staircase, he gazes up at the skylight on the top floor. His eyes look up and down the stairway's multiple steps and levels, the activity suggesting that he is simultaneously measuring the depth of the various steps or levels within his own psyche. Archetypally, a series of ascending stairs is associated with ladders, particularly with Jacob's ladder, a sign of communication with the divine sphere—which is another metaphorical way of expressing the idea of intercommunicability between the unconscious and conscious worlds. To look upward, until now, has meant for Brydon dependence on rationality alone. At this point, however, it signifies preparing the way for a wilder, more inclusive view, for an increase in perspective and awareness, a readiness to penetrate the world he most fears—the instinctual domain. His ascent by implication paves the way for his descent, for the plunge into the collective unconscious.

Nevertheless, Brydon still needs the reassurance of the rational sphere, with its constructs, its limitations, its circumscribed vision, to use as a stepping-stone before his "reach" can transport him back still further to the small servants' rooms, which "multiplied, abounded in nooks and corners, in closets and passages, in the ramifications especially of an ample back staircase" (p. 621). What was jungle and uncultivated area in the hunter metaphor has now been transformed into an ordered domestic region able to feed and nourish his ego sufficiently to give it the strength needed for a real plunge into subliminal spheres.

Brydon looks to the rooms above, where he knows that the "other" force—his shadow—is awaiting him. "He's *there,* at the top . . . the fanged or the antlered animal brought at last to bay" (p. 623). The rational principle, the thinking factor, Brydon's pride and joy until now, recedes; dismay, doubt, dread, anger, are called forth. Brydon literally feels that "other" entity alive, lurking "somewhere unseen" within the empty house. He wonders whether he will have enough courage for the encounter. Although he claims he is not afraid, the phrase "the state of holding on" indicates the contrary, as do the words "stood firm." Mental reservations block his progress. Brydon closes his eyes as if blotting out the exterior world, gaining time to compose himself, to face "the terror of vision" (p. 624), the reality existing above. Reminiscent of those ancient Greek mystery rites when the waters of Lethe (forgetfulness) and of Mnemosyne (recollection) were imbibed prior to the actual enactment of the ritual of death and rebirth, Brydon feels himself slowly and painfully moving into the deepest and darkest of regions—a world inhabited by all sorts of venomous shapes that are capable of holding him in their grasp forever.

Having ascended to the top of the staircase many times before this last, decisive time, Brydon has learned that if he limits himself by thinking, probing, explicating, rationalizing, he will only prevent action and ensure stasis. His instinctual and spontaneous realm—that natural, impulsive world—must be left untouched if hidden dimensions are to reveal themselves. Only then will Brydon advance to "another station" and step forth from the crossroad before him (p. 628). Nevertheless, fear again intrudes. The "spell" lifts, as does the magic of the moment. Brydon cannot resist turning toward the outer world for solace; he starts his descent to the front entrance rather than opening the closed door leading to the fourth room—where he feels sure the encounter will take place. The comforting remembrance of the empirical realm takes hold; the rational sphere intrudes, allowing him to "hold on," rather than yield to the dizziness of imponderables.

Moments later, however, he realizes he must pursue his course, divest himself of all "profane" aids, which prevent him from searching out that living presence within him. He ascends. He feels himself to be in the "*most* immediate presence of some inconceivable occult activity" (p. 633). He descends several stairs, walks into another passage, experiencing a searing sensation, as if light beams were shooting through him, their silvery nimbi flooding him with powerfully shifting and expanding assaults. Darkness grows denser as he advances; penumbra takes on form and being. Then suddenly:

> Rigid and conscious, spectral yet human, a man of his own substance and stature waited there to measure himself with his power to dismay. This only could it be—this only till he recognised, with his advance, that what made the face dim was the pair of raised hands that covered it and in which, so far from being offered in defiance, it was buried as for dark deprecation. (P. 633)

Brydon faces his shadow, his adversary. He gapes at "his other self," and when he sees that, just as on his own hand, two of the specter's fingers have been cut away, dread overwhelms him.

> Horror, with the sight, had leaped into Brydon's throat, gasping there in a sound he couldn't utter; for the bared identity was too hideous as *his*, and his glare was the passion of his protest. The face, that face, Spencer Brydon's?—he searched it still, but looking away from it in dismay and

denial, falling straight from his height of sublimity. It was unknown, inconceivable, awful, disconnected from any possibility—! (P. 635)

The encounter is far too powerful for Brydon to view it equably. It seems impossible for this monstrous face, this "stranger," this unknown quantity, "evil, odious, blatant, vulgar," this "life larger than his own," this archetypal image, to be integrated into Brydon's psyche. The confrontation is of such a character as to eclipse Brydon's ego. The collective unconscious takes over with tidal velocity. No longer does darkness enclose Brydon's eyes, as in earlier images, but the doors to consciousness shut firmly. He faints dead away.

REBIRTH: THE SHADOW'S PARTIAL INTEGRATION

When Brydon returns to consciousness sometime later, the first thing he hears is the voice of Mrs. Muldoon. He then realizes that Alice Staverton, who is seated on the lowest step of the staircase, is holding his head in her lap, the position indicating the hold this anima figure now has upon him. A mediating force, suggestive of Dante's Beatrice and Petrarch's Laura, Alice Staverton symbolizes goodness and understanding for him; she is a warm and all-encompassing maternal figure—not out of keeping with the image of Mary in Michelangelo's *Pietà*, holding the dead body of Christ in her arms. Medieval iconography also comes to mind: the unicorn whose head rests on the lap of the virgin, underscoring the bridling and channeling of the instinctual realm by the supportive and innocently youthful feminine figure.

Brydon rests in the warmth and security of the anima figure. He has survived the "interminable grey passage" (p. 636) and returned from his "prodigious journey" with expanded "consciousness" and a strengthened ego, cleansed and purified by the inner waters of the collective unconscious. He gazes at Alice Staverton and understands for the first time the meaning of the heart—which is not only the rhythmic pulsating organ on which all human life depends but an archetypal entity that reaches deeply into the very essence of being, enabling relationships to take root, fostering emotional responses, allowing egotism and loneliness to dissipate now and then and be replaced by understanding, warmth, and gentleness. "Yes—I can only have died. You brought me literally to life," he tells her as she bends over to kiss him. "Oh keep me, keep me!" (p. 637) he pleads, still weak from loss of consciousness. Brydon has awakened not only to an awareness of his shadow but also to the positive nature of the eternal feminine principle so long ago severed from his conscious life.

The anima figure of Alice Staverton does not represent for him a concrete maternal force but rather a transpersonal archetypal being, welcoming both his conscious and unconscious spheres, healing the long separation between intellectual and instinctual. She has known from the outset, from the very first moment Brydon entered his home, that he would "persist" in his attempt to know his shadow. "You came to yourself," she utters and she "beautifully" smiles as she speaks. "Ah I've come to myself now—thanks to you, dearest" (p. 639), he replies as he recognizes and accepts the role she has played in his life: mediatrix, guide, inspiration—the one force that has helped him not only to find himself but to transform his arid world.

The breach, however, is not completely healed. Psychologically, Brydon still cannot accept that "brute, with its awful face—this brute's a black stranger. He's none of *me,* and even as I *might* have been" (p. 639). Alice Staverton, however, in her clear, loving, and compassionate way, has always understood that, like everyone else, he is a composite of opposites and that perhaps his dichotomy has proved to be more painful to him because of his great sensitivity. She cannot really conceive of any part of him as representing "horror," because she has for all these years loved him *plain.* "I had accepted him," she gently says; and then, when she realizes he does not accept himself completely—not yet at least—she murmurs to him, as if to a child, "And he isn't—no, he isn't—you!" as he draws her to his breast (p. 641).

In this technically perfect tale, James, using the archetypal image of the house, takes his readers on a literary and psychological pilgrimage to the center of being. The house, with its multitudinous rooms and chambers, large and small, its corridors and inner stairways, provides a perfect metaphor for the protagonist who seeks to come to terms with what he has abandoned and most fears: his shadow world, which for Brydon means the unexplored, eruptive, uncontrollable side of being. He is impelled into his inner regions by his anima, that feminine principle also neglected and cast aside by him, so busy has he been in shaping a persona for the European community with which he sought to associate himself. Drawn ever deeper into the coils of that vacant, gaunt shell of his old home, he finally succeeds in encountering its former occupant, and, as a result, a traumatic reshuffling of unconscious contents takes place. After regaining consciousness, Brydon gazes into the empty space before him, recollecting once again and recognizing those fragmented factors within his psyche. More warmly disposed to them than ever before, he says simply, "I was to have known myself" (p. 639), summing up with graceful understatement the pain that accompanies understanding.

FOUR

Ansky: "The Tower of Rome"

An Architectural Archetype of the Self-Made Man

"The Tower of Rome," by S. Ansky, has been described as "a fearful and wondrous tale about a magic tower with four portals and an iron crown and blades of grass that did not wither."[1] Religious doctrines are secreted within the archetypal tower image: those of Hebrew mystics in general and the Merkabah religious sect in particular. A psychological experience is also hidden in Ansky's tale: the dangers involved when the ego of the self-made man no longer evolves but inflates. Unable to learn from experience, he reacts mechanically to the events in which he participates, in keeping with his personality type. In so doing, he vanishes as an individual and what remains is the collective force: the archetype of the ever-demanding and possessive, power-hungry transpersonal ruler.

Ansky, whose real name was S. Z. Rappaport (1863–1920), was born in Vitebsk, Russia. Moved by the suffering, poverty, and persecution of his people and of humanity at large, he joined the Haskalah, a movement of enlightenment among Jews of Eastern Europe. Influenced by the political and economic doctrines of the *narodniki,* who were agrarian socialists, he decided to live among the Russian peasants. He worked at various jobs until, in 1892, he was forced to flee Russia for political reasons. He went to Germany, Switzerland, and France, remaining in Paris for six years as secretary for Piotr Lavrov, a revolutionary philosopher. In 1905 he returned to Russia and joined the Socialist Revolutionary party, but spent his leisure time writing tales based on the legends he heard around him. From 1911 to 1914 he traveled to numerous villages in Volhynia and Podolia (which are now in the Ukraine), gathering material on the Jews as people, an occupation that brought him great satisfaction.

"The Tower of Rome" deals with an eternal problem: that of maintaining balance when worldly success has been achieved. As such, it is mythical in stature. The story takes place "ages and ages" ago in Rome, the capital of Edom, a city founded by Esau's descendents (Gen. 36:1) and not to be confused with the capital of Italy. According to historical and biblical texts, the Edomites were known as the traditional enemies of the Israelites. Ezekiel excoriated them (25:12–14), as did Jeremiah, when he predicted that the House of Edom would be consumed like a flame (25:15–29). In a mystical context Edom was said to be ruled by Samael, the Celestial Prince of Darkness, associated with Satan, whereas Israel was guided by the Celestial Prince Michael. With the coming of the Messiah, it was believed—after Edom's fall— the Holy One would deliver the multitudes to his radiant light.[2]

"The Tower of Rome," then, is replete with Merkabah mystical symbology and imagery. Few facts are extant concerning the origins of this hermetic religious group. We do know that the sect existed during the period of the Second Temple and that the doctrine of the Merkabah mystics revolved mainly around Ezekiel's vision: the perception of the mysteries of the Throne Chariot and the Divine Glory.[3] (See Ezek. 1.) The Throne Chariot, as described in Ezekiel's vision, refers to the "pre-existing throne," or archetypal throne within which all forms of creation exist.[4] When, therefore, the soul of a mystic ascends to the celestial court (after practicing such disciplines as prayer, fasting, study, and meditation) it perceives the Throne Chariot and the Divine Glory and experiences religious ecstasy. (Mystics speak of ascending or descending as the same, since linear time concepts do not exist in the space/time continuum in which the visionary undergoes the numinosum.)

The archetypal tower in Ansky's tale is of "indescribable beauty," and its "four portals facing the four sides of the world" (p. 3) represent a mystery. Since time immemorial these portals have been shut "with iron bolts, and locked with iron locks." Each new emperor, in keeping with tradition, hangs "a new lock on each portal," symbolically assuring the nation's continuity and security. One day a "man of common descent" who has "raised himself from the dust to the highest rank" is asked by the princes, lords, and stargazers of the land to become the next emperor. He agrees, providing they yield to a request that he will disclose to them only after his coronation. So firmly do they believe in the wisdom of this self-made man, and in his ability to bring prosperity to their land, that they concur. He is made emperor, after which he informs them of his intent to enter the tower. Although they fear punishment for such transgression, those who chose him to be their emperor have no other alternative but to yield to his demand and call a locksmith. The emperor enters alone.

The archetypal tower in Ansky's tale is a living mystery, a formalized perception of the godhead. That access to it should be denied all the people of Edom including the emperor is perfectly understandable, since they are unacquainted with the religious disciplines involved in the initiation rituals affording access to higher spheres. To reveal the cosmological and cosmogonic systems contained within the tower would be to court disaster. Such arcana might be misinterpreted by the unindoctrinated, and the knowledge gleaned could be used for the benefit of one rather than for humanity at large, thereby distorting the very essence of the lessons to be learned.

Viewed psychologically, the tower may be looked upon as an image of the Self: the totality of the psyche. As such, it is a complex of opposites, endowed with the ability to see into the world of contingencies and beyond it, into the invisible and nonmaterial domains that flow into it from both above and below. Let us recall that for the mystic everything within the universe is linked: "The Lord made this world corresponding to the world above, and everything which is above has its counterpart below . . . and yet they all constitute one mystery."[5] The ego (the center of consciousness), if aware of its strengths and weaknesses, psychologically speaking, may penetrate the collective sphere, the Self (the totality of the psyche), and be nourished by such an encounter. Then it can bring balance and harmony to what previously might have been a distorted or chaotic sphere. During such a period of interchange, the ego's latent qualities, of which it is still unaware, may be brought to consciousness. But dangers are also present. When the ego is either unprepared or weakly structured, it may not be able to deal with the Self, an infinite power; it may be submerged by this force. An eclipse of the ego, or a drowning of consciousness, may lead, as we have seen, to insanity or death.

That the emperor seeks to enter the tower indicates a need on his part to expand his consciousness so that he is not dominated by his power drive. It also suggests a desire on his part for additional conquest and in this connection is reminiscent of the tower of Babel myth, in which the intention to build a link between earth and heaven is a metaphor for humankind's desire to rise above the common level and reach deeply into divine spheres.

The emphasis on the number four in Ansky's tale is significant. Numerology was an important factor in Merkabah mysticism. The four portals facing the four sides of the world represent the four letters of God's secret name: YHWH, or Yahweh (the Tetragrammaton), the supreme mystery revealed to no mortal. From a psychological standpoint, we may say that the four letters standing for God's secret name may, under certain conditions, activate energy charges, originating in the archetypal nature of the letters and their equivalent numbers.

When such powers are triggered, spiritual light flows forth into the worshiper's being; in like manner, the Self is said to energize the ego. From a mystical standpoint, we may assume that if the charge is overly powerful, the soul attempting to witness an epiphany will be struck down by this very force. If the worshiper is initiated into the arcana of the supernal spheres through prayer and meditation—the "knots" and "garments" binding and protecting the soul—he will most likely not be swept away by the tremendous force of the numinous experience. The ego must be protected, and must always be aware of its rightful place within the totality of the psyche, so that the energy embedded in the archetypal letters and numbers, rather than flooding the ego, will decant its radiance slowly, allowing the individual to absorb it in nourishing portions. The mystic, prepared to receive and perceive the Throne Chariot and the Divine Glory, as depicted in Ezekiel,[6] will benefit from the ecstatic experience granted him; so, too, will the inroads made by the ego into the Self expand consciousness and endow it with the awareness of latent attributes, which may now be concretized in the empirical world.

The number four used throughout "The Tower of Rome" may also allude to four religious ways of approaching the Torah, a document referring, strictly speaking, to the first five books of the Bible, which the orthodox believe were given both orally and in written form by God to Moses on Mount Sinai. Mystics, however, consider the Torah as containing God's revelation; as such, it is a living organism within which exists divine life.

The four religious approaches to the Torah—literal, moral, allegorical, mystical[7]—may be complemented by four psychological equivalents, C. G. Jung's four types: thinking, sensation, feeling, and intuition. The literal path leading to the Torah experience may be compared to the thinking approach, which calls upon the intellect and its formulas to guide the way to a deeper understanding of the work studied. The moral road may be identified with the sensation approach, which adapts to conventional reality and adheres to its dicta. The allegorical road proceeds through feeling: it is sensitive to human needs and envisages relationships in terms of images and symbolic figures. As for the mystical attitude, it may be said to be closest to the intuitive way. A person with this attitude perceives connections among elements that to others seem unrelated and envisages the whole universe as a cohesively linked phenomenon.

Emphasis on the number four may also indicate yet another need: to experience the fourfoldedness of the psyche, that is, its archetypal foundations. Based on the quaternity principle, such an image may serve to balance what is imbalanced, to reestablish an "original order" that exists within every psyche but must be discovered by each individual in his or her own way.[8]

By any measure, the religious and psychological condition of Ansky's emperor and his people leaves much to be desired. The lords, princes, and stargazers who have chosen their new emperor—a self-made man—to be their leader, without reflection, have indicated an abdication of their thinking function. It is no wonder that they feel anguish and terror when the emperor reveals his intention to overthrow the status quo. They have leaped into a situation they are unprepared to handle; they have behaved headlessly, so to speak. To follow such a course is to divest oneself of a most precious attribute: consciousness. It is this factor that makes it possible for an individual to become aware of himself, to discover his roots, identity, and way of life. Without questioning, and simply on faith, the Edomites hope that one man will enhance their empirical situation. That is, they resort to a kind of hero worship, attributing divine qualities—those of a redeemer—to a flesh-and-blood being. The Edomites have thus indulged themselves in a way strictly forbidden to Jews. And so, Ansky's story is an added warning to Jews, who have too many times been led to spiritual oblivion by false messiahs: one of the most dangerous being Sabbatai Zevi (1625–76).

The emperor who seeks to rule the world may be envisaged in Ansky's tale as the ego identifying with the archetype of the Self. By seeking greater power through yielding to his unconscious drive, he is relinquishing human life experience, divesting himself of a sense of himself as an individual and thus courting disaster.[9] To cut oneself off from earthly and personal needs and to live exclusively in the transpersonal sphere encourages a condition of alienation. As a thinking type, in the narrowest sense of the word, the emperor understands and figures out, in the most methodical manner, the steps necessary to reach his goal. What he fails to view, however, is the picture as a whole, the dangers involved in the course he has chosen to follow. He enters the tower alone, despite the warnings and fears of the people who chose him, and during the course of his four visits to the four portals he has four visions. These are designed to alter his state of consciousness, to heighten his awareness, so that he may experience both a subjective and objective view of life, thereby allowing the individual (ego) and the emperor (collective) to function in the most positive way throughout the life process.

THE FIRST PORTAL: THE IRON CROWN

When the emperor enters the first portal of the tower, he sees an inner space reminiscent of the Garden of Eden, with trees and plantings all about. Unlike the paradisiac image, however, the center area has a pool of blood, upon which floats an iron crown. Hands, interwoven "like the roots of an ancient oak tree," reach out toward this symbol of authority from the ground surrounding the pool of blood (p. 5).

In the first vision, nature is beautiful, as it is in the Garden of Eden: ordered, contained, representative of the patriarchal sphere, where continuity and a sense of serenity prevail. The cultivation of a predominantly vegetal kingdom, as the trees and plantings indicate, represents the beginning of a cycle, an unevolved psychological level that may be associated with uroboric existence: the ego living in a *participation mystique* with the Self. Under such conditions, the ego is cared for, nurtured, wanting nothing. It contains, however, the potential for evolution. This garden or *pardes* scene refers, for the Hebrew mystic, to a domain in which superior or esoteric knowledge is concealed; the entire destiny of both the individual and the collective exists within this domain, and it is incumbent upon the emperor, in this instance, to discover and probe this hermetic knowledge and make it his own.

Never varying in his ego-driven ways, however, the emperor fails to stray from his single focus, his earth-oriented *idée fixe*. He will, therefore, look upon the scene in a *literal* fashion: his approach will be that of a *thinking* person, experiencing everything at face value, without ever attempting to understand those elements contained *within* or lying beyond the image or object per se. Never once does he consider what is invisible or hidden within the structure of the forms he sees. He is always an outsider, an observer of an unfolding spectacle, detached from the profound meaning of what is taking place. His thinking function in this context is therefore restrictive, limited to increasing his obsessive need for power and hence blocking out a whole other frame of reference. His entire life is based on a minuscule obsession, but for him it is all-encompassing.

The emperor's eyes are drawn progressively to the center of the vision: to the most highly charged area, the pool of blood. Representing life, passion, sacrifice, the irrational, blood is considered the sun's earthly counterpart. As such, it is a catalyst, an energizer, psychologically speaking, driving one on and on. The most precious of all offerings when spilled in war or during religious rituals, symbolically or otherwise, this energy brings enlightenment to some when it is channeled, but when unguided, it leads to death. (The meaning of the pool of blood will not be revealed to the reader at this point.)

The iron crown floating on the pool of blood stands for power and energy and refers to the throne symbolism of Merkabah mystics and Kabbalists (students of esoteric knowledge) in general. According to their cosmological and cosmogonic beliefs, based to a great extent on the *Sefer Yetsirah* (Book of creation) and the *Zohar* (Book of splendor),[10] the crown alludes to the Ten Sefiroth (see fig. 1). The Sefiroth are viewed as emanations of an unknowable and hidden divinity *(En-Sof* in Hebrew) in the manifest world. The crown is the first and the highest of the Sefiroth. The ten Sefiroth (or ten elementary or primordial numbers) represent the deepest layers of mystical consciousness, for it is within them that God exists in his infinitude, without qualities or attributes. The ten numbers, or emanations, allow humankind to perceive or experience God (the absolute) in the differentiated sphere. Conceived as a process, the Sefiroth, or the ten aspects of God's hiddenness, may be understood in their limitless nuances and gradations; each individual approaching these spheres of being reacts to them according to his or her own psychological type and the depth of the projections involved.[11]

The highest Sefiroth, then, encompassing all of God's mystical qualities, is referred to as the "Crown of the Holy King" or the "Supreme Crown" *(Kether Elyon)* of God. As the supreme emblem of divinity, it is a metaphor for an unmanifested force, an unfathomed aspect within the psyche. In that the crown usually sits on the head, on top of the body, it stands for consciousness—preeminence. A diadem that shoots out its beams or rays of light in spiritual and psychological energic patterns exists as a mediating force between celestial spheres and is thus incomprehensible to mortals—except to the most evolved, and even then, only in glimpses. What may be comprehensible to the mystic on an occult plane, and to the ordinary person on a psychological level, are the feelings and thoughts these *scintillae,* or sparks of light, emerging from the crown image trigger during the course of a numinous experience.

In that the crown represents divinity (the Self, psychologically), it stands for the world of the absolute: transcendent, circular, and eternal. Its visible form, however, exists in the empirical world, and as such it unites spiritual and human domains. So, too, may the exposure of the ego to the Self activate what exists in a potential state within the individual's unconscious. In such a limitless space it may bathe in wonderment, expanding consciousness and awareness. By the same token, it may also be blinded by this supernal force.

That the crown is made of iron rather than of gold indicates the role it is to play in Ansky's story. Metals are usually associated with planets, and iron is attributed to Mars, the god of war. Violence then, may be expected in "The Tower of Rome": enormous activity, a power struggle, perhaps even a cataclysmic event. Such an assumption is given greater credence by the fact that the crown lies atop a pool of

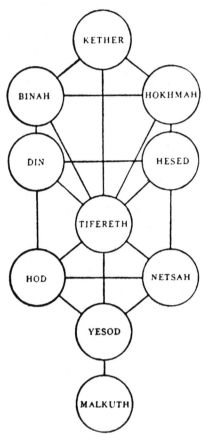

FIG.1. The Ten Sefiroth. The ten spheres of divine manifestation, in which God emerges from his hidden abode. (1) *Kether Elyon:* the "supreme crown" of God. (2) *Hokhmah:* the "wisdom" of the primordial idea of God. (3) *Binah:* the "intelligence" of God. (4) *Hesed:* the "love" or mercy of God. (5) *Gevurah* or *Din:* the "power" of God, chiefly manifested as the power of stern judgment and punishment. (6) *Rahamim* or *Tifereth:* the "compassion" of God, to which falls the task of mediating between the two preceding Sefiroth. The name *Tifereth* ("beauty") is used only rarely. (7) *Netsah:* the "lasting endurance" of God. (8) *Hod:* the "majesty" of God. (9) *Yesod:* the "basis" or "foundation" of God. (10) *Malkuth:* the "kingdom" of God, usually described in the *Zohar* as the *Keneseth Israel,* the mystical archetype of Israel's community, or as the *Shekhinah.* (Chart reprinted by permission of Schocken Books Inc. from *Major Trends in Jewish Mysticism* by Gershom Scholem. Copyright © 1941 by Schocken Publishing House, Jerusalem. Copyright 1946 Schocken Books Inc., New York; Copyright © 1954 Schocken Books Inc., New York. Copyright renewed.)

blood, indicating the locus of the creative energy involved in the image: "the expansive principle of power."

The hands reaching toward the crown express extreme activity: stretching, yearning, attempting to grasp something. Hands are the sign of dominion, justice, power, aggression, and when invoked by a spiritual force, they take on magical or religious value. To be touched by God's hand is to acquire divine power: Yahweh's hand touched Jeremiah's mouth before he preached; when Elijah was on Mount Carmel he saw a light cloud arising from the sea and felt Yahweh's hand upon him. In such images, the hand is comparable to the eye, indicating knowledge and energy.

For the emperor, the seeking and pleading hands reaching toward the crown—that central point—indicate ego striving to apprehend a forbidden "sublime" power. In that they all point toward one direction, one goal, channeling their efforts toward an area outside of themselves, they are expelling libido through projection, seeking a symbol, an object, upon which they may heap all their miseries and needs. To concentrate on the creative center outside of oneself (in meditation, for example) sometimes brings equilibrium after years of spiritual discipline. Here, however, the hands reaching forth seem to be divesting individuals of libido, emptying out what is essentially theirs: weakening their egos. These hands, we should mention, are minus heads and bodies—nonhuman. They are reaching out into God's hiddenness, or divine presence, as it exists in the iron crown: an inaccessible zone.

That the hands are interwoven like the roots of an ancient oak tree indicates the complexity of their needs. The tree, representative of a triurnal sphere, reaches down into the earth, that is, the unconscious; its trunk stands visible in the terrestrial sphere, encouraging one to become conscious of one's earthly existence; its branches and leaves, however, are stretched heavenward, disclosing a desire to relate to divinity. The tree, therefore, represents sustenance, strength, stature, security, and continuity, and plays a role in connecting earth and heaven, the spiritual and the real, the conscious and unconscious domains. But the hands the emperor sees emanating from the earth do not rise straight as does a tree. On the contrary, they are horizontal, indicating their inability to encounter the world of air and spirit. In that they lack heads and bodies, they are devoid of proliferating and generating power, as well as perception and *gnosis* (knowledge). As such, they remain enslaved to their blindness—rooted in their obsessive *idée fixe*.

The vision as a whole (garden, pool of blood, crown, hands) is round and hence takes on the attributes of a mandala: a metaphor for the state of wholeness or psychic integration the emperor and his people so badly need. By moving into the center of an image (or of a problem, psychologically speaking), one transfers one's attention from exterior to interior questions, from the multiple to the unified, space to spacelessness, time to timelessness. The mystic, as he centers on the crown metaphor, the innermost point within the concentric circles envisaged here (garden, pool, crown), penetrates another sphere of being and in so doing gains nourishment. As viewed by the emperor, however, the iron crown may not be an emblem of God's hiddenness (or the Self's limitlessness) but a power that he identifies with and seeks to arrogate to himself. The Bible warns against such inflation: "For he said, Thou canst not see my face: for there shall no man see me, and live" (Exod. 33:20).

THE SECOND PORTAL: THE FLAME AND THE MYSTERIUM TREMENDUM

In sharp contrast to the first experience, which was filled with light, the emperor gropes his way into an inner sanctum that is bathed in darkness. He bends down and feels human bodies beneath his feet; much to his surprise, they are warm and odorless.

The darkness prevailing here may be equated not with gloom or evil, but with undifferentiated matter, primordial chaos, a germinal condition that mystics allude to as nothingness (*obscurum per obscurius*). It is, psychologically, the lowest of experiential conditions, a paradigm for undeveloped potential. Hands were visible in the previous image; here there are only motionless bodies, functionless blobs. That these bodies are still warm indicates their livingness, but they are existing in a dormant state, unconscious of their condition. Like animals, they lie on the ground, underscoring how unevolved and passive they are. Without the flame of divinity, without that energic factor which takes one inward, leads one to the discovery of one's individuality and the mystery of existence, these human masses of bones and flesh know nothing and therefore may easily be trod upon.

Suddenly the emperor sees "a host of candles burst into flame," and the blackened inner space is transformed into light. A temple "of wondrous splendor" appears, its cupola pointing heavenward, and the dead rise to their feet and begin praying. Their ardor is such that "their faces ... blaze and sparks [fly] from their lips."

The blazing flames are an emergence of supernal light: an epiphany. Psychologically, the immense energy involved in the vision flows forth, activating spirit and psyche, sublimating what had heretofore been merely terrestrial valuation and preoccupations and passive existences. The numinosity of this dazzling radiance (the spiritual power known as *pneuma, ruach*) represents the outpouring of enormous feeling, transforming dormant or dead factors within the psyche—potential—into active and positive forces. Passion is born where a once lifeless condition had prevailed; ecstasy, where indifference had dominated. The medium within which energy is dispensed in this vision indicates the power of the archetype: man in prayer (ego), longing for nourishment from divinity (Self).[12]

A temple where God is received and honored is revealed during the visionary experience, underscoring the depth, rootedness, universality, and timelessness of the emotions triggered. According to Philo and Flavius Josephus (and this was the orientation of the Merkabah mystics as well), a temple—Solomon's temple being the prototype—was a figurative representation of the cosmos: the seat of worldly and celestial rapprochement and experience.

What is of extreme significance in this second vision is the resurrection of the dead during the prayer sequence: a paradigm of the Kabbalist's belief in transmigration of the soul—the *Gilgul*—that aspect of Judaism which gives the devout hope of overcoming their dreadful terrestrial conditions in a future existence. In Ezekiel we read: "I will open your graves, and cause you to come up out of your graves, and bring you into the land of Israel" (37:13). Physical as well as spiritual resurrection will come about for the righteous because they are inhabited by an inner fire—the divine *scintillae*. Psychologically, one may say that those who are catalyzed, those who seek to experience greater awareness and deeper penetration into the Self through continuous probing and questioning, will experience insight and enlightenment radiating from the divine sparks that permeate their inner world. It is in this manner that increased consciousness is brought to them and that psychological evolution comes to pass.

That prayer may become fire, that inactivity and a deathlike condition may be transformed into fervor and livingness, is a spiritual and psychological truth: "And I shall put my spirit in you, and ye shall live" (Ezek. 37:14). The psychic energy invested in praying became such a powerful force for the limp bodies in the inner sanctum that it ignited into flame. In the Bible, fire is associated in many instances with the word of God: "The voice of the Lord scattereth flame of fire" (Psalm 29:7); "Is not my word like as a fire . . . ?" (Jer. 23:29). Words do burn, sear, activate those who listen, feel, and understand. The incredible intensity of words, their pith and pitch, and the libido aroused by the archetypal image of beings in prayer, paved the way for the epiphany: this powerful vision of a Redeemer. Such an image, psychologically speaking, is a symbol of the Self; it reflects and concretizes an inner generative force that belongs to the worshiper and is brought out into the differentiated world as a result of the ego/Self tension: the mortal attempting through prayer to gain access to transcendental spheres.

Prayer may be likened at times—and is in this second vision—to prehypnotic autosuggestion. Under such conditions the ego's rational and conscious views are obliterated, and the barrierless unconscious or collective aspects of the psyche take over. The recitation of prayer, particularly when accompanied by certain breathing techniques or the sounding and pronouncing of specific words or numbers, leads some acolytes to participate directly in an ecstatic experience. It is at this point that the irrational and numinous bring on a *mysterium tremendum*.[13] The "awful mystery" surrounding God's majesty, as revealed in the *Zohar*, fixes itself in the spirit and pysche of those present. "In every word [of the *Zohar*] shine many lights."[14] Such luminosities become visible to the worshiper, act upon him, trigger excitement within his psyche. Prayer in this instance becomes a magical key; the words unlocking the doors leading to pleromatic spheres—the center—thus allowing the soul to ascend/descend into its own outwardness/inwardness in the godhead (Self).

A strange psychological situation comes to pass during such heated religious experiences. The energy activated during prayer fluidizes what is fixed, thereby enabling it to reconnect in fresh patterns. During this powerful archetypal experience, the ego is exposed to the divine life underlying creation—the Self; not as an alienated force, but bathing within its nutritive or "baptismal" waters, experiencing sustenance and exposing itself to new ways in which it may approach the life process once consciousness returns.

The angels the emperor sees in his second vision are carrying "in their wings a splendid man in white garments," whose "face is radiant"(p. 6). Viewed as messengers, divine spirits, incorporeal intelligences, and formed from the breath and power of God, angels are hosts of the Great Spirit, presences in his celestial court.[15] As such, they are considered intermediaries between God and his creation, synthesizing lower and upper spheres, functioning in both a changeless and changeable world, transpersonal and empirical realms. At home in divinity's domain, they function accordingly in a nonmanifest manner: as psychological impulses, feelings, intuitions, insights. When experienced in the empirical world, as in this vision, these winged pneumatic beings, souls of sorts, help humankind work out events, and thus they may be looked upon at times as patterns of behavior or archetypes.[16]

Angels have been associated with the Torah. Both were mystically conceived; both are the "living incarnation of divine wisdom which eternally sends out new rays of light" in keeping with the universe's cosmic laws.[17] Like the hiddenness within the Torah, which is exteriorized to some extent when divinity is reacting to the needs of individuals or groups, so angels are brought into being in response to spiritual and psychological lacunae. In the case of the emperor and his people, the vision of the descending angels indicates a fundamental inability to relate to the upper spheres; psychologically, this is a separation of consciousness from the unconscious domains. Ego-driven, the emperor functions impulsively, dominated as he is by the archetype of the self-made man. In so doing, he rejects the wholesome life experience, his commitment to himself and humanity. He also reveals an inability to cope with the here-and-now, always projecting outward, interested only in his next conquest or port of call.

The being in the "splendid white garments" could be identified with the Messiah as described in Ezekiel: "upon the likeness of the throne was the likeness as the appearance of a man above upon it" (1:26). So powerful a need and expectation that God would reveal himself was involved in the experience that the worshipers, psychologically speaking, were emptying their conscious minds of all extraneous material, transferring empirical attitudes and notions into the collective unconscious and hence activating archetypal images in huge, wavelike force. The vision of the godhead was thus concretized: a concentration of libido directed the energies of the worshipers inward, to the depths of their unconscious, stirring those inner waters and ejecting certain powers outward in the form of archetypal images. When a person interiorizes or exteriorizes libido so powerfully, it dredges up humanity's archaic heritage. In the process, what is amorphous may be transformed—and is in this image—into a religious or psychic reality, ushering the God-figure into being.[18] A "world of punctiform lights" is born in this epiphany.[19]

For the Merkabah mystics and Kabbalists, garments represent the outward appearance of divinity's inwardness: a concrete image used to cover what is hidden within the godhead. Garments, then, are metaphors used to clothe the name of God (as this is experienced in letters, sounds, numbers, rhythms). God's name in this case is woven into the very texture of the white garment worn by the being the angels bring to earth, endowing it with secret knowledge and power: the thread of the fabric underscoring the interrelatedness of phenomena, the web of illusion spun by the world of sense impression. Each worshiper, therefore, approaches the garment as he would a sacred force or object, always in keeping with the depth of his feeling and the degree of his understanding.

Just as the radiant being in this vision is clothed in a white garment, and letters or numbers are used to denote the godhead, so the Torah is covered with cloth. Within its infinite layers of material existence are White Fire and Black Fire, representing the greatest mystery of all. For the Merkabah mystics and Kabbalists in general, the original text of God's word given to Moses on Mount Sinai was revealed in White Fire and remains invisible to mortals. Only the letters made visible in the oral Torah may be made known to human beings: by impressing Black Fire, or black letters, on the white parchment of the torah scroll. After the coming of the Messiah, the White Torah, or White Fire, will be revealed.

The fervor and excitement of the prayer experience has made the epiphany possible. When the prayers cease, darkness again permeates the atmosphere. Many repetitions of this supernal experience will occur during morning and evening prayers, thereby reinforcing the cyclical death/rebirth phenomena occurring in nature and in human life. It is then that the great cosmic cycle (Shemittah) that Hebrew mystics believe in creates and re-creates an endless and changeless world of emanation that pursues its course in every level of experience in a space/time continuum.[20]

THE THIRD PORTAL:
THE TREASURE HARD TO ATTAIN

The emperor now enters a circular room; the walls are inlaid in black stone and in the center lies a golden coffer worked in the most wondrous of ways. Circular spheres may indicate celestial regions, implying that which is universal, eternal, without beginning or end. The mandala image viewed in this third vision is somewhat reminiscent of the pool, crown, and hands of the first vision and corresponds to a continuous round, a psychological process: the inner being always in a state of *becoming*. Like the wheel of Ezekiel (1:15–19), a rotating sphere leading to the godhead, the image seen here concentrates on channeling emotion, encouraging spirit to move within and not outside of itself; to evolve from biological to geometrical spheres or from corporeal to spiritual zones, from disorder to order.

The black stone of the walls brings cohesion and fixity to the previously fluid images of blood, hands, flame, and the resurrection of the bodies. Stone reconciles opposites: it is hard, durable, and when compared with dust, sand, or splintering crystals represents strength, unity, and firmness. Stones are also hierophanies: the Ka'aba in Mecca, the *omphalos* of the Greeks, the Beith-El for the Hebrews (Gen. 28:22), the philosopher's stone for the alchemists. Each is an image of a complex of opposites: mortal/divinity; ego and Self. Embedded in the stone as a hierophany is a sense of magic, of the sacred, the durable, indicating its ability to fix the volatile, to terrestrialize the sacred, and unify the fragmented.

The blackness of the stone may represent the shadow cast from the light of the previous images. The bipolar visualization—underscoring black as opposed to white in each of the tower's portals—makes whole what is divided, thus unifying on a spiritual plane the concepts of good and evil. Psychologically, such a process endows a splintered psyche with wholeness. The Hebrews, unlike the Christians, consider deity a complex of opposites endowed with thirteen attributes that humankind, living in the differentiated world, may interpret as negative and positive or good and evil (Exod. 34:6–7). It is wholeness that comes into being when black and white emerge in the vision, uniting the disparate and fragmented components of both the spiritual and psychological experience in a cohesive whole. Circularity, then, includes multiplicity, and in this case, a regrouping of what has been dispersed around a former oneness, thereby preparing for the discovery of the treasure.

This treasure, the gold coffer in the center of the inner space, underscores the *temenos:* the sacred area in which nonhuman knowledge is contained. Reserved for the creator, alluded to by Aristotle as the "Unmoved Mover" and by the Chinese as the *Pi*, it is the area of non-being or the mystic's nothingness. It is within this central point that energy, rather than gliding outward, now streams inward, in keeping with the ebb and flow of ever-diminishing radii.[21]

That the coffer is made of gold is in itself a manifestation of divinity. Because gold does not tarnish, it is considered the closest representation of the unchanging eternal God in the physical world.[22] Therefore the gold coffer contains all the spiritual and physical attributes and elements within humankind: heart, brain, womb—life's very course. Such a receptacle also contains secret knowledge comparable to that within the ark of the covenant: a wooden chest that Moses was commanded by God to construct, containing the two tablets of the law (Exod. 25:10.12), God's secret word. Lined inside and outside with gold, the Ark was carried by the Levites throughout Israel's wanderings. When stationary, it was placed in the Holy of Holies within the tabernacle.

In this third vision, then, one is in the presence of the most sacred of objects. Identifying with the all-powerful, the emperor, revealing his own ego-driven needs, commands the box to open, and it does. Inside he sees "all kinds of blades of grass, torn out by the roots" yet still "green and fragrant" (p. 6), bound in sheaves of ten and numbering 60,000.

Grass in its fertile and fragrant states, as represented here, stands for virility, hope, and joy, but not merely of an earthly nature. In this context it is to be understood as a supernal experience: the greenness that God brought into existence during the third day of creation: "The earth brought forth grass and herb yielding seed after his kind" (Gen. 1:2). The grass contained within the golden coffer in this third vision lives in a transpersonal sphere and, as all else does in the world, experiences the many cosmic cycles. That the grass has not withered indicates its succulence and the power vested in it, its ever-burgeoning thought and feeling as manifested in a continuous condition of becoming.

Reminiscent of the green pastures in the Twenty-third Psalm, the color of the grass stands for youth, excitement, newness, birth, humidity that fructifies everything emanating from the earth. Let us recall also that green has a healing or medicinal quality: a mediating tone between yellow and blue, heat and cold, high and low, its colorations are as reassuring as water.

Nourishment is given the grass in part because it is bound in sheaves of ten, a number already discussed with regard to the Sefiroth—God's ten emanations. The science of numbers (*Gematriah*) practiced by Hebrew mystics revealed sacred qualitative and quantitative conditions in numbers. The calculation of numerical values of Hebrew words indulged in by the Kabbalists was an attempt to search for connections with other words and phrases of equal numerical values. Numbers are archetypal and thus endowed with their own energic value.[23] The number ten of the Sefiroth is one of the most sacred and powerful of values and represents the universality and timelessness of creation. The All is ten and is derived from ten; it returns to ten in keeping with the eternal rhythmic cosmic process.

There are 60,000 sheaves or bundles. That they are bound together represents the binding or knotting factor so important in spiritual as well as empirical existence. It is this linking or tying of disparate parts of the spiritual or psychological components within an individual that is so important in containing what could erupt, shatter, or simply drain off in emotional energy. The number ten sealed into the 60,000 sheaves binds a personality so that it can function; unites a nation that might otherwise be dispersed. For the mystic, the soul must be bound within the body as it enters the pleromatic spheres; only after its difficult journey has been completed and it has experienced the godhead may it be unfettered and liberated from its sensual garments.[24] In psychological terms, the ego must likewise be clothed in identity, which will strengthen its vision as well as enable it to know its limitations. If not, the ego could be flooded or seared by the divine stream or the Self. As a dam confines but also protects the water contained within its walls, so human experience must be embedded or surrounded in order not to be destroyed by the overpowering luminosity and energic power of divinity (Self).

The emperor's ego remains unprotected as it glimpses the secret knowledge of the grass and the sheaves in the golden coffer. It has been exposed to the divine experience but has gained nothing from it, nor has it been seared by it; it has remained an observer, never becoming a participant.

THE FOURTH PORTAL: THE SEVENTH SPHERE AND THE MIDNIGHT HOUR

The emperor now sees a "palace of red marble" decorated with gold, silver, pearls, and precious stones. He walks through six rooms and then arrives at the seventh, more splendid than all the others, for it is here that "the royal throne carved out of pure sapphire" stands in all its glory.

The most sacred place or inner palace for the Merkabah mystic is located at the junction of six directions of space, or the six days of creation, and the seventh, standing for the center—the space reserved for God. It is in this sacred area that the divine king, the Holy of Holies, the *mysterium tremendum,* the numinosity contained in the heart, spirit, mind, consciousness, and unconsciousness, exists. It is here that the soul rises through the seven planetary spheres, fighting off during its trajectory whatever evil forces assault it from the outside.

The throne carved out of sapphire is mentioned in Ezekiel: "And above the firmament that was over their heads was the likeness of a throne, as the appearance of a sapphire stone" (1:6). The perception of the phenomenon of the throne and its chariot without the understanding of the true nature of good (since this is impossible for a mortal) was instrumental in activating a component within Ezekiel's spirit and psyche, leading to the vision that allowed him to witness the mysteries contained within the throne and the divine glory.

Sapphire is identified with celestial azure, air, lightness, transparency; it is the deepest and most immaterial of colors. Though opaque, it seems transparent, like a diamond and other crystals, giving the impression of being empty, since one can see through it, but pure in its absoluteness. Yet it is hard, cohesive, durable, resilient, firm. Thus sapphire is a composite of opposites, a repository for divinity's hidden nature, and it is understandable that mystics used it for meditative purposes, its mirrorlike power attracting disparate thoughts and feelings, fusing the fragmented libido into a single unity, thus encapsulating a soul on its pilgrimage toward ecstasy.

The emperor also sees tables of silver upon which golden cloths have been laid, as well as the finest foods and wines. Yet there is not a living soul in the palace. What the emperor fails to understand is the nature of the food offered. It is not living food of the material world, but spiritual food given to those penetrating the seventh room: "But thou, son of man, hear what I say unto thee . . . open thy mouth, and eat that I give thee" (Ezek. 2:8; 3: 1-4). It is within the seventh room—another layer within the unconscious—that the transformation ritual is undertaken. The material is transmuted into the immaterial; what has been digested by the ego penetrates the sacred rooms of the Self.

The sun suddenly vanishes; noises, trumpets, horsemen are heard; joy flares and blares. Soldiers, princes, captains wearing gold-embroidered attire enter the hall, and at their head marches "a man in royal attire with a crown on his head" (p. 7). The noise and commotion are virtually deafening, arousing in those present, who have formerly been well-ordered and serene, great fervor and impetuousness. Such noise and disruptive elements announce the oncoming of a great cosmic event, as attested to, for example, by Joshua's battle: when his trumpet sounded, the walls of Jericho came tumbling down. Whenever a cataclysmic event takes place, be it terrestrial (e.g., a war or storm), spiritual (the Last Judgment), or psychological (a trauma), a conjunction of elements is unleashed: winds rise, tidal waves surge forth, eruptions of all sorts emerge as chaos—not cosmos—spills over into the empirical domain.

Although the man wearing a crown who enters the divine hall is an anthropomorphic image, he is not a visualization of divinity in its fullness or of supernal light; nor does he flow forth from "primeval space . . . like a beam of light." What the emperor sees is a mirror image of himself: a human being wearing a crown, a man being honored by followers who bow and scrape as he walks forth during a festive occasion. As midnight approaches, this same man asks that the iron crown be placed on his head. No sooner has this request been made than all present leap upon the man, drag him from his royal throne, tear off his royal attire, and rip him to shreds, after which everything disappears (p. 7).

Mystics consider the hour of midnight to be of utmost importance. It is at this time that God enters paradise and rejoins the righteous. Hymns are sung and tears shed, sins depart, sparks are carried to earth, embedding their radiance in the pious, who, after studying God's words in the Torah until dawn, ascend to heaven, so filled are they with spiritual strength. In the midnight scene just described, however, the kingly figure is too impatient to pursue the task of completing God's work through meditation upon the symbolism of the throne. Instead of meditating and eating divine food, thus paving the way for spiritual and psychological evolution, the king (a representation of the ego) rushes ahead and asks for the iron crown: the power vested in the godhead (Self). Inflation marks this act, and, as a result, the hordes of angels present who are carrying out God's words use their powerful energies to tear asunder the impostor's soul/psyche. No longer a spiritual entity preparing to absorb divine intelligence, the king experiences a dismemberment and is symbolically returned to earth, to the world of contingencies, where he will lie dormant until he is reawakened—which, for the mystic, means until he is redeemed—in keeping with the great cosmic cycle, the return of all creation to nothingness before it is born anew.

THE EXPLANATION

Devoid of spirituality and intuition, the emperor is at a loss to understand the meaning embedded in the four visions. He asks his stargazers to explain them to him. They cannot. Only the father of one of them, an old man on the verge of death himself, is capable of doing so. He tells the emperor that Nimrod built the tower after conquering the world. Fearing that his dominion might be usurped after his death, he resorted to witchcraft: the iron crown became immovable, indicating the eternality of his dominion. After Nimrod's death it was rumored that any contender to the throne who could place the iron crown on his head would rule the earth. Numerous contenders presented themselves, and a bloody combat ensued. The contenders were all killed, and their hands alone, as in the first vision, remained aboveground. The archetype of the greedy reaching out for power they are ill equipped to handle is evident, as are the dangers involved when one is anchored to an *idée fixe*, an earth-oriented need to possess and dominate everything around, thereby cutting out all other aspects of the life experience and stunting the psyche's potential for development.

King Nero, long after Nimrod's demise, decided he wanted to possess universal power. He called Egyptian sorcerers to his kingdom and told them he wanted to know Nimrod's secret. They suggested that it was concealed under a heavy rock on a high mountain called the Mountain of Darkness. They told Nero to have an eagle caught, then to attach the severed head of a man to a pole and place it in front of the eagle. Nero followed the orders and reached the Mountain of Darkness. After he opened the door of the cave that held a great wind captive and tied himself to a peak to avoid being blown away, as the wise men had suggested, the wind blew fiercely and the rock rolled off a tablet, after which the eagle was guided back to earth. In accordance with the instruction written on the tablet, which Nero took back with him, he called all the nations peopling the earth to the tower. Because each attempted to win the crown, everybody killed one another. The dead bodies of the second vision, upon which the emperor stepped as he entered the portal, attested to the reality of the event that took place.

That the eagle was chosen to fly to the Mountain of Darkness indicates the power residing in this bird, which can fly above the clouds and stare directly at the sun. The king of birds was capable of carrying the emperor to heights where primitive powers, in the form of wind, were unleashed. When the door was opened, releasing the wind, the divine spirit or power unleashed was incomprehensible to Nero. He misunderstood its profound message, and therefore, the results were nefarious. Psychologically, the emergence of such a powerful wind (or spiritual force) might also confuse an individual who is not sufficiently initiated into the world of the mystic. An archetypal situation may thus come into being in which the sacred word is misread or misinterpreted: calling forth a purely subjective or ego-centered attitude rather than putting one's energies toward fulfilling a humanitarian goal and enlarging one's perspectives. The tablet discovered by Nero on the Mountain of Darkness was not the tablets of the law designed to teach humankind its potential and limitations. Nero's tablet dealt with matter, undifferentiated mass, unevaluated entities. The wind made it possible to snatch the tablet, but it was not divine *pneuma*— which breathed a living soul into Adam—nor was it the cosmic breath or the word of God. It represented instability and agitation of the most intense kind, creating a condition of chaos.

Strictly speaking, Nero did not ask all the earth's nations to gather together, since seventy was the traditional number and he called only sixty-nine. So the crown remained immovable. Since the seventieth nation, Israel, possessed no land, Nero thought it was not a true nation, although he was told that it was because it was still ruled by the House of David. Since he failed to obey the law, he was given another alternative: to invite ten Jews. It was thought that they would reach for the crown and in the process the treasure would be lost and Nero would acquire it. The Jews were invited, but they refused to take the crown. They wanted no material rewards, only spiritual beatitude. So angered was Nero that he tied the Jews up with copper chains. They prayed with such fervor, however, that the walls of the temple in Jerusalem rose around them, as in the third vision. Light infiltrated from the heavens as angels flew about asking the Messiah to come down to earth. It was not to be, however, and so the worshipers again fell to the ground, returning to their previous condition.

Nero was then told to kill all the Jews. Only then would he succeed.

> Everyone of the children of Israel has his blade of grass in the world and as long as the blade grows and stays green and has its lovely scent then the Jew is alive and sound. But when the roots of the blade go dry, and it bends and turns yellow, and loses its scent and sap, then at the same moment the life-spirit leaves the body of the Jew, and his flesh is like dust. (P. 17)

Nero had his men hunt down sixty times ten thousand blades of grass, tearing them all out by their roots. Upon their return, the blades of grass "tied themselves up in sheaves of ten" by their own volition. The metaphor indicates that when one binds things together, energy is channeled rather than dispersed, increasing the power and authority needed to dominate a situation. To bind, under certain circumstances, helps develop an inner attitude, as it did here in the case of Jews. As an archetype of containment, it represents strength.

Nero placed this grass in the golden coffer, as described in the third vision, and let it stand a year, after which time he opened it up, expecting the grass to have withered. It had not, however, and was as green as it always had been. Its roots so deeply entrenched within the earth had allowed the sap to rise; mystically speaking, the grass was inhabited by divine *scintillae*.

The grass viewed by Nero was a supernal emanation stemming from the Root of Roots, the Self. As such, it offered the ego power, nurtured vision, and protected these forces when called upon to do so. Unaware of the power vested in the grass, Nero was enraged and had the Israelites killed, who "melted like wax at a flame" (p. 18). At this point he entered the "palace of red marble" in the fourth vision, saw the feasting and the kingly figure torn to shreds after asking for the iron crown. It is also at this juncture in his explanations of the four visions to the emperor that the old stargazer dies, his last words being, "If emperor Nero had separated the . . ." (p. 20).

Intent upon acquiring the iron crown for himself, we learn at the conclusion of the tale, Nero acts impulsively: he rushes back into the tower and begins tearing the threads binding the sheaves—his ego in this instance simply runs amok. While he is working so feverishly, a two-headed calf leaps out at him—not the sacrificial animal of old or even the golden calf, but a powerful and fearsome creature who fixes his gaze upon Nero and gives out a deafening bellow, like the roar of a lion. When Nero hears it he dies. As for the tower, it is consumed in smoke, and the bloody pool begins "rocking furiously with crashing waves," and the iron crown turns over and plunges to the bottom (p. 20).

The emperor of Edom, a thinking type, was dominated by his ego, which sought to forge ahead and become the authoritative figure throughout this world and the next. By disobeying the dictates of his fathers and grandfathers, by seeking to unlock the doors, he was granted access to revelation but was unable to experience its message. Although he refused to remain contained in the patriarchal sphere of his ancestors, he could not expand his vision or alter his manner of functioning. No time was devoted to meditation, examination, probing into spiritual folds of life. Compelled to acquire more and more power, his ego was forever identifying with the Self.

That "The Tower of Rome" reveals the anatomy of a psychological process, that of a man having reached midlife, is of utmost significance. It is at this point, Jung has repeatedly stated, that one's course is usually altered, that a religious or expanded point of view evolves and that maturity encourages one to look within oneself as well as outside—experiencing life as a process and in keeping with one's own development.

To unlock the portals of the tower is to open up the ego to the Self, the individual to the godhead. Insufficient understanding and preparation to receive the godhead (Self) as an energetic charge leads to destruction: insanity and death.

The emperor (ego) who sought to acquire the power of God (Self), the people who abdicated their identities and their commitment to life—out of fear of persecution in many cases—revealed themselves to be spellbound. Rather than attempting to understand the "crown of the holy king," psychologically the Self, that is, one's potential, they limited their vision: the emperor, to his need for power; the people, to their need to assuage their fear by opting for a messianic figure without thinking about the consequences. The archetypal tower vanished and all was enshrouded in darkness. Another great cosmic cycle returned everything in the differentiated world to the womb and to nothingness, to be born anew during that midnight hour—when God's glory radiates throughout the universe and his fragments of *scintillae* awaken the dormant, the lifeless, the withered—this time, one hopes, expanding their consciousness in the re-created being or the renewed psyche.

FIVE

Kafka: *The Castle*

The Archetypal Land Surveyor

In his novel *The Castle* Franz Kafka (1883–1924) focuses on a veiled and mysteriously elusive spatial archetype. A transpersonal image, spelled with a capital C, the Castle may be considered a metaphor for the Self: the totality of the psyche. During the course of Kafka's novel, the protagonist, alluded to simply as K., seeks to penetrate the Castle, which is a complex of opposites and includes within its portals human and nonhuman beings, ideal and real concepts, good and evil forces. Each time K. observes this spatial archetype from afar, it alters in configuration, depending upon the depth of his projection and his need for whatever unconscious contents it represents at the time. Psychologically, K. is the alienated ego: the ego being defined as the center of consciousness and as that factor which determines the individual's subjective identity. As an ego attempting to grow and determine its place and destiny within the Self, K. strives to establish an ongoing relationship with the Castle and its authorities.

The reader realizes from the outset of Kafka's novel that the Castle, a coveted and prized universe, is a symbol for K.'s psychological, aesthetic, and cultural experience. A spatial archetype that is described first as a single, blurred, vaguely defined entity, and then as a conglomerate of buildings including a rounded tower, and later is personified as a silent and meditative force, the Castle is to some extent comparable to the Great Rounds of ancient times.[1] Knossos in Crete or Stonehenge in Great Britain were holistic sanctuaries set apart from the rest of the world—not necessarily good or evil, but sacred areas where one came to meditate or commune with cosmic forces. A numinous source in that it promises Kafka's protagonist spiritual salvation, as did the Grail Castle for the one who succeeded in passing through the ordeals required for initiation, Kafka's edifice bears some of the characteristics of the Garden of Eden and the New Jerusalem. As a cosmic center, it could be equated with the Forbidden City of the

Chinese (Peking). Indeed, in Thomas Mann's "Homage" to *The Castle*, he suggested that his multiple, hidden, and forever mysterious edifice

> represents the divine dispensation, the state of grace—puzzling, remote, incomprehensible. And never has the divine, the superhuman, been observed, experienced, characterized with stranger, more daring, more cosmic expedients, with more inexhaustible psychological riches, both sacrilegious and devout, than in this story of an incorrigible believer, so needing grace, so wrestling for it, so passionately and recklessly yearning after it that he even tries to encompass it by stratagems and wiles.[2]

As a deity in the religious sense of being all-encompassing, and as the Self in the psychological sense, the Castle is a focal force, an organized and dynamic center that not only exists outside the ego but also includes it. This power guides, directs, and orients K.'s very existence. Yet it is also that very factor which prevents him from experiencing a community of feeling, from knowing the warmth of acceptance; it forces him to remain outside the community, alienated from it—a pariah. We may assume that if K. succeeds in penetrating this edifice, thereby creating a working relationship between ego and Self, his fractured and segmented psyche will be healed.

Kafka's Castle is, then, an autonomous complex that takes on reality for the observer in exact proportion to the power of K.'s projection. The Castle defies definition, as does any sacred area; it is a house of imponderables. When Samuel Beckett was questioned as to the identity of Godot in his play *Waiting for Godot,* he replied that Godot was what each one believes him to be. The same is true of Kafka's spatial archetype—the Castle.

Kafka may be said to possess the psyche of a displaced person. Born in Prague when this city was still part of the Austro-Hungarian Empire, the son of a well-to-do Jewish merchant, Kafka was educated in German-speaking schools, including the city's German university, from which he earned a law degree in 1906. Considered a Czech by the Germans, a German by the Czechs, and a nonbeliever by the religious Jews, harboring antagonistic feelings toward the bourgeois ideas of his father, Kafka knew alienation and hostility in almost every area: social and psychological.

Hypersensitive, Kafka was frequently overwhelmed by feelings of isolation and desperation. He belonged nowhere: neither to a nation nor to a religious group, not even to his family—nor to himself. He was forever seeking ways and means of experiencing a deeper understanding of the reasons for his anguish, hoping that he would perhaps learn to cope with or even heal it. Ego-centered, his attempts to communicate and relate to others were usually unsuccessful, leading to ever-increased introversion. There was only one certainty in his life, one way of earning fulfillment insofar as he was concerned: by writing. Yet even here the struggle for recognition was an ordeal—known not only to Kafka but to all artists whose works remain unappreciated and whose sentiments of solitude and helplessness during and after the writing process increase an already excoriating sense of aloneness.

Kafka's strength, nevertheless, resided in the confidence he placed in his writing ability, his dogged perseverance, his determination to dredge up from within his inner being those personal and collective experiences which are the source material of masterpieces. He realized he could not support himself by his pen alone and took a job as an official in a worker's accident insurance company. Although he was diagnosed as tubercular in 1917, he continued to work until 1922. Then he left his job to seek continuous treatments. It was at this juncture that he began to plan *The Castle*.

Strangely enough, Kafka almost welcomed his illness. It gave him the necessary leisure to write. It liberated him from what he felt to be a need to conform to the fashions and responsibilities of his times and the demands made upon him by his conventional family, whose credos were anathema to him. Nor did his amorous relationships bring him security, stability, or satisfaction. On the contrary, they caused him despair. In 1922 he broke a second engagement to Felice Bauer, whom he purported to love. He could not marry her any more than he could any other woman with whom he had had amatory relations. He was unprepared to make the commitments required by marriage. Writing came first. It was primordial—his lifeline. It fed his despair, nourished him in uncertainty, and gave him definition.

Kafka's mind was always teeming with activity, thoughts, feelings that he then decanted in disciplined and ordered ways. "I don't describe people. I tell a story. Pictures . . . only pictures," he wrote.[3] The visual element, as attested to in his statement and in *The Castle*, was for Kafka of prime importance. Unlike traditional novelists, Kafka never has his narrator impose his views on the flow of the protagonist's thoughts. Instead of coloring situations with his own judgments, he depicts only their outlines. Kafka's writing, therefore, remains ambiguous, enigmatic, like so many flat-surfaced visualizations imbricated into the spatial archetype. Divested of psychological explications and moral valuations, facts alone are given, clusters of detached thoughts interwoven in complex designs. Since Kafka's style is both imagistic and divested of interpretation, it has been compared to that of an artist and also a newspaper reporter. Lucid, precise, devoid of sentimentality, his verbal depictions are bone-hard, at times overly cold and aloof, as the increasingly tenuous march inward proceeds. *The*

Castle's actionless plot is paradoxically filled with the protagonist's ceaseless activity, which leads nowhere. The perpetual routine of talking, talking, enduring, infused as it is with a sense of futility and doom, is a perfect example of a psychological condition of conspicuous alienation: the ego severed from the Self, desperately attempting to find some common denominator, some way of reconciling the breach.

The surface events of *The Castle* are simple. K., given only an initial and not a name, and therefore divested of identity, arrives at a village, perhaps by chance, perhaps by design. The day is snowy. He sees a Castle in the distance, veiled by a cloud of white flakes. He makes his way to the village and comes upon an inn, where he seeks lodgings for the night. His identity papers and work permit are requested by the authorities. He has neither and tells them that he has been hired as a land surveyor by the count of the Castle. The rest of the novel, with its subplots, its seemingly unintelligible, detached, and illogical happenings, its multiple phantasmal characters, details K.'s unsuccessful attempts to make contact with the Castle. Were he to succeed in his endeavor, his credibility with the villagers—and in his own mind—would be established. To be accepted by the community would give him identity and add purpose and orientation to his life.

K.'s failure to confront the bureaucracy, his inability to get closer to the mysterious Castle run by a complex of unapproachable and evanescent functionaries, produces alternating behavioral patterns. At times he is aggressive, at other moments obsessive or obsequious, but he is always intent upon gaining some kind of recognition or some definite answer from the authorities as to whether his position as land surveyor is fact or fiction. K. is willing to sacrifice anything and everything to gain entrance into the Castle, thus confirming his existence and giving him status in the community. His wanderings about the village with its bridge and inn, its schoolhouse, its peasantry, are seemingly illogical, unpremeditated, planless, and fruitless. Yet he never ceases in his quest. He writes letters, phones, uses the influence of the women he meets, begs officials to help him. Frustration and futility result. The turmoil he feels, however, is always controlled, repressed. Nor is K. despondent, despite his repeated failures—at least not overtly so. Such pathos as there is resides in the black humor, the sardonic and macabre epithets incised into the story. The hopelessness of K.'s quest—his inability to deal with the lying, scheming, hypocritical, ignorant, and inefficient organization that prevents him from gaining entry into the Castle grows in dimension and power like a threnody until it fuses the disparate parts into a whole, overpowering, leaden mass.

Although *The Castle* was never completed, Kafka's notes left to Max Brod indicate that K. never reached his destination; he remained a stranger, an outcast, unacceptable to the villagers and to himself. His function and his relationship with the spatial archetype—the Castle— were never clarified. As for the metaphor itself, the Castle remained a mystery, a void mirroring the protagonist's own emptiness and desolation, issuing its cryptic forebodings in elusive ways. K., the wandering ego, pursuing his turmoil-ridden course, is reminiscent in a great many ways of those physically distorted beings and edifices slashed onto the canvases of Chaim Soutine. Extreme distress, the pain of being, is the message of the pariah artist.

FIRST VISION

The first description of the spatial archetype alluded to as the Castle is given upon K.'s arrival to the village.

> It was late in the evening when K. arrived. The village was deep in snow. The Castle hill was hidden veiled in the mist and darkness, nor was there a glimmer of light to show that a castle was there. On the wooden bridge leading from the main road to the village, K. stood for a long time gazing into the illusory emptiness from above him. (P. 3)

The Castle appears as if it has emerged from a dream; it is a phantasm, a hallucinatory vision. It stands in the center of nowhere, detached, veiled in mist, curtained off, closed to the wanderer or intruder—like a disembodied object floating about in a Magritte painting. From the very outset, the reader knows that a condition of *separatio* is to be experienced: a division, a fissure, a fracture between the one and the whole, the inside and the outside, consciousness and the unconscious—ego and Self (see fig. 2).

K. looks longingly at the archetypal image of the Self/Castle, its "illusory emptiness from above him" mirroring the inner aridity of his psyche, its need for nourishment, its desire for warmth, understanding, and relatedness. There is nothing inviting about the Castle, situated as it is in deep snow, its whiteness and grayness, lightness and distance, constellating so many foreboding and frightening sensations. Since the Castle is set on the *other* side of a bridge, K. must symbolically complete a rite of passage before earning entry into this Castle/Self.

Because of the barriers that exist for K. from the outset—a bridge, an obscurity, the slope of the hill—sensations of doom and failure are immediately evoked. Let us recall that Kafka had already had recourse to metaphors of impediment: the wall, for example, in his

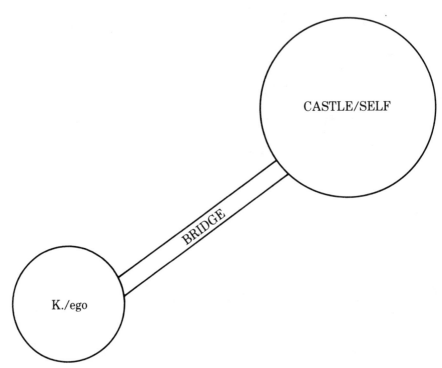

Fig. 2. Kafka's archetypal land surveyor—the wandering ego

short story "The Great Wall of China." Here, however, there seems to be a "main road" that leads from the Castle to the village, implying the possibility of access and flow between the two points. In this regard, one may perhaps associate the Castle vision as it appears here and in subsequent images with the Cambuluc, the city constructed by Kublai Khan in the thirteenth century, which became his capital. Built "in a grid of eight miles on a side reflecting the traditional Chinese magic square," this spatial archetype consisted of three enclaves: an Inner City, an Imperial City, and a Forbidden City.[4] Although the Forbidden City was inaccessible to the collective, certain individuals, if deemed worthy to the honor and only after completing their initiatory process, were invited into this fabulously exciting secret world. Such was K.'s goal: to penetrate an arcane sphere known to mystics and conquerors.

The colors used in this first vision—white and gray, with its dark and shadowy textures—determine K.'s desolate mood. Gray, the color of fog and ashes, indicates for Hebrews and Christians alike protracted pain and sadness; poets also associate it with melancholia and ennui. The layers of snow that becloud K.'s vision, like opaque gauze and mat chromatic tones, parallel yet-to-be discovered layers in his subliminal world. The whiteness of the snowflakes, a color counter to blackness, represents both an absence and a summation of colors: the beginning or conclusion of an initiation, of a passage into profounder spheres of being. The color of the untouched, the virginal, the as yet unlived—but also that of death—absorbs the whole of K.'s attention and holds it in its grasp. For Kandinsky and for K., whiteness represents the color of oblivion, extinction, absolute silence—a world *in potentia,* where phantoms breed and erupt into being at a moment's notice, where the unincarnated are injected with energy so that activity may give birth to color and unborn whiteness to life.

After K. enters the village and learns he needs permission to spend the night at the inn, a strange phone call is made on his behalf to the Castle authorities. Inexplicably, he is granted permission to remain, at least for the time being. During the sequences that follow, K. moves about the town with its Piranesi-like baroque intersections, its light and black shadows following him at slow or rapid paces, its intertwining houses and labyrinthine rooms, attempting all the while to clarify his own state of affairs while seeking access to the Castle.

When questioned about his profession, K. tells those in charge that he is a land surveyor hired by the count in the Castle. As previously mentioned, he himself does not know if it is fact or fiction. K. might just have said the first thing that came into his mind when questioned as to his function. Nevertheless, that he identifies himself with the role of land surveyor is in itself intriguing.

Land implies earth, the Mother Earth archetype, and suggests involvement in the workaday and existential realm, reality and solidity; it also indicates a link with and need for the feminine principle, that nourishing and sustaining force. As for "surveyor," the profession deals with certain geometrical and mathematical procedures; it is preoccupied with location and form, with boundaries and tracts of land, with determining specific angles and measurements of houses or land masses. Surveying or telescoping a whole system or area in order to determine, structure, and orient its height, depths, and general view is exactly what K. is attempting on a psychological and spiritual sphere. To be a surveyor, then, requires both mathematical knowledge of earth surfaces—symbolically, a relationship with the feminine sphere—and an ability to understand ascents and airy or celestial realms, which are identified frequently with the masculine domain. Air, as viewed in terms of spatial archetypes, is a volatile element, invisible, dissolving into nothingness. Blended with earth, however, it may take on concretion and visibility and appear and reappear at certain junctures, as it does in the Castle archetype in Kafka's novel. The spatial forms that are concretized when land and air, feminine and masculine principles, cohabit—the village, the Castle—attract the wandering ego, mesmerize it as it floats perpetually about from one area to another, one object to another, one person to another. The Castle is perpetually surveyed by K., as is the village, in his determination to understand each of the steps he takes. By superintending, overseeing, administering, examining all passages, all hidden and vague paths, K. performs the function of the land surveyor. What he does not understand is that he is a pawn of that ruling authority as represented by the Castle—the Self.

In this first image and throughout the novel to various degrees, the Castle emerges as a kind of no-man's-land, an organism that encapsulates everything and anything, intrudes and detaches itself from K.'s life as it acts and interacts with the other forces and beings around him. No common denominator, however, seems to exist as yet between K. and the other protagonists with whom he later becomes involved.

Each character may be considered a facet of K.'s psyche, a faceless presence related in some unfathomable way to the protagonist. As K. pursues his search down roads and crossings, into houses and rooms in sequences of dislocated and fragmented incidents, his rootlessness seems ever greater, his turmoil more profound. He is sometimes led to believe that he will discover a way of making real contact with the Castle, now looked upon as a secure and solid force. Meanwhile, the chasm existing between subject and object, ego and Self, grows wider. The greater the efforts made by K. (the ego) to locate the place himself, the more detached and alienated he feels. Indeed, perhaps as a protective device, K. loses himself more deeply in his introverted, empty, and agitated inner world. Still, he endures the turmoil; never does he grow passive. Like Job, who said to the Deity, "Though he slay me, yet will I trust in him. . . . But I will maintain my own ways before him," so K. goes on, struggling and forging ahead. Unlike Job, however, he does not experience greater understanding or serenity; nor does he achieve that communion between man and God that Job knew at the conclusion of his labors. Comparable also to Kierkegaard, K. searches for truth, not as an objective fact, but as a way of experiencing greater awareness in his relationship with the transcendental force that is God. Like Kierkegaard, K. sacrifices the peripheral world, with its possibly anxiety-free temporal existence, to explore a new, remote, mysterious, and dimensionless realm. Bleakness enshrouds him, as it had Abraham in Kierkegaard's *Fear and Trembling,* when he contemplated the sacrifice of Isaac, then departed to a new land. Pain and struggle await the one who seeks to bring innovation to the world, the fresh, the unknown into existence.

THE SECOND VISION

Another description of the Castle is offered shortly after K.'s arrival in the village. Though still veiled, the spatial archetype is given some form and substance, thus appearing to K. to be less remote, unreal, and dim.

> Now he could see the Castle above him, clearly defined in the glittering air, its outline made still more definite by the thin layer of snow covering everything. . . .
>
> It was neither an old stronghold nor a new mansion, but a rambling pile consisting of innumerable small buildings closely packed together and of one or two stories; if K. had not known that it was a castle he might have taken it for a little town. There was only one tower as far as he could see; whether it belonged to a dwelling house or a church he could not determine. Swarms of crows were circling around it.
>
> With his eyes fixed on the Castle, K. went on farther, thinking of nothing else at all. But on approaching it he was disappointed in the Castle; it was after all only a wretched-looking town, a huddle of village houses, whose sole merit, if any, lay in being built of stone; but the plaster had long since flaked off and the stone seemed to be crumbling away. K. had a fleeting recollection of his native town. It was hardly inferior to this so-called Castle, and if it was merely a question of enjoying a view, it was a pity to have come so far. (P. 11)

Once unified and whole, this new view of the Self seems fractured, separated, cut into pieces. Conglomerates become visible: vacant streets, two-story houses, buildings with cluttered rooms, each set against the other in a haphazard and confused manner. Yet each is clearly dependent on and related to the other, as are the protagonists who surge forth in what seems to be an equally illogical manner. The small city that has now been projected into the Castle archetype reminds K. of his own village. Evaluation comes into being at this juncture; consciousness and awareness are being born. When comparisons are made, past, present, and future become distinct entities and are no longer embedded in a *participation mystique.* K., the ego, is taking stock of itself and its condition.

The "glittering air" seems to confirm K.'s psychological evolution. Light helps K.'s vision to take on contour. The Castle, once viewed as a blurred whole, is now viewed as a composite entity made up of multiple elements. In this context, we recall Noah, who sent the raven out to see if the flood waters had receded (Gen. 8:7). When the raven did not return, he realized that land had been sighted: psychologically speaking, consciousness had surfaced from the subliminal spheres. In K.'s image, we see "swarms of crows circling around" the spatial archetype, helping him distinguish the structure of the buildings in the distance and his relationship to them.

The "glittering air" in the vision may also be identified with the mystic's *scintillae,* or seeds of light, representing the onset of awareness, greater lucidity. Luminosity enables the Castle to come forth from the snow, from the dimness of the unconscious, and take on consistence. Knowledge is born when subject and object leap into existence, when the power to evaluate takes hold. Now K. is able to distinguish between what he had formerly believed to be the ideal or sacred realm and the present reality. Disappointment marks his countenance as he observes the "wretched-looking town," which, he now realizes, is on the verge of disintegration, with its "crumbling" stone structures. What is decaying and breaking up is K.'s childlike fantasy world. Reality is intruding now that the luster of the first vision is flaking off and the numinous is taking on the contours of the everyday.

Still, the stone buildings in the Castle compound, although eroding, merit some admiration. Stone is what K. needs: strength and durability to compensate for his fragile ego. Stone symbolizes hard and long-living qualities, those usually not subject to the laws of birth and decay—at least, not to the same degree as the flower. Stone is the antithesis of dust and sand and represents psychic strength. It is also representative of the foundation of religious feeling (the Hebrew *Bethel*, or House of God), thereby infusing the believer with solid faith and an inner power. In K.'s case, however, a flaking off or dispersal of this once-solid stone suggests a disintegration of his former view of the uniqueness and ideal aspect of the Castle community. K.'s perhaps unilateral belief is now breaking up; a slow annihilation of those forces that have given him the strength to pursue his search is occurring. What K. had thought of as an eternal and all-encompassing archetypal image—the Castle—is mortal and human. K.'s capabilities as land surveyor permit him to observe life with greater clarity than before: to measure, cut, probe, define the object of his search in engineer-like fashion.

The Castle—a vast, impersonal spatial archetype representative of a social hierarchy, which belongs to the Count of West-West in Bohemia—has become more accessible in K.'s mind's eye. As he peers at this image, more and more shapes and forms come into view, as if he were indulging in active imagination. Jung defines such a process as "an active evocation of the inner images *secundum naturam*."[5] What is significant during such periods is the attempt on the individual's part to understand the impact of "the inner object in its quality of a faithfully reproduced mental image."[6] K. is now able to structure his vision, to set it in a specific framework, around centers of energy such as houses, crows, a tower. In this measured and confined area, he feels assured of some kind of solid—or relatively so—stonelike security that he can fall back on when he is confused or disillusioned. Such cluster images may also act as a repository for feelings of fear and frustration, functioning as defense mechanisms that will help him surmount moments of anguish. The tension between ego and Self still exists, but in this image it appears to diminish in severity.

K. seems infused with strength and a *raison d'être* when penetrating the spatial archetype in this second vision. A kind of New Jerusalem for him, it gives him the protection, both physical and spiritual, for which he longs. It may, however, also be a negative quantity, imprisoning him still further in his role as voyeur, encouraging him to look outside of himself rather than within for solace, thereby prolonging a condition of stasis.

As K. pursues his vision, a towerlike structure rises "above him" in the Castle compound, its red tiles and broad roof reminding him of the church tower in his home town.

> The tower . . . was uniformly round, part of it graciously mantled with ivy, pierced by small windows that glittered in the sun—with somewhat maniacal glitter—and topped by what looked like an attic, with battlements that were irregular, broken, fumbling. . . . It was as if a melancholy-mad tenant who ought to have been kept locked in the topmost chamber of his house had burst through the roof and lifted himself up to gaze at the world. (P. 12)

Light which broke out of the gray and dismal hues in the previous depiction takes on greater radiance now: it becomes a "maniacal glitter," characterized by ungoverned frenzy and excitement. Such brilliance may be likened to Parsival's blinding vision when encountering armed knights on his path out of the forest. Their shields glittered so powerfully that he thought he was in the presence of the godhead. K.'s vision could also be termed extraordinary, even apocalyptic, for the glitter emerging from the windows virtually dazzles him as it sheds light on the buildings in the Castle compound, their irregularities, their "broken" and "fumbling" aspects. That ivy surrounds the tower is further evidence of the fecundating nature of the Castle archetype and its environs. Ivy, however, though green and ushering in fertility, is identified with the Phrygians and their god Attis, who castrated himself for love of the feminine principle, Cybele. It is a force in need of protection and warmth, also of death and rebirth. So, too, is K., in his pursuit of a *raison d'être*.

The tower image, so frequently associated with patriarchal and celestial spheres, as well as with the phallus because of its form, represents the energic force in nature. By reminding K. of his home-town church tower, it draws him back to his familial past, to a spiritual sanctuary for the soul that he knew in childhood. K.'s edifice is not unlike the tower Jung had built for himself, which could be considered a metaphor for psychic integration, but for K. the tower still remains inaccessible and unattainable—an object outside of himself and not in harmony with his psyche. It floods him, however, with some semblance of security. But this vanishes rapidly. He regresses as he persists in his scrutiny of the Castle archetype and then concludes that such a vision might have emanated from "the trembling or careless hand of a child," perhaps his own, or might be the result of madness—also his own. In either case, it is likened to an eruption, a release of repressed forces that only a child or insane person may reveal without knowing shame.

Ascensional archetypes, such as the hill upon which the Castle is placed and the tower image, may be likened to watch towers, belfries, and spires in ancient times. These were built to look out for enemies, to halt their attacks. Such high edifices protected towns, but they also suggested spiritual elevations, as does a ladder, for example, in the biblical story of Jacob wrestling with the angel. These structures were also an attempt on humanity's part to discourse with divinity. A universally known example is the Tower of Babel, a ziggurat of brick and asphalt located in Ur, Abraham's native land. Because of humanity's inflated ego, God transformed the tower's once-harmonious community of builders into a confused group of individuals. Two ideas, then, are implicit in the tower image: the fear and trembling identified with Abraham when he departed from the comfort of his own country, and the energy involved in discovering the new, the untried. In either situation, there is discomfort and malaise. K. must likewise struggle in his endeavor to do away with the social and hierarchical armature that seeks to prevent him from fulfilling his destiny, from forging ahead and creating a niche for himself.

As K. *surveys* the world about him, its stone buildings and other structures, such objects help him fix on something solid rather than allowing his eyes to wander restlessly about. Again and again he stares at the Castle, frequently at the small windows of the tower. Mystery is embedded in these "eyes" set in the concrete—arousing his curiosity but also his despair. Because windows look out onto the world, they represent freedom, and K. desperately seeks freedom from stress, from guilt, from everything that seems to corrode his psyche. However, windows may also represent imprisonment, especially windows in towers, where legendary prisoners were often kept. Let us recall in this regard the bronze tower in which Danaë, Perseus's mother, was incarcerated, and the tower room in which the Sleeping Beauty lodged until she was rescued by Prince Charming.

The Castle with its tower is a sanctuary, and hence access for the intruder is difficult. Like many sanctuaries, it is built on a height; K.'s gaze is always wandering up "above" the rest of the countryside to see it. Such a mountain archetype implies sacrality, as it does in so many religions: Mount Olympus for the Greeks, Mount Moriah for the Hebrews, the Mount of Olives for the Christians, Mount Caf for the Muslims, Mount Meru for the Hindus, and Mount Salvatch, which houses the Grail. Sanctuaries encourage meditation and inner probings, endowing those who remain there with serenity as well as feelings of power. The ego is not alone or cut off but is linked in communication with nature as a whole, the transpersonal and cosmic element.

In contrast is K.'s wandering ego as he looks lovingly at the Castle archetype, aspiring to penetrate its confines. Whether the Castle as metaphor for the Self represents good or evil is really of no consequence. It is a living and concrete appendage of K.'s psyche that alleviates his pain and ennui. Everything and everyone else he encounters is unable to help him at all. The puppetlike figures with whom K. deals in the village and whom he summons into existence when his ego demands their presence appear and vanish according to an inner logic and not the rationale of the workaday person. Nor is there any feeling of morality encountered in K.'s relationships or in the ideas he enunciates. Nor are emotions felt between man and woman: the women for the most part are already the mistresses of other men from the Castle or village and no one really seems to care. What is also disconcerting is that whenever K. stumbles into an impasse or a difficult situation, he falls asleep, perhaps out of desperation, boredom, or simply a desire to block out what he cannot deal with or integrate into his personality. Dozing, psychologically, may indicate an eclipse of the ego, an inability on K.'s part to further investigate his situation.

THE THIRD VISION

Alienated and dejected, K. pursues his course. He keeps suffering rejection and reversals each time he attempts to cope with the Castle officials. They procrastinate and thwart his every move. They hand him documents that prove to be completely useless; they prevent any real communication between him and those he believes can help him. The atmosphere grows increasingly oppressive as K. weaves his net, ceaselessly, through the confines of the village. Reminiscent in its intricacies of some of Henry Fuseli's visions, particularly *The Nightmare*, with all of its phantomlike qualities, cruelties, and macabre realities, it is also laced with celestial nuances, an inner glow, a dynamism infused with serenity, a detachment that is no longer cold and arid but reveals understanding and strength.

> When K. looked at the Castle, often it seemed to him as if he were observing someone who sat quietly there gazing in front of him, not lost in thought and so oblivious of everything, but free and untroubled, as if he were alone with nobody to observe him, and yet must notice that he was observed, and all the same remained with his calm not even slightly disturbed. . . . (P. 125)

The energic factor injected into the Castle metaphor is in keeping, perhaps, with K.'s increasing need for self-realization. He must prove his abilities and function as land surveyor, thereby giving credence to his identity and status to his life. The personification of the Castle humanizes the image; it also endows it with a kind of tranquility that K. so desperately needs, a transpersonal quality, as found in Rodin's statue *The Thinker*. Above and detached from the madding crowd, this individual that K. sees in the Castle complex is "free and untroubled," set apart from the masses of discontented and anxiety-ridden individuals. In Schopenhauerian aloofness, having integrated every polarity within the psyche, this transpersonal force exists as a welcome relief from the chaotic qualities infused in previous images and K.'s own searching, seeking, painful ennui.

This individual who sits in meditation remains silent, fixed, as he studies the world about him, following the subtle and nuanced inner movements of K.'s existential condition. Like God's eye, he pursues, scrutinizes, encompasses, and engulfs. K., in contrast, follows, wishes, longs to be part of this sphinxlike entity, impassable, impenetrable, existing in splendid isolation.

K. responds deeply to the singleness of purpose of this arresting being, untroubled and alone. Like an impregnable fortress, the Forbidden City or the New Jerusalem, this Castle/divinity is both object and subject blended into one. Like the God of the Kabbalists, the deity sits alone as he observes what he has brought into existence: the created world with its struggling, pained, fighting, deformed beings.

K., the antihero, looks on, the recipient of chaos and conflict, attempting to digest the polarities that are wreaking havoc within him.

He plods alone, hovering always on the brink of catastrophe. The antihero saves no one—unlike the great heroes of old such as Roland, David, Bayard, Arthur—not even himself. Introverted, egocentric, seeking to understand his own desires and needs, he is forever focused on his own being, his own pains and sorrows, and the purposelessness of his futile, static, fixated condition. His entire vision, like Wagner's "twilight of the gods," can be said to be "lost in the twilight" of his own fungal and regressive realm, ready to be plowed under, in darkness, into oblivion—death.

As a symbol of the unconscious, the Castle, like the Self, is a centrality, a center, a mandala of sorts, representing order and wholeness. According to Jung, mandalas appear in dreams when people are in the throes of chaotic psychic states, when disorientation and panic strike them.[7] The purpose of the mandala is to help them sort out their present confusion, to balance what is traumatic. For Tibetans and Westerners alike mandalas represent balance and completion, and usually activate a religious or numinous thought or idea. One understands why Kafka wrote that he proceeded pictorially, that images were of great significance to him. The Castle configuration, the tower as it rises high above the rest of the edifices, its roundness, the personification of the entire spatial archetype in the last vision, endow the entire proceedings with a kind of magical quality, as if Kafka had depicted sequences of icons or hierophanies. As such, the Castle area may be looked upon as a sacred space—a *temenos*—isolated from the rest of K.'s world, distant and inaccessible, yet paradoxically linked to it in tenuous and nuanced ways. His vision of the Self transcends the individuality of the ego, yet, like religious cities and sanctuaries of old, is incorporated within it as well.

Though K. struggles along throughout the novel, there is little psychological evolution on his part. The first question he poses upon his arrival in the village—"Is there a castle here?"—may again be asked at the conclusion of his trajectory. Unlike Parsival, who goes through strenuous initiations to earn his knighthood—the title of *chevalier,* which symbolizes "master of the horse," that is, of the instinctual realm—K. discovers little about himself. His function, his identity, remain unknown. Nothing is really clarified. Object and subject still remain divided; each views the other in a perpetually unsatisfactory relationship, seeking the impossible, which is harmony between ego and Self.

Yet some differentiation does come to pass in the ego's fogged vision of the Self. The visual configurations of the buildings, their patternings and colors, their strength and shape, are no longer idealized.

Reality does intrude, adding an increasing burden to K.'s futile and pointless journey. But he never relinquishes his constant roving; plodding from one house to another, in and out of relationships, he keeps in touch with nothing really, either in the animate or in the inanimate world—except for the spatial archetype of the Castle/Self.

K. lives in a void, in an empty space, in an innocent relationship with himself. Uncommitted, he accepts the consequences of his obligations and acts but does not really know what that means, why such and such should happen to him. Yet, like Sisyphus, he is relentless in his struggle, pushing, forcing, intent upon discovering his place and rank, his clear-cut position in society, although he knows, like the Greek hero, that he shall never accomplish what he wishes to do. As he attempts to fix the fluid, to understand the imponderable, to penetrate the archetypal image embedded in and outside of his psyche, he is reminiscent of Beckett's creatures in *Endgame* and *Happy Days*: their activity is perpetual; it is also essential to the life process. So, too, K. deploys his energy in every way, to give sustenance and substance to his earthly sojourn. If he were not continuously active, he would think more deeply, despair more trenchantly, and death or insanity would overwhelm him.

Activity, one might say, *occupies* K. during his lifetime. His egocentricity, however, prevents him from really seeing the larger factors involved: the transpersonal realm, the objective psychic dimension. He sees something, but always blurred in the distance; never does an aspect of it become integrated into his personality, adding solvency to his being. Perhaps the very failure of his mission, however, helps him accept his disappointments. One feels that K. has a kind of fatalism; that further travail will bring *dissolutio*, the fracture of his already splintered ego.

Some critics have called Kafka a mystic, and indeed, judging from his conversation with Rudolf Steiner, as reported by Mann, he was. The Czech novelist suggested that writing allowed him to experience certain "clairvoyant states," and that as a result he offered his readers "a new secret doctrine, a cabbala" (p. ix). Unlike the Merkabah mystics, who experienced their ecstatic visions after passing through difficult initiation rituals, proceeding through seven paths to the palace, rooms, and chambers, where they heard the "whispering hymns and songs,"[8] K. never completed his initiation. He did, however, hear the sounds emanating from the Castle, like whispers and musical tonalities. Whereas the Merkabah mystics ascended past the gatekeepers, the archons, the fiery torches, the sealed doors, which they unlocked as a prelude to experiencing the *mysterium tremendum*, K. remained incarcerated in his own spatial archetype, imprisoned in the Castle community with its village, its crumbling houses and tower, never really unburdening the enormous weight he carried with him from day to day, hour to hour, minute to minute. Isolated, detached, never disentangling himself from his function as land surveyor, he could never realize a linkage with a larger scheme of things.

Perhaps there was no answer for such a sensitive and introverted spirit as Kafka. His inner abyss was nurtured by a profound dissatisfaction with the world of the positivist and realist, as well as the man of religion. Nothing seemed to be able to overcome an inherent fear, a turmoil, an inability to accept the vagaries of destiny and the impotence of the individual when confronted with collective forces. Assailed by terror and doubt—perhaps even about the quality of his own talent—Kafka was a wandering ego, pursuing a solitary course, unable to take that final leap into the pleromatic sphere, the Castle, so as to experience the transpersonal realm from which he would emerge cleansed, purified, and nurtured.

SIX

Lorca:
The House of Bernarda Alba
A Hermaphroditic Matriarchate

The House of Bernarda Alba (1936), a tragedy in three acts by Federico García Lorca (1898–1936), is concerned, as the title indicates, with a structure, a symbolic image that may be viewed as the concretization of a psychic condition. It is within this structure that Bernarda Alba rules and seeks to maintain her matriarchate. With great skill and a marked economy of images, words, and actions, the playwright explores the means by which this archetypal and domestic tyrant uses her absolute power to preserve the most regressive of traditional conventions. The tribal primitivism of those involved, Bernarda Alba's obsession with outer ecclesiastic forms rather than with truly spiritual matters, her ferociously sanguinary thoughts and deeds, are all centered on the role and function of virginal chastity and marriage, as is the unconscious rejection by her daughters of her immaculately experienced—bloodless and semenless—sadomasochistic sexual views.

Born in Fuentevaqueros, near Granada, Lorca himself was the son of a well-to-do landowner and of a cultivated mother, who taught him his alphabet and gave him music lessons as well. He displayed his love for both composing and writing early in life, and later frequently incorporated musical forms into his ballads, poems, and plays, even collaborating instrumentally with the great twentieth-century composer Manuel de Falla. Although Lorca earned a law degree in 1923, he never practiced this profession, preferring to devote his time to travel and the arts.

Lorca's fascination with the theater evinced itself when he was still a child. As a small boy, he used to entertain his sisters, his brother, and the family servants by reciting the liturgy of the Mass, standing behind an altar he had improvised and decorated with flowers for the occasion. In time, he became drawn to puppet shows, even building his own marionette theater. "The theatre was always my vocation,"[1] he stated. In 1932 he became associated with La Barraca, and as its director he carried out the company's goals, touring through Spain producing the works of Lope de Vega, Calderón, Tirso de Molina, and other dramatists of that nation's Golden Age.

Lorca's own dramas are said to have been influenced by the social satires and comedies of Jacinto Benavente, most specifically by *The Passion Flower*, which is similar in theme to Lorca's own *Blood Wedding* (1933). There are other playwrights who may also have pointed the way for Lorca's development as a dramatist: Ramón del Valle Inclán, who used his surrealistic vision to scorn and deride what he felt to be aesthetically and socially unacceptable; Jacinto Grau and Antonio and Manuel Machado, whose plays frequently dealt with themes from ancient Spanish folklore and mythology. Nevertheless, Lorca's dramas are unique. The stark restraint of their lyricism, the simplicity of their plots and setting, the bone-hardness of their archetypal characters, and the way in which music and poetry are intertwined to heighten emotion are his alone. In *Yerma* (1934), for example, a drama revolving around the plight of a barren wife and the searing emptiness of her rural life, the pain within her is underlined by the portrayal of her yearning on the stage as dreams accompanied by cradle songs.

Bernarda Alba *is*, in effect, her house. The house reflects her consciousness, her rule as chthonian mother, a woman who has never awakened to the dormant possibilities within her own being. The house is accordingly a restrictive, corrosive construction—not a home where gentleness, love, and relatedness are encouraged. The house controlled by Bernarda Alba serves to imprison her five unmarried daughters, aged twenty to thirty-nine years. It cuts them off from all contact with the outside world, and with men in particular, who she believes might sully them. Her goal is to guard her daughters—projections of her own psyche—from the world, especially from sexuality, which she considers evil unless used for procreative purposes.

In that Bernarda Alba has denied her daughters the right to be themselves, forcing them to fit into the mold of her preconceptions, she has by the same token blocked her own energies through her obsessive lust for power and possession. Her ego has overridden her maternal instincts. Instead of expressing her love for her offspring, she uses what nature has bestowed upon her as a weapon to dominate and scourge her daughters. Instead of her energies being directed by the *eros* principle, seeking relatedness and affection, her whole being is focused on combative, tyrannical ways, on fulfilling an unrelenting power drive that often yields to sadomasochistic behavior in an attempt to control her environment. Her blind urges—comparable, psychologically speaking, to the mythical dragon figure in ancient days—reach back to an *illo tempore:* an ancient time when titanic beasts spewed forth fiery breath, scorching their sacrificial victims—usually helpless maidens. But in those days there was a Saint George to rout these destructive primordial forces.[2] Nothing can stop the drive of Bernarda Alba, as revealed in Lorca's play.

The house of Bernarda Alba is a paradigm of an attempt to force a static condition upon others. The matriarch requires that her daughters remain sexually undeveloped, encouraging in this way a degenerative and insalubrious climate to fester. In alchemical terms, *putrefactio* may be said to be operational here. It is not surprising that in Bernarda Alba's house, along with this stifling, stultifying atmosphere, incidents of voyeurism and sadomasochism multiply.

Bernarda Alba's house is a repository for restrictive, outworn rituals. It has become a breeding ground for unbalanced and unacknowledged inner frustrations, for covert instincts and emotions resting somnolent in the darkened world of the unconscious. Her medieval views of Mariolatry may be considered in part the outcome of the romantic notions held by Spaniards in general concerning women. Indeed, the subtitle of Lorca's tragedy is *A Drama about Women in the Villages of Spain.* For centuries, Spanish women were idealized as willing saints and martrys, passionately desirous of devoting their entire lives to their savior God, or else they were envisaged in diametrically opposite terms—reviled as whores, worthy of hell and damnation, torture and burning.[3] For Lorca, such views were not only without validity; he considered them calamitous, preventing any possibility of growth, either along individual lines or in terms of collective development. To idealize such a moral absolute—woman as sacrificial victim—as the Spanish masses did and as Bernarda Alba does, is to live outside of oneself through projection. On a psychological level, such activities encourage a condition of stasis and the repression of eros factors and the ability to live in a warm human relationship.

In Bernarda Alba's world, woman is a vessel, a container: a procreating agent to be fertilized. Germination of the woman's individual personality is of no consequence and is therefore not to be considered. All innovative, creative, joyous sexual factors—outside of giving birth—are to be extirpated from a woman's life. The joys of girlhood, of youthful romance and love, are forbidden; they are to be cut short, crushed.

As an archetypal figure, Bernarda Alba is transpersonal, a collective mother who functions according to traditional modes of behavior. Ruling her domain with an iron hand, she acts like a tyrant who would not hesitate to kill in order to defend her terrain. Indeed, one of her servants, who shares similar views, remarks: "You have to fight like a man."[4] A composite of opposites, Bernarda Alba harbors within her being both male and female attributes and thus may psychologically be said to possess a hermaphroditic, rather than an androgynous, psyche.

The androgyne, as defined by Plato in his *Symposium*, was regarded as the gods' first creation, incorporating in its physical being both male and female characteristics and reproductive organs. Examples of such primal beings in other ancient cultures are Quetzalcoatl, Siva-Sakti, and Adam, before Eve's creation. Each of these primordial beings is self-sufficient, whole, functioning in harmony with itself. Hermaphroditism, on the other hand (psychologically speaking), represents sexual opposites in one body that are at odds with each other and therefore unbalanced. Each vies for dominance; each remains unsatisfied and hence abnormal and monstrous. Such intersexual beings, as they are sometimes termed, were looked upon in ancient times as freaks of nature and were killed at birth. Mircea Eliade writes in this connection that "the actual, anatomical hermaphrodite was considered an aberration of nature or a sign of the gods' anger and consequently destroyed."[5]

Psychologically, Bernarda Alba is such a mutant. Possessing both male and female drives and components, she is a composite of blocked, repressed, and perpetually dissatisfied opposites. Her libido (psychic energy) does not evolve into creative acts; eros, for example, which could foster a climate of love and relatedness, is unknown in her home. She is a *ravisher* of life and brings her daughters no emotional support whatsoever—only frustration and suffering. Her energy is always closely linked with her determination to maintain her own rule over her possessions. There is, therefore, no room for anything beyond her drive for power and position.

Bernarda Alba's psychological hermaphroditism is so extreme that any deviation from what her ego—her ruling consciousness—considers the right path is punishable by stoning, flaying, burning, or any other method that will prevent the slightest digression from her way. So possessed is she by her vision of Roman Catholicism—its beliefs and traditions—that she is not in touch with her religion, nor with her own spirituality, which remains dormant within her psyche. She lives her beliefs directly out of the archetype,[6] never thinking about her own actions and statements and their effect upon others, never wavering or attempting to delve into herself to search out the deeper meanings interwoven into her credo. Assuming the powers of high priestess, which such a being exercised in ancient matriarchal times, she is driven by her vision of asceticism, repulsed by the thought of sexuality, which for her is the hallmark of evil. As a result, her world is devoid of all feeling, all understanding for her daughters—and for what she considers to be taboo, the natural sexual urge. To this end men are only referred to in Lorca's play; they never appear on the stage.

Houses are usually associated with the feminine principle because they are containers and protectors; here the house serves to preserve Bernarda Alba's hermaphroditic matriarchate. Here darkness rules and latent diseased urges dwell, ready to erupt at a moment's notice.

The stage sets are simple and stark. What is of utmost significance is the emphasis on whiteness: "A very white room in Bernarda Alba's house" is the setting for Act I. Whiteness, or purity, in the context of Lorca's play, symbolizes the home's stifling sterility. Indeed, the very name *Alba* (white) reinforces this notion of absolute noncolor, thereby encouraging the continuation of lives without growth and development, without variation or change in activities or feeling.

Whiteness has since ancient times also been associated with the moon, that celestial feminine orb which has no light of its own to cast but reflects the rays of the sun, disclosing with its unearthly pallor a frozen silver world. Although the moon is empowered to provoke storms, thereby linking whiteness with the transformation process in nature and with seasonal fertility, in Bernarda Alba's house life is not renewed; it is devoid of blood, warmth, growth. The underside of the moon is what prevails in this house, the domain of Hecate, the goddess of the underworld, of ghosts, and of sorcery, who sends forth her demons to search for sacrificial victims to assuage her appetite. Emptiness and longing prevail in this white house, where nothing ripens. Only infection is encouraged to grow, to spread its poisons insidiously, behind a façade of immaculate whiteness and a barrier of stillness and seeming serenity. But concealed by this camouflage—even from lunar rays—there exist visible signs of unrest. Underneath, a whole unrecognized chaotic world pulsates, ready to overthrow and tear asunder the marsupial force, the psychological aberrant that is Bernarda Alba and her house.

The "arched doorways" of the home, so typical of the architecture of southern Spain, support the feminine imagery. The arches open onto the daughters' rooms, enclosures that are breeding grounds for repressed rage and powerful sexual urges.

Later we learn that outside the house the summer sun is burning, parching the earth, scorching the land. Inside, too, all new and fresh ideas are desiccated, struck down: "Life without secrets one from the other," says La Poncia, Benarda Alba's maid (p. 158). Yet the house is apparently radiant as it stands in seeming brilliance and health, the hot sun flooding it with celestial fire; it is clean, neat in all visible ways, symbolizing righteousness and the collective ideal—the highest religious concepts. But just as the overpowering heat outside stifles all that burgeons, encouraging the ascendance of passivity, regression, and even death, so within Bernarda Alba's house a suffocating atmosphere prevails: the suppression of all fresh air, all activity. The house is tightly sealed.

"A great brooding silence fills the stage" (p. 157), the directions read, corroborating the mood of staleness and suppression. All extremes, of course, indicate the existence of their opposites. Something, therefore, seems to be kept back, restrained—an untold story, an unlived life that remains to be experienced. The only sound heard, nevertheless, as Act I opens is the tolling of church bells, vibrations filling the atmosphere with death, not life. The funeral of Bernarda Alba's second husband is taking place in the local church; she and her daughters and the village mourners will soon return from the ritual.

ACT I: THE WATER SYNDROME

The stage is empty as Act I opens, but almost immediately, sixty-year-old La Poncia, who has worked for Bernarda Alba for half her lifetime, enters, talking to one of the other servants. She castigates the "mumbo jumbo" of the priests taking part in the church services and refers to Bernarda Alba as a "domineering tyrant." She even curses her: "May the pain of the piercing nail strike her in the eyes" (p. 158), using the stark imagery of the nails holding Christ to the cross to emphasize her point. Such an iconographic representation of one of the wounds of the crucified Christ accompanied moments of religious ecstasy for worshipers like St. Theresa of Ávila: the vicarious experience of nails sinking deeply into the flesh provided the supernal pleasure of being initiated into the realm of saintliness and martyrdom. Similar instruments, nails and sharp cutting objects, were used by Thracian women to scratch in their tatoos, thus endowing them with their supernatural distinguishing mark. In both cases, these phallic-shaped piercing instruments aroused erotico-mystical pleasure. For La Poncia, the two (erotic, mystical) are unconsciously linked, underscoring in this way the ambivalent emotions she feels toward her mistress. She despises her, yet, like a "good watchdog," she is faithful to her in her fashion. She spies for her on the neighbors and on her daughters, ready to root out any secrets, infractions, or subversive elements lurking within the dark recesses of the house.

Innumerable references are made to water, to washing, and to cleanliness during this opening dialogue—indeed, throughout the play in general. "Scrub, scrub," La Poncia tells the servant; dishes, cupboards, floors, pedestals, and everything else in the house must be immaculate. The idea of washing, of cleansing, to safeguard a person from sin is understood in Bernarda Alba's house in the same way as it is implicit in the *benedictio fontis*, or baptismal ritual that absolves the Christian. The white garment worn during the baptismal ceremony symbolizes the birth of a new, impeccable personality—rebirth and renewal through the primordial element of water. Let us also recall that water of the baptismal font, associated symbolically with the uterus of the Mother Church, represents all that is unsullied, all that was originally incorporated in God's pure creation.[7]

But such an emphasis on washing, on water, on the minutiae of cleanliness in daily life is a denial of all that is living, growing, reproducing, and changing. For in each stage of existence, as life takes unto itself, it also gives off unwanted elements. To overemphasize the danger of contamination is to kill all duality—any incipient male and female interchange. Any deviation from Bernarda Alba's circumscribed dicta, from her limited and limiting ideas, acts, and rituals, is considered a threat, a contamination of her own pristine ways. To retain a spirit of godliness and sanctity in her hermaphroditic matriarchate requires continual cleansing, constant separation from any source of infection, severance from all that is tainted—from the "human herd."[8]

No conflict, therefore, exists in Bernarda Alba's mind; there is no tension in her world. She remains immured in her own closed domain. Unable to relate to others or to her own unconscious self, she is desensitized and feels no true emotion for anyone. Unfeelingly unaware of her mistreatment of La Poncia and the others in her household, she lacks any notion of guilt or repentance; such emotions never take hold. Nor does she understand the repercussions her threats and humiliating orders have on her five daughters. She is neither surprised at nor interested in the fact that her second husband's family despises her, or that, as La Poncia says, after her father's death "people stopped coming to her house." On the contrary, such a situation has enabled her to remove herself still further from any outside interference; she withdraws, progressively, into her own unencumbered, uncluttered, unchanging sphere, increasingly discouraging all contact with the outside world. "She doesn't want them to see her in her domain," La Poncia states (p. 158). Locked in her own crystalline purity, sealed in her own secure medieval vision of Catholicism, isolated from free-flowing interchange with the outside world, she has banished all life-giving factors from her existence.

The pristine cleanliness and whiteness of the house make a stunning contrast with the black dresses of the throng of mourning women when they enter after they return from the funeral. The diametric opposition in coloration creates an abrasive atmosphere: no nuances, no shadings, only harsh and rigid extremes. Black, like white, is an achromatic tonality. While white symbolizes the unlived, sublimated, aerated, and unreal world, black represents primordial, undifferentiated, chthonian darkness. Let us recall that when Adam and Eve were cast out of Paradise, they were clothed in black garments—entering as they did into the world of sin, the adulterated earth. Yet it is within this so-called defiled realm that the seed is nurtured and life is generated; in psychological parlance, blackness ushers in the nocturnal world of dreams and visions—a whole secret and silent domain that exists *in potentia*.

The black-and-white duality, paralleling day and night, the sun and the moon, consciousness and unconsciousness, is dramatically used by Lorca to subvert and destroy the seeming harmony that exists. Just as whiteness in its pallor searches for life, growth, activity—the non-virginal and nonimmaculate tones that will transform a spectral condition into a life-giving force—so, too, does blackness—the shadow world, the primitive and instinctual domain—need clarity to channel its urges, to bring the fruit of its endeavors to a higher state of consciousness.

In keeping with the theme of whiteness and the water ritual, La Poncia serves the mourning women with lemonade in "little white jars," attempting in this manner to purify and cleanse the atmosphere, to wipe away the *dirt* brought in by outsiders dressed in black (p. 162). The men are served their refreshments on the patio, underscoring the fact that matriarchal forces rule within the house in a powerful way.

Bernarda Alba despises men and "the dirt they track in." She also states in no uncertain terms that "women in church shouldn't look at any man but the priest—and him only because he wears skirts," symbolizing the sacrifice of the priest's virility for the sake of God (p. 162). A woman hater as well as a man hater, she becomes progressively more identified with her own closed world, where she reigns unopposed, governing her subjects with an iron rod, crossing herself when she should, giving alms when called upon to do so, spouting her prayers, litanies, and religious sayings in automatic sequences. "Rest in peace with the holy company at your head," she says to the assembled mourners. "With the Angel Saint Michael, and his sword of justice," she adds, ushering in cutting and bruising imagery with phallic ramifications (p. 163).

Hatred and resentment are the fruits of her constricted, loveless world—her empty life. These destructive characteristics fill the void of her psychologically bereft, possessive rigidity. A sterile woman, despite the birth of five daughters, she does not know the meaning of fulfillment as mother, friend, or simply warm companion. When her thirty-year-old daughter, Magdalena, starts to cry because her father has died, Bernarda Alba beats with her cane on the floor, drowning out symbolically all feeling and emotion. Like a scepter, the cane represents impersonal power and authority. Tears are always to be restrained in her house, as is any other show of emotion.

Once the mourners have left and Bernarda Alba has received their gifts of charity, she expresses her hostility toward the entire "cursed village." These people "fill my house with the sweat from their wraps and the poison of their tongues" (p. 164), she stated unequivocally. Indeed, each time she is constrained to surround herself with outside acquaintances, resentment and anger flood her being. Separation—physical as well as psychological—is her byword, along with cleanliness and fixed order.

Bernarda Alba informs her daughters that for the required eight years of mourning her house will be sealed to the outside world. "Not a breath of air will get in this house from the street," she states. "We'll act as if we'd sealed up doors and windows with bricks" (p. 164). Not one of her offspring is to go outside. Life is to be lived within the walls of the house. As the hermaphroditic high priestess of her own religious cult, she is convinced that she is carrying out inherited patriarchal obligations: "That's what happened in my father's house— and in my grandfather's" (p. 164). Her daughters are to spend their time sewing their hope-chest linens.

Magdalena refused to adhere to her mother's dictum; she says that she prefers to carry sacks to the mill rather than to remain cloistered within these darkened rooms, this insalubrious, hate-filled enclosure. Bernarda Alba merely repeats her orders, adding that a woman's mission is to serve: "That's what a woman is for" (p. 165). An object, a collective figure without any personal value, a woman is used to mediate and procreate. She is a function—nothing more. "Needle and thread" are for women. "Whiplash and mules" are for men, underscoring their obligations as laborers, providers, inseminators. Man lives his life in the open spaces of the outside world; woman, in contrast, is confined to her uterine function, her condition of containment, her vessel-like existence.

The heat grows so oppressive that Bernarda Alba asks for a fan. Adela, her twenty-year-old daughter, hands her mother her green one with red flowers. Angrily Bernarda Alba hurls it on the floor. Colors are not suitable for a mourning widow; only a black fan will do.

Twenty-four-year-old Martirio gives her black fan to her mother. Martirio's personality is the antithesis of what her name implies (martyr). Like her mother, she appears to be calm and rigid, acting and behaving automatically, without thought. "I do things without any faith, but like clockwork" (p. 169), she says. Unlike her mother, however, she sometimes attempts to rationalize her apprehensive attitude toward the opposite sex: "God has made me weak and ugly and has definitely put such things away from me" (p. 170). In time she will yield to the resentment and even rage surging within her; she will lust for the phallus, the Dionysian in nature, that thwarted urge toward life.

Like their mother, Bernarda Alba's daughters are archetypal figures, each in their own way representative of transpersonal and eternal forces in nature. Restrained, inhibited, despising the rigidity of their mother's system, one by one they try to sever themselves from her suffocating and enclosed world. Their frustration leads to constant bickering, fighting, discontent. Angustias (the name implies anguish), who is now thirty-nine years old, is perhaps the most fortunate. The daughter of Bernarda Alba and her first husband, she is being wooed by twenty-five-year-old Pepe el Romano. Magdalena is bitter over this state of affairs, as are the other sisters. "We rot inside," she says.

Within the house and psyche, the sisters yearn for contact with the male stud, the phallic idol, and in the course of the play their antagonism toward each other grows more and more overt, each desiring Pepe el Romano for herself. Only Adela, the youngest sister, is actively rebellious, reaching out to life no matter what the cost. She has put on her green dress, the one she made for her birthday, and has gone to the chicken coop to be admired by the animals. Upon her return, she says: "Chickens! Chickens, look at me!" (p. 171). The pathos of her statement is mordant. Deprived of all human contact, she can relate only to lower forms of life. "They presented me with a few fleas that riddled my legs" (p. 173), she continues, dejected. Although the green dress represents hope and fertility, frequently Adela's view is destructive: chickens are spreaders of dirt and parasites. Her world is already imbued with her mother's retrograde vision—yet not completely so. A drive to experience what is natural in the world is expressed in her spasmodic and frenzied cry: "Tomorrow I'm going to put on my green dress and go walking in the streets. I want to go out" (p. 173). The extreme eroticism of her statement excites her to an even higher emotional pitch and hence arouses her rage.

Only one woman in this cloistered matriarchy speaks freely of what is on her mind: Bernarda Alba's eighty-year-old mother, Maria Josefa;

she is senile and kept locked in her room. During the course of the play, however, she manages to escape from her prison several times. At the end of Act I, she appears "decked out head and breast with flowers" and asks for her mantilla. Like the fool and jester of old, she is the only perceptive being in this stultified, stifled family; the only one who relates to nature, to the Dionysian factor, to the delights of joy and love. Intuitively she sees into the situation and predicts that not one of Bernarda Alba's daughters will marry. As for herself, she longs to escape from this fungal realm: "I don't want to see single women, longing for marriage, turning their hearts to dust. . . . I want a man to get married to and be happy with! . . . I want to get away from here! . . . To get married by the shore of the sea—by the shore of the sea!" (p. 176).

ACT II: SEWING AND THE KILLING INSTINCT

Act II opens on a domestic scene: the sisters are sewing hems and embroidering monograms on Angustias's trousseau linen. Traditional feminine arts, sewing and embroidering are looked upon as creative activities, since they refine and shape what is considered crude, un-aesthetic, and unserviceable. Such activities are considered a transfor-mation ritual, with physico-erotic ramifications.[9] The phallic piercing action of the needle, and the touching, palpitating, feeling process of their work, help to arouse dreams in the girls as they prepare their sister's sheets for her bridal trousseau.

As the girls sew and embroider, in effect they are stitching their own lives together, each in her own way attempting to mend what has been torn, to place within a framework what has been dislocated, to fill what has remained blank. Beneath this vision of feminine harmony lurks repression and suppressed violence of the most powerful kind. "I'll soon be out of this hell," Angustias blurts out (p. 177). As for Martirio, her ways are more subtle and far more destructive and deadly in their intent than those of her sisters—her very name indicat-ing the extent of her mother's projection upon her. She follows Adela everywhere, refusing to leave her alone for even a moment. Unrelent-ing and rightly suspecting her of having an illicit relationship with Pepe, she says, "My head and hands are full of eyes where something like this is concerned" (p. 182).

Eyes, whether those of Martirio or La Poncia, play a significant role in Lorca's play. Frequently the eye, the organ of vision, is equated with the sun, with light, intelligence, and understanding. Here, however, it stands for law, rigid and unyielding as it encircles the individual, seek-ing to catch the guilty one and hunt her down, spying on every act, thought, feeling. Martirio, like La Poncia, sees everywhere—into the most secret and shaded areas of the household. Hunted down and haunted by Martirio's gaze, Adela can find no refuge, no place within the home that she can call her own; she feels stifled, hounded. The eye of God has its satellites, and in her case, it is Martirio who intends to fumigate the mephitic areas in which she believes Adela lurks. Her powerful vision burns out the instinctual forces that prowl about, those sexual urges with which nature in its lustful joy has endowed all living creatures. Martirio, unlike her mother, a proponent of ascetic Christianity, is catalyzed by her own passion for Pepe, her jealousy of Adela. She would like to be the one to experience sexuality, not her sister.

It is through references to the eye that Lorca introduces the psychological condition of voyeurism. The cloistered atmosphere, the sealed, repressive lack of love in Bernarda Alba's house, encourages the growth of this perversion. La Poncia tells Bernarda Alba, for example, of the "evil" woman in town whose husband has been tied up by some men so that they may take her "to the depths of the olive grove" and there enjoy their pleasure with her. Bernarda Alba condemns such behavior, but she is obviously agog when she speaks of the incident, visualizing the entire situation clearly, powerfully, her sadomasochistic joy blazing at the thought of the woman's fate.

Later, as the five sisters listen to La Poncia telling the same story and others equally sordid, they are aroused to hitherto unknown erotic heights. Visualizing the lascivious acts, they, too, vicariously experience erotic thrills. Unable to understand the meaning of the biological drive they feel, each of them secretly lusts for a symbolic representative of heterosexual life—for a phallic lord; for Dionysus in the form of Pepe el Romano. According to J. J. Bachofen, Dionysus is "a woman's god in the fullest sense of the word, the source of all woman's sensual and transcendent hopes, the center of her whole existence."[10] Created and revealed by women, the cult of Dionysus was propagated and celebrated by them in ancient times as a weapon to fend off the patriarchal society then in power.

The same cult may be said to prevail in Bernarda Alba's house. Shut up in their chaste, frigid world, enlivened only by La Poncia's stories— which principally revolve about women dressed in "sequins" dancing and being enjoyed by men in olive groves—they passionately yearn to take the place of the women in question. But La Poncia, by the same token, forces reason upon them: "Men need things like that," she says (p. 185). Adela, the youngest, the freshest, the most outspoken of the sisters, the one who longs the most forcefully for life, rages at such injustice: "Everything's forgiven *them*." Her sister Amelia agrees: "To be born a woman's the worst possible punishment" (p. 185). In such an atmosphere a woman is obliged to spend her life preserving the man's world, thereby inflicting continuous punishment on herself; she must remain relentlessly obedient, subservient, enslaving herself to her hallowed master.

As the girls bitterly ponder their fate, song pours into the house from the outside world, and the dichotomy between the cloistered and the free world becomes even broader.

> Throw wide your doors and windows,
> Young girls who live in the town
> The reaper asks you for roses
> With which to deck his crown. (P. 186)

The atmosphere turns dense, cruel, ugly. Innuendos and recriminations begin anew. Bursting into the room in a frenzied display, Angustias accuses one of her sisters of having stolen the picture of Pepe that she kept under her pillow. Martirio is the culprit, it is discovered. Her excuse? Just to play a joke on her sister. "Hypocrite! Troublemaker!" Angustias screams (p. 189). Later, Martirio tells of the noises she heard the night before. It was Adela entertaining Pepe el Romano after he had been wooing Angustias outside her window.

La Poncia's native insight reveals a greater truth: Martirio is "lovesick"; a "grave" situation is brewing within the house, she warns her mistress. Interestingly enough, Bernarda Alba sees nothing, so anchored is she in her own narrow domain, her own unrelated world. Blind to the forces smoldering in her clean house, she says with certainty to La Poncia: "Fortunately, my daughters respect me and have never gone against my will!" (p. 193).

Yet the feud between Martirio and Adela over Pepe continues to strengthen in its savagery. "I'll tear you out of his arms!" Martirio informs her. "None of us will have him!" (p. 195). She would rather see her sister dead than allow Adela's love affair with Pepe to continue further.

Tumultuous shouts from the street are heard. There is the sound of a woman shrieking. Bernarda Alba enters along with La Poncia, who is informing her of what is happening. An unmarried girl has had a child, and "to hide her shame she killed it and hid it under the rocks, but the dogs, with more heart than most Christians, dug it out and, as though directed by the hand of God, left it at her door. Now they want to kill her" (p. 195). The townspeople are dragging the girl through the streets. "The men are coming, shouting so the fields shake" (p. 195). Bernard Alba thrills at the thought of the chastisement the

girl will receive. Let them all "come with olive whips and hoe han-
dles—let them all come and kill her!" (p. 195).

Adela, panic-stricken, holds her belly, unable to cope with her feelings, using gestures to reveal the terror that overcomes her. "No! No!"
she cries, stunned as she listens to her mother shout out with un-
paralleled ferocity: "Hot coals in the place where she sinned! . . . Kill
her! Kill her!" (p. 195).

ACT III: SILENCE AND RETRENCHMENT

The four white walls of the interior patio of Bernarda Alba's house
are described as "lightly washed in blue," pointing not only to the time
of day but to the nonmaterial nature of the events that are to take
place in Act III. Purity, coldness, and deprivation prevail in an endless
expanse, an airy domain, an empty sky. For Kandinsky, the color blue
most frequently represented a solemn note, as if all earthly entities
had been transported to a dematerialized sphere where infinite purity
reigned, divested of contrast, tonalities, individuality.

Bernarda Alba and her daughters are eating supper. Food, representing an interchange and a communion in the religious sense that
the *agape* symbolized for early Christians, can be a spiritual love feast
expressing God's feeling for humans and theirs in turn for all things
and beings. A spontaneous and altruistic communal sharing, an *agape*
is the complete antithesis of the spirit reigning at Bernarda Alba's
board. Here venom, hatred, jealousy, and insidiously dictatorial
powers prevail. Here is Hecate's dominion in all its deadly, aggressive
force. "A daughter who's disobedient stops being a daughter and becomes an enemy," Bernarda Alba states (p. 197) in her endeavor to
maintain her control over the situation—as if with sword and needle
in hand.

A loud blow resounds from one of the outside walls. The stallion
locked in its stall is kicking; it wants to be free. A facile symbol used by
Lorca to represent natural urges struggling to break out from a constricted atmosphere, it is taken into the corral on Bernarda Alba's orders. The stallion's function is to inseminate mares; this brings the
family money, power, and position and provides it with food. Since
Bernarda Alba is the provider and the protector of her brood, she is,
to all intents and purposes, the patriarchal ruler of the house.

Meanwhile, the house continues to be a "battleground" for the con-
niving, scheming, jealous sisters, each attempting to root out the
others' secret urges. Martirio, "a pool of poison," continues her proddings, her calumniations of her sister. Adela can no longer stand it.

I can't stand this horrible house after the taste of his mouth. I'll be what he wants me to be. Everyone in the village is against me, burning me with their fiery fingers; pursued by those who claim they're decent, and I'll wear, before them all, the crown of thorns that belongs to the mistress of a married man. (P. 208)

Maria Josefa enters, having once again escaped from her room. This time she bears a lamb in her arms and sings gently to the animal as if it were her child. "It's better to have a lamb than not to have anything," she tells Martirio, then informs her that "Pepe el Romano is a giant. All of you love him" (p. 206).

Commotion again sets in, and when Bernarda Alba hears the chaotic sounds, she returns. Adela is ready for the great struggle now. She grabs her mother's cane and breaks it in two: "This is what I do with the tyrant's cane. Not another step. No one but Pepe commands me!" (p. 209). Unaccustomed to such rebellious ways, Bernarda Alba runs to get her gun. She is certain Pepe is in the garden and shoots in that direction. Thinking that Pepe is dead, Adela runs into her room. Martirio, who had seen Pepe ride away on his horse to safety, refrains from telling her sister. Moments later a thud is heard. La Poncia tries to open the door leading to Adela's room, but is unable to do so. Finally she forces the locked door open, enters, and screaming, backs out.

Adela has hanged herself. Her suicide—a symbolic crucifixion—is a willed return to the Earth Mother, where the cessation of all conflict is realized.[11] That she has hanged herself may also be viewed as a kind of castration, a severing of life, a cutting off of all desires, not merely physical but psychological ones, which was in part Bernarda Alba's aim in incarcerating her daughters in the house. Adela's psyche had to be separated from her body; it could no longer function in an atmosphere so prejudicial to the body that housed it. Only through death could she escape from the imposition of her mother's moral code: a *sacrificium intellectus* had to occur—a mental detachment, a return to the *prima materia,* to rebirth and renewal.

There are to be no tears, no recriminations, no emotion, Bernarda Alba orders. Only one factor is important:

My daughter died a virgin. Take her to another room and dress her as though she were a virgin. No one will say anything about this! She died a virgin. Tell them, so that at dawn, the bells will ring twice. . . . Death must be looked at face to face. Silence! . . . We'll drown ourselves in a sea of mourning. She, the youngest daughter of Bernarda Alba, died a virgin. Did you hear me? Silence, silence, I said. Silence! (P. 211)

Such an atmosphere of sterility and repression can only lead to an impasse, to defiance, to useless sacrifice, to the perversion of all that is natural in life. Bernarda Alba's archetypal house, a sanctuary for a tyrannical, retrogressive code of morality, harbors and prolongs a suffocatingly unhealthy view of life. Unthinking, unfeeling, the transpersonal figure of Bernarda Alba thrives on power, knows fulfillment only when crushing others in her grasp. A *vagina dentata* type, she is in effect a female Kronos who rules her home in absolute whiteness; an Agave in her hermaphroditic matriarchal theocracy—rigid in her virginity, grim in her dogmatism, guarding her power and possessions with tenacious ferocity, ready to trample upon anyone who attempts to escape her sway. *The House of Bernarda Alba* possesses the simplicity and cumulative power of classic Greek tragedy as it slowly, inexorably, builds itself to climactic heights and reveals its blood-drenched, harrowing conclusion.

SEVEN

Borges: "The Library of Babel"

The Archetypal Hexagonal Gallery

"The Library of Babel" (1941), by Jorge Luis Borges, is a mystical and psychological meditation that focuses on a library housing endless hexagonal galleries, inner halls, spiral staircases, and vast air shafts. The author tells us that this library represents the universe. As an archetypal image, it may be alluded to in psychological terms, as the Self (the totality of the psyche), in that it incorporates both space and spacelessness; the finite, in the form of concrete shapes and forms; and the infinite, those mysterious essences which pulsate in known, undefined, transcendent regions. The books within the library also exist in a dual world. When inhabiting a linear time scheme (the letters, words, commas, periods, numbers imprinted on the page, thus involving these visualizations in past, present, and future events, that is, the workaday world), they may be associated, psychologically, with the ego (the center of consciousness). These same glyphs may be considered ciphers of unrevealed and hidden spheres: atemporal schemes dwelling in the collective unconscious (the deepest layer of the unconscious, which is inaccessible to awareness). As the narrator of Borges's story, in his role as individual and mortal, wanders about the geometrical constructs within the labyrinthian library, he exists as ego. As an archetypal figure emanating from the collective unconscious, he stands for an eternal and immortal being—Everyman!

Borges's short stories may be viewed both realistically and symbolically; as, for example, the burning bush in the Moses experience. Was it simply a brush fire? Or was it an epiphany? In either case, the account of the event triggers a mood of wonderment—also anxiety. What agitates and perturbs when one considers Borges's fiction emblematically is the subtle way he has of introducing the unexpected, the chance factor, the idle thought or sensation—an unknown world—into a neatly unfolding, plotted, and ordered baroque tale. The reader is then suddenly faced with the unknowable: endless abysses, swirling masses—the infinite, the very real possibility of losing footing and equilibrium, perhaps dying in the process. Psychologically, such a condition can lead to the dissolution of one's identity (ego) in the churning waters of the collective unconscious, leading to insanity.

Borges's approach to storytelling is unique. His architectural archetypes in "The Library of Babel," "The House of Asterion," "Death and the Compass," and so many stories are brilliantly faceted—Poelike. His *mazes amaze*. But what makes his fiction outstanding is his ability to combine fantasy with the numerical and alphabetical systems used in the meditative practices of the mystical Hebrew Kabbalistic tradition. In Kabbalah, emphasis is placed on visual and oral arrangements, rituals and disciplines designed to encourage an initiate (pure in heart and in soul) to concentrate upon certain ideograms. In time, and depending upon the depth of his feelings and his psychological projection onto the visual images and sonorities, he may undergo altered states of consciousness and experience the godhead. During such moments, the spirit of the meditator may be said to be moving forward or backward, evolving or devolving in a space/time continuum. Unlike the Kabbalist, however, the Argentinian writer introduces doubt and humor into his painstakingly wrought archetypal image: symmetrical and replicating hexagons, transversal cutouts, hallways, spiral staircases, and smaller linear patterns in the form of letters, commas, periods, and numbers. The combination of structure and its opposite, chaos, encourages readers to question the meanings and truths of the protagonist's statements and conclusions. Indeed, at one point he suggests that the entire web he has spun out may be fallacious. Or is it? In either case, readers are invited to question vast cosmological schemes and themes in what could be called Borges's puzzling parables.

Borges's neatly joined configurations are consistently uniform in arrangement. As if they are opening so many Chinese boxes, the one set into the other, readers follow him into his reality, believing all the while that they are firmly anchored in the workaday world. They are, in fact, being caught unawares. What they believe to be their reality is being progressively effaced and undermined by Borges, the psychopomp who takes them into forbidden territories where all rests on quicksand and speculation. A wry, subtle, piquant, and frequently macabre sense of the absurd is interwoven into the very fabric of Borges's tale, heightening its fascination, its muted and subtle tones dilating the impact of its terror. To wander about endlessly in meandering archetypal architectural constructs is tantamount to being lost in space forever—powerless, floating about in an empty world. Are the readers pawns in one of Borges's labyrinthian schemes of things? Or is the tale simply one of his homiletic games?

Jorge Luis Borges, born in 1899 in Buenos Aires, came from a well-established bourgeois family. His father, who was a writer, jurist, and linguist, taught him English; his mother spoke Spanish to her son. Both encouraged him culturally. It is not surprising that the young lad developed a love for books early in life.

World War I caught the Borges family in Switzerland, where they remained for the duration. Borges attended a fine secondary school and became fascinated with the writings of the French symbolists and the German expressionists. He started to write his own poetry. In 1919 he traveled in Spain and associated with the *Ultraísta*, a group of writers who, like the dadaists, surrealists, and expressionists, reacted strongly against nineteenth-century literary values. When Borges returned to Buenos Aires in 1921, he continued his collaboration with experimental poets such as Guillermo de Torre, Rafael Cansinos Assens, and others; he also published his own verses. As poetry evidently did not answer all of his literary and emotional needs, he branched out and began writing essays and short stories. His collected works include *Inquiries*, 1925; *Dimension of My Hope*, 1926; *El Aleph*, 1949; and *Ficciones*, 1935–44.

Rarely, if ever, did Borges mention his personal life in his writings. His poems, essays, and fictional works were objective in nature. We know, therefore, little concerning his feelings and relationships. It is common knowledge, however, that after his father died in 1938, Borges took a full-time job as a cataloguer in a branch of the municipal library in Buenos Aires. We also know that he lived with his mother until 1967, that he married a widow eleven years his junior when he was sixty-eight, and that they separated three years later. Though Borges's library position was dull, routine, and uninspiring, and his colleagues were uncultured, the job did have redeeming features: it was undemanding and gave him sufficient leisure to do a lot of reading and writing. Borges remained with the library for nine years, which he described as "years of solid unhappiness."[1] It is this library, perhaps, that is at the root of his fantastic, fearsome architectural archetypal image in "The Library of Babel"—a library that is the source of an overwhelming mystery—or game.

HERMETIC ARCHETYPAL FORMS

We might question from the very outset of Borges's tale his use of the biblical image of Babel in his title. Was it his way of assessing the Westerner's drive for achievement? His way of showing readers how people want to "make it to the top"? We may recall that Noah's descendants were convinced that if they could build a tower high enough to reach heaven, they could perhaps become the equals of God (Gen. 11:1–9). Aware of their condition of hubris, God caused them suddenly to speak a variety of languages. No one was able to understand anyone else. Confusion resulted. Psychologically speaking, one may conclude that people should not attempt to surpass their human condition. To do so disturbs their psychological and spiritual equilibrium and upsets society's order. Yet—and this is the paradoxical nature of the human species—to want to reach out in life, to be ambitious, to try and try harder to attain greater heights in one's chosen domain, is the way of the world. The need to attempt to change one's frame of reference and further one's knowledge, be it scientific, mathematical, architectural, or otherwise, has enabled humankind to build empires and cities, create new philosophies and religions. Implicit in this inner fire that compels people to push on is a passionate desire to prolong life through scientific and religious means. Unconsciously, and consciously as well, mortal beings seek to live on eternally. In so doing, however, they are negating their human condition. Eternalness is the prerogative of divinity. Still, the struggle to discover the mystery of existence—though to do so is impossible—goes on and on. Those who seek to achieve such a goal are perpetually frustrated. In the twentieth century, the ailment has been diagnosed as *metaphysical anguish.*

The narrator in Borges's tale is introduced and begins to recall his past youth and idealism, his ambition to increase his understanding of the world by making his way into deeper folds of the library: those architectural archetypal constructs—fronts for a hermetic level of being—for a whole universe (Self). When he was young, the narrator believed he could destroy the barriers preventing him from leaping into immortal spheres and divining God's secrets. Only later on in life did he understand that success could never be his. Even so, he still wants to know more and more.

That Borges, an introvert, chose the image of the library as a metaphor for the universe is understandable. Iconographically speaking, the library as depicted in his work may be looked upon as a great globoid—a mandala—representing an unknowable reality that every person seeks to understand. It is a sphere, Borges writes, "whose exact center is any one of its hexagons and whose circumference is inaccessible."[2]

Libraries house the treasures of the intellect; they represent people's desire to know, to experience, to amass. The fact that they are enclosed, protected, womblike, inspires feelings of security. Here, too, time and space may be circumscribed and arrested, knowledge fixed in the written word. For Borges, the book became in time a cult object, a kind of hierophany: a sacred force that nourished him perpetually.

To read and write was his way of life—perhaps also an *escape* from the rigors of the workaday world, which were not always to his liking. The domain of the mind, the imagination, was preferable to him, for within his own domain he would fashion a universe—a library tailored to suit the imperatives of his temperament.

An analogy may be made between Borges and the Kabbalists, whose cosmic vision so fascinated him. The Kabbalists also centered their world on the *book*, which they venerated and considered an instrument of divine will. Their book, the Torah, unlike Borges's literary, philosophical, scientific, and other tomes, was strictly religious in nature. The Torah (the first five books of the Bible) was and is for the Jew the most sacred of religious works: it is the *Book of Books*, for within its pages and ciphers is contained the living presence of God. The book is of utmost importance in both traditional and mystical Judaism: "Seek ye out the book of the Lord and read" (Isa. 34:16); "Thus Speaketh the Lord God of Israel, saying, 'Write thee all the words that I have spoken unto thee in a book'" (Jer. 30:2).[3]

Borges was drawn to Kabbalah because of its symbolistic and analogical approach to words, letters, and numbers. Along with later Christian mystics, the Kabbalists believed these glyphs contained deeper realities and untapped mysteries. It was the unrevealed meanings behind the ideograms and imprints that bewitched and haunted—tantalized—Borges, accounting in part for the unusual quality of "The Library of Babel," which is to be viewed as a kind of decoding narrative, like the life process.

Each book in this library, we learn, is adorned with a face and a spine; each is alive with energy, pulsating with activity, igniting those who peer into its depths and absorb its arcana. Some will *know* spiritual ecstasy during their disciplined meditations and become inundated by an inexplicably radiant inner light, succumbing at this point to the ebb and flow of the transpersonal realm. Others will remain aloof, detached, as they view unending maws, and they will wear the smirk of the unbeliever. Yet they, too, yearn to decipher, to explain the laws that lie just beyond their reach.

Borges's narrator is well versed in Kabbalah, having spent his life burrowing deeply into the books contained in the endless hexagonal galleries within the library. Its nooks and crannies, its hallways, closets, air shafts, are known to him for the treasure trove of secrets that lie buried within them—unseen, impalpable, preexistent!

The library (universe, Self), is envisaged as follows (see fig. 3):

> The universe (which others call the Library) is composed of an indefinite and perhaps infinite number of hexagonal galleries, with vast air

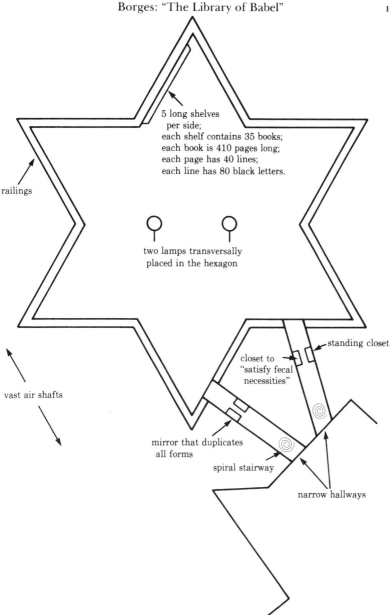

5 long shelves
per side;
each shelf contains 35 books;
each book is 410 pages long;
each page has 40 lines;
each line has 80 black letters.

railings

two lamps transversally
placed in the hexagon

standing closet

closet to
"satisfy fecal
necessities"

vast air shafts

mirror that duplicates
all forms

spiral stairway

narrow hallways

FIG. 3. The hexagonal gallery. Library = universe as well as divinity and the Self. It is unlimited and cyclical; infinite. Orthographical symbols in the books are twenty-five in number: twenty-two letters of the Hebrew alphabet, comma, period, and open space surrounding each of the blackened verbal or numerical ciphers.

shafts between, surrounded by very low railings. From any of the hexagons one can see, interminably, the upper and lower floors. The distribution of the galleries is invariable. Twenty shelves, five long shelves per side, cover all the sides except two; their height, which is the distance from floor to ceiling, scarcely exceeds that of a normal bookcase. One of the free sides leads to a narrow hallway which opens onto another gallery, identical to the first and to all the rest. To the left and right of the hallway there are two very small closets. In the first, one may sleep standing up; in the other, satisfy one's fecal necessities. Also through here passes a spiral stairway, which sinks abysmally and soars upwards to remote distances. In the hallway there is a mirror which faithfully duplicates all appearances. Men usually infer from this mirror that the Library is not infinite (if it really were, why this illusory duplication?); I prefer to dream that its polished surfaces represent and promise the infinite…. Light is provided by some spherical fruit which bear the name of lamps. There are two, transversally placed in each hexagon. The light they emit is insufficient, incessant. (P.51)

That the library consists of "an indefinite and perhaps infinite · number of hexagonal galleries" indicates the crucial nature of the number six in Borges's tale. Before explicating the meaning and function of digits in this tale—the six in particular—let us first broach their meanings in two of the most important Kabbalistic texts: the *Sefer Yetsirah* (Book of creation) and the *Zohar* (Book of splendor).

The *Sefer Yetsirah,* which modern scholars believe was written between the third and sixth centuries A.D., describes the creation of the world and the ways in which humanity can share in a divine process that lies both within the linear scheme of things and outside it, in a cyclical space/time continuum. In the *Sefer Yetsirah,* the stages of creation are associated with the ten primordial numbers and the twenty-two letters of the Hebrew alphabet. Together they form the "Thirty-Two secret paths of Wisdom" leading to God.[4] Each number is endowed with depth, weight, intensity, and significance. Some of them will appear in "The Library of Babel" and will be discussed as they are mentioned. The *Zohar* is made up in part of a second-century mystical commentary on sections of the Bible presented in the form of discussions between scholarly rabbis and their leader and guide, Simeon bar Yohai. The main part of the *Zohar,* it is believed, was written by Moses de Leon, the fourteenth-century Castilian Kabbalist. It was he who elucidated still further the numerical and verbal symbolism implicit in the religious text, thus revealing glimpses of arcana buried within the visible forms of letters, words, and numbers. The impact of the various combinations and convergencies of letters and numbers, in addition to the sequences of spectacular imagery in the *Zohar,* redolent with beauty and power, brought on numinous experiences for some Kabbalists.

Numbers are not only important to the mystic but as already mentioned in chapter 4, have a numinous quality and appear frequently in works of art or religious tracts when individuals suffer from some psychic disorder or anguish. They symbolize a need to compensate for a chaotic inner state. Numbers were not invented by the conscious mind but emerged from the unconscious, spontaneously, as archetypal images, when the need arose. The Pythagoreans based their philosophical and metaphysical arguments on astronomical, geometrical, and numerical calculations. In their theocentric universe, astral movements, they were convinced, were circular and eternal, and therefore divine (eternity is an attribute of divinity). The "intelligent," rational, circular, and uniform movement of the heavenly bodies was juxtaposed with the "irrational," erratic, and disorderly paths of terrestrial entities. The Pythagoreans further observed that terrestrial motion was rectilinear, and therefore limited (the object moves, rises, falls, then remains immobile).[5]

Numbers, then, have both a religious and psychological connotation in Borges's tale. Six, as in the hexagonals that make up the Library of Babel, is the most important of digits. According to the *Sefer Yetsirah* (itself divided into six chapters), the universe "is sealed on all six sides with the six permutations of the name YHWH" (Jehovah).[6] In the *Zohar,* as well, we learn that heaven is a complete unit, since it has six sides "which extend from the supernal mystic essence, through the expansion of creative force from a primal point."[7] Six has other meanings for the Hebrew mystic, standing for the spirit of both servitude and effort: God created the world in six days and then "rested on the seventh from all his work which he had made" (Gen. 2:2). The notion of totality and completion is also to be identified with the number six as it is manifested in the six-pointed star (also called the star of David or the seal of Solomon), composed of two interlocking triangles. The origin of this archetypal image is unknown; it is, however, present in Hebraic, Arabic, masonic, and alchemical writings.[8] Let us also mention the significance of the number six in the mantic procedures of the *I Ching,* whose trigrams and hexagrams symbolize "the original psychic structure common to all mankind."[9]

The hexagonal galleries in Borges's tale, he tells us, are infinite. Each parallels and replicates the others *ad infinitum.* Shaped like a six-pointed star, they represent a union of contraries, a totality, a microcosm of the macrocosm. Each includes the personal or individual sphere (ego), in its capacity as digit in the workaday computations, and the impersonal and multiple domain (the collective unconscious), which corresponds to the number considered symbolistically or analogically. The hexagrams, then, allow for an integration of the mortal and divine spheres: a fusion of what is disparate.

We also learn that the hexagonal galleries are separated by "vast air shafts": open spaces that physicists and mystics alike know are not empty, but are, on the contrary, a plenum filled with unmanifested, invisible matter. As the narrator pursues his trajectory through the outer and inner contours of the library, these infinite etherlike areas seem boundless, arousing feelings of vertigo and angst. He does not know where these areas lead, nor does he know what to expect. Quickly, however, Borges allays his narrator's fright by returning to a safe and tried sphere: concrete, ordered, measured, and structured forms. Indeed, throughout the tale—and this is one of Borges's literary techniques—he shifts from unstable quicksandlike terrain, which arouses trepidation or even dread, to the relatively safe territory of numbered, framed, and organized glyphs, ushering in moments of serenity and well-being.

The image of vast air shafts existing in the immensities of space arouses tension and panic in our narrator (and in the reader also); their philosophical and psychological import triggers feelings of dread and awe. Air or breath (*pneuma* in Greek; *ruach* in Hebrew), is associated in religious literature with male spiritual force: an active breath, a wind, and the sublimated sphere of divinity. Let us recall that God "breathed into [Adam's] nostrils the breath of life; and man became a living soul" (Gen. 2:7). For the Hindus, Vayu, the god of wind, represents cosmic breath. In the Gospel of John, breath is equated with the Word: "In the beginning was the Word, and the Word was with God, and the Word was God" (I,i). Masons, such as the eighteenth-century Claude de Saint-Martin, consider air to contain invisible life; it is a universal purifying agent. Mystics in general equate air with light: it becomes visible through its color and vibrations and acts as an interplanetary way of communicating between heaven and earth, a means of uniting the finite with the infinite, of welding disparate parts into a single unit. The air shafts, then, in Borges's tale, serve as sublimating forces capable of blending, mixing, transmuting, altering what is manifest and unmanifest within the cosmos; and in the psychological sphere, they serve to associate the conscious with the unconscious. They combine what is disparate, and as such are catalysts.

That each of the hexagonal galleries is "surrounded by very low railings" indicates the barriers that must be surmounted if the narrator (or any other librarian inhabiting these spheres) is to pass from one level of experience to another. In mystical literature, barriers, or rites of passage, act as protective devices and as obstacles. Placed in the path of those who seek to forge ahead, they are designed to test the depth of the hierophants' perseverance and gnosis. As protective devices, they prevent them from leaping into Kabbalistic or other mystical arcana without being sufficiently prepared to sustain the onslaught of powerful energies. Psychologically speaking, seekers who are unaware and undisciplined might lose their way, and the disorientation that would follow might lead to an alienation of the ego or perhaps insanity. These railings, then, like Borges's other architectural forms, his numbers, and his letters, warn and steady those who might be unprepared to face a plurality of worlds, and so prevent them from being sucked up or down by supernal spirals or churning abysses—wafted away into pleromatic spheres.

Visibility, the narrator notes, is interminable from any of the hexagons: that is, for one who can *see*, whose sight is directed to those endless expanded spaces—both inward and outward spheres. In time, and with prolonged study, the narrator realizes that he and his fellow librarians, as mortal beings, can only detect aspects or parts of the whole. Psychogically, they admit to the fact that the ego is not strong enough to experience the effulgence of the forces inhabiting the collective unconscious. It would be blinded in the process. Nor can the narrator even imagine the immensities of an infinite universe/divinity/Self. As a human being, he understands that he must work within a certain framework: a Piranesi-like baroque hexagonal structure. Only then can he approach the unending mazes one at a time, absorbing their treasures in small doses. In so doing, he may integrate the interplay between light and shadow, the known and the unknown within his soul/psyche. As he describes his wanderings, the narrator's entire being fills with awe and apprehension, as he attempts to encapsulate lower and upper hexagonal spheres in his mind's eye.

Returning once again to the safety of numerical forms as fixed concretions, the narrator tells us that the galleries are all constructed in an identical fashion: five long shelves line four sides of each of the walls, and two sides are kept empty. The number of shelves adds up to twenty.

The number four, identified with the four points of the compass, the four seasons, the four elements, is a quaternity that has come to represent the world of manifestation: earth, terrestrial space. Psychologically, it stands for rational organizational systems, for equilibrium and balance in telluric situations and relationships. The contents of the books, therefore, which line the four sides of the hexagonal galleries reveal humankind's need for serenity as well as a need for further information concerning its destiny in the finite world. The heavenly sphere, which, as we have seen, is six-sided, is not mentioned in this arithmetical grouping. It remains, therefore, beyond human comprehension.

The Kabbalistic device of calculating numerical and letter values for religious purposes is known as *Gematriah*. It was adapted by Borges in his fictional tale and used as a literary technique. Gematriah is designed to calculate the numerical value of certain words in order to probe hidden meanings of other words or phrases of equal digital value, thus enabling the seeker to decipher hidden mysteries. Let us not forget that for the Kabbalist, God wrote numbers and letters. He "drew them, hewed them, combined them, weighed them, interchanged them, and through them produced the whole creation and everything that is destined to be created."[10] Because of the emphasis placed on number symbolism in "The Library of Babel," each cipher may be said to be a metaphor for something else. Such an analogical approach to arithmetical dispositions allows Borges to link, relate, exploit, and poetize images and thoughts that emerge from his words, clauses, and sentences.

The numerical values subsumed from the four sides of each of the library walls, we understand, represent earthly equipoise. As for the two sides leading to the hallways, they stand for binary opposition—conflict, duality—and as such are equated with the earthly domain in its provoking and tension-producing capacity. Opposition in life brings to mind the echo, the reflection, the moon, evil, the unconscious, since all of these entities possess their counterparts. Because everything within the cosmos is linked, all is subject to duality—a *complexio oppositorum*.

The hexagonal spheres in the library, then, as well as their contents, exist in both the manifest and unmanifest world. As concretion, they undergo periods of ferment and completion, then back to disruption, growth, and so forth: four and two. The dual number, being the catalyst, sets the four aflame, spelling activity, excitement, destruction, and construction. Psychologically, the narrator and the librarians are forever bombarded by duality; they are, therefore, never satisfied with their lot, yearning to know more, compelled by some inner glowing flame to leave their hexagon and go to a hallway that will take them to other hexagons, hoping all the while to discover some more information embedded in one of the remote galleries. They are active and dynamic forces as they pass from the "narrow hallways," each identical to the first, on to other spheres or levels of consciousness. The vigor they display may be looked upon as a paradigm of people's need to pursue their search in the eschatological domain, and in so doing, participate in a cyclical scheme of things. Psychologically, the animated ego seeks nourishment—perpetually—from the fertile waters of the unconscious, as mortals do from their deity.

That the four sides of the hexagonal galleries are lined with five long shelves adds yet another digit to our puzzle, another aspect to our religous and fictional tale. Five represents a *hieros gamos:* a union of three and two. Three is a celestial number for Christians in that it brings to mind the Trinity; for the Jews, it refers to the three highest Sefiroth—God's ten emanations or unfoldings into matter. Two, as we have already pointed out, represents the material world of conflict, birth, growth, and decay. But five, particularly in medieval times, stands for a superior stage: that of body/mind completion. Images of a man (or woman) with outstretched arms and legs, plus a head, appear frequently in drawings from the Middle Ages and Renaissance, implying that the intellect (or the spiritual aspect of being) is not only united with the physical but controls it. The head is *above* the body; it orders its functions, as it is hoped that wisdom (or spirit) determines worldly activities. Such visualizations indicate heightened consciousness or awareness of one's role in life. Such awareness is the goal of the narrator and the librarians who wander in and out of various hexagonal galleries, reading and studying countless mystical terms—in search of the five, the guiding force leading to mind vitality, mind activity, mind operation, and mind animation. Only then, do they believe, will they be able to transcend the world of duality and experience the ineffable.

That the shelves add up to twenty indicates an actualization of the notion of death and rebirth: the cyclical or eternal nature of the universe (Self, deity). In Tarot, which many historians believe to be based on Kabbalah, the number twenty allegorizes the idea of spiritual and physical renewal. The Tarot card for this number features the image of the angel of the Apocalypse sounding his trumpet as he flies above six naked human beings: three emerging from their graves in the foreground and three others in the background. The noise of the trumpet is so deafening that it awakens the dead. Sound experienced as vibrations is the manner in which cosmic breath is now being diffused throughout the universe, thereby activating what is dormant. Kabbalists and Orphicists (the latter basing their beliefs largely on Pythagorean numerical systems and concepts) refer to the *music of the spheres:* a type of interplanetary sonority that may not necessarily be heard by the naked ear but is more likely to be heard by an inner hearing system that the mystic feels and senses once he has experienced transcendence. Through prayer, incantation, swaying bodily movements, and the repetition of sacred words, the initiate sets off rhythmic and sonorous waves, devices within himself that correspond to cosmic movements; in so doing, he may pass beyond an inert to a spiritually active state—from death to life or vice versa. That the Tarot card for twenty is labeled "Judgment" is significant. Judgment, according to Kabbalah, is identified with *Gevurah* (or *Din*), that factor within the Sefiroth, or the godhead (by extension the human psyche), that indicates the power of decision, evaluation, authority, the settling of controversies. In the number twenty, as viewed in the Tarot image, the rational function is called upon to work side by side with the sensory world. In Borges's tale, we learn that the narrator and the librarians are also awakening to an *inner wisdom:* they have tapped sources within their collective unconscious after having completed specific disciplines, which encourage cooperation between body and mind, in keeping with the number five, mentioned above in connection with the person with a head and outstretched arms and legs. They are beginning to evaluate their role in the world, to understand and perhaps accept their limitations as well as their assets.[11]

Each of the numbers in Borges's tale is given both personal and impersonal values, quantitative and qualitative natures, ranging from unity (one) to diversity (twenty). The greater the number, the more involved it is in the material world and the less embedded it is in spiritual domains. But there are other factors involved in numerical symbolism and geometrical patterns: they become for the narrator ways of communicating with the outer world—with the reader in particular; ways that allow for further speculation and the delights derived from these mental activities and/or homiletic games. For Borges, such activities are both entertaining and challenging.

Playing with number and language, one of Borges's favorite pastimes, is his way of relating to the outside world: organically, viscerally, aesthetically, and spiritually. Leading the cloistered life he always did—even though he no longer works as a card cataloguer in a small municipal library or shares a small flat with his mother—he clearly lives in his mind—nearly exclusively so. That he has grown increasingly blind during the course of time has cut him off still further from the mainstream of existence. It is through his writings that he shapes his personalities, establishes his situations and identities, constructs edifices and objects that he can view and penetrate with his inner eye. Such is Borges's way of participating in the life experience: his *engagement* in the world of reality. Metaphors help him concretize the amorphous and convey his intensely poetic visions.

In the Borgesian construct, play has cultural, psychological, and religious dimensions. It sets up multiple realities, and as we follow the narrator into the narrow hallways leading to augmented or diminished treasures, depending upon his (or our) levels of sensitivity and understanding, we penetrate more deeply into arcana. We are told that two closets are situated on either side of each of the hallways: one is large enough to allow a person to sleep standing up; the other serves to satisfy an individual's "fecal necessities." The first closet may be looked upon as an inner chamber of the mind, where the narrator or the librarians may withdraw to dream, meditate, pray, or play standing upright. We may regard this position as another metaphor for the number five (mind and body working as a whole), or for a tree, its branches reaching upward toward heaven as it yearns for spiritual fulfillment. The second chamber permits biological needs to be focused upon: a person must be fed through and by earth; instinct must be awakened. An earthly or perhaps a more ego-centered experience is in order in this closet, rather than a mystical or transpersonal sequence.

A spiral staircase is also to be found in each of the halls. Such an image of verticality announces the possibility of ascension to dazzling climes or descent into abysmal depths. The narrator and the librarians are thus given a directional choice: free will. Or is this another illusion? Can they really determine their destiny? Or can they do so to a certain extent? If so, where will they go? What will be their choice in life? Such a decision may arouse tension, libido, agitation—ups and downs. For mystics such as Blake, Rembrandt, Boehme, Piranesi, and the like, stairs involve schematic images of evolving and devolving universes: a rotating earth, cosmic relationships between the world of unity (the absolute) and multiplicity (the material world). Metaphors for high and low, good and evil, ego and the collective unconscious, point the way, symbolically speaking, allowing the wanderer to choose his or her path—the one that best answers a spiritual and psychological need.

The spiral staircases in "The Library of Babel" come to represent levels of experience and of consciousness. Let us recall that in the Egyptian *Book of the Dead* Osiris was often referred to as "He who stands at the top of the steps," because from this vantage point he could see into the distance and view the activities of all the other gods. Steps, be they those of the Sakkara pyramid in Egypt or the ziggurats of Mesopotamia or the *teocalli* of the Americas of pre-Columbian days, stand for humankind's need to transcend, degree by degree, to supernal spheres. In the *Zohar* and the Bible, Jacob's dream, in which he sees a ladder with seventy-two rungs reaching up to heaven and disappearing in the clouds, reveals a yearning to immerse himself in divine domains. Archetypal images of this type indicate enormous psychic activity: an intense desire to fluidify communication between earth and heaven, spirit and flesh, the conscious and the unconscious.

The spiral as a form has other ramifications. As an image of a coiled serpent, it represents motion, movement, enterprise, a need to reach a goal. It also signifies eternity: like the snake that sheds its skin yearly, the spiral denotes not a one-time situation but rather a continuous condition. In that the spiral represents activity and continuity, it stands for fire and energy. In Kundalini yoga, for example, the snake is said to rest at the base of the torso: as disciplines are practiced and accomplished, the fire from this animal (or energy) rises until it reaches every part of the body: from animal to spiritual spheres. The snake comes to represent flux in nature, flame forcing an interplay between disparate elements within the cosmos; transformation from the multiple to the one and its dispersion once again in never-ending cyclical patterns. So, too, are the inner workings of the narrator's and the other librarians' psyches sparked. Each in his own way probes, evaluates, fired by some burning desire to realize himself, to ascend the spiral staircases without toppling cosmic balance.[12]

The enormous surges of spiritual, physical, and psychological activity that come into being in "The Library of Babel" as a result of the power of the archetypal image of the spiral staircase are powerfully increased by another visualization, that of the mirror, which "faithfully duplicates all appearances." Like never-ending prismatic images—diamonds cascading about—the mirror reverberates its patterned sequences throughout the library/universe. Glimmerings, radiant luminosities, scintillae, sparks, have been equated by the mystic with wisdom, intuition, knowledge, allowing meditators to cogitate, evaluate: thus is light shed. Let us recall in this regard that the Latin word for mirror is *speculum;* mirrors, then, encourage speculation, contemplation, understanding—and narcissism. The intellectual interchange that can emerge from increased consciousness brought to a person through speculation may help to bring about an integration of these insights, those fiery intuitions, or *Einfalls,* rather than their fragmentation and dispersal.

The mirror, however, is not merely an aid to the intellect, the spirit, and the psyche but invites the body—the earthly sphere—to join forces with enlightenment. Let us recall, in this regard, a Japanese myth: Amaterasu, the sun goddess, had withdrawn into a cave because she was so angered by what she considered to be her brother's offensive actions. In so doing, however, she deprived the world of sun. Attempts to entice her out of her dismal haunt were to no avail. Only when one of the goddesses decided to dance in the most humorous and erotic of ways, eliciting uproarious laughter from the other divinities, was Amaterasu curious enough to step out of her cave. As she looked into the mirror in front of her dwelling place, which reflected the dancing, she too was caught up in laughter, thus returning light to life. The mirror, then, was that instrument which depicted certain antics that encouraged the sun to come out of hiding—as light dispels ignorance. It is through the intellect in Borges's tale—light bringer—that the narrator and the other librarians are emotionally stirred, bringing soma and psyche into balance, as in the Japanese myth.

Another vibratory image sheds further illumination on Borges's superbly constructed fictional work. "Light is provided by some spherical fruit which bears the name of lamps." Concentrated and densified in this metaphor, as opposed to its diffusion in the mirror image, luminosity exists as beacons embedded in blackness. Their glowing lights mobilize energies as they transmit wisdom in unending phosphorescent patterns. Their spherical shapes indicate the eternality of this need to know and to teach the next generation. That Borges compares these lamps to spherical fruits brings us directly to the Garden of Eden legend and the forbidden fruit: knowledge.

Lamps, we learn, are placed transversally in each of the hexagons. Their placement, then, not only underscores the geometric nature of the enlightenment process—that is, the importance of numerical values—but also accentuates their power as luminous forces, crossing from one side to another, or transversally, setting up patterns of activity. Light and shadow, therefore, replicate each other, shimmer, blaze, glitter in sequences and series of levels: up and down as well, illuminating supernal as well as abysmal spheres. Let us recall that Hermes Trismegistus, the alleged founder of alchemy and the builder of the first Egyptian pyramid, was also believed to be the incarnation of the Egyptian god Thoth. In his work, *The Kybalion*, he stated: "As above, so below; as below, so above."[13] The earth (and the human being by extension) is a fragmented and imperfect replica of celestial creation; it is in constant touch with it. Hence the narrator and his fellow librarians are able to absorb some bewildering forces, dazzling though frequently confusing, which at times heighten their awareness but at other moments blind them to the true notion of reality. Each approaches knowledge in his own way.

The narrator, who has spent his whole life traveling from one hexagon to the other, through hallways and closets, sucked up by air shafts or descending into the blackest of depths, now informs us he is old. As he looks back upon his youth in a kind of anamnesis, he recapitulates the changes effected throughout his lifetime—metaphorically. He does so by examining the course of his personal history, but that of all nations as well. In his youth, he searched aggressively and energetically for truth and reality, as is the prerogative of boyhood and adolescence. He was convinced at that time he would succeed in divining the information existing in the book of books or "the catalogue of catalogues"; that he would understand and experience the godhead (the Self)—if not completely, then at least in flashes, in intuitive experiences. Now, however, he knows that gnosis yields only an infinitesimal part of the mystery of creation: the size of an atom as compared to the cosmic mass.

The narrator's use of the word "catalogue" is of interest; from the Greek *katalogos*, a combination of *kata*, meaning "down" and complete; and *legein*, to "count" or "say." We are once again in the presence of a methodical, ordered, rational approach to existence. Everything the narrator has learned throughout his youth has been conveyed numerically or alphabetically: uniformly, painstakingly, punctiliously, as in a catalogue. The digits, letters, words upon which he meditated in the various books he consulted enabled him to unravel some of the arcana embedded in the invisible world, to fathom fragments of the unlimited sphere surrounding him. His longing to discover that undefined primal state, that unrealized condition which contains everything, indicates an intense need to give conscious form to what lies in an amorphous state in his collective unconscious. He needs to increase his conscious awareness: to make knowledge more accessible. In Orphic mysteries, numbers, words, and letters are prototypes of everything that is and is not. Like the Orphic egg, or the seed—in the narrator's case, the letter or digit—each visualization or sonorization is a potential force. So, too, is the book, since it contains hermetic knowledge. It is from the book that the narrator will be nourished. Not just any book—only one that has been catalogued, for then and only then does it enjoy a specific place and function in a hierarchically structured universe. Cosmos and not chaos answers the narrator's needs.

As the narrator grows increasingly old and his eyes weary and dim, he sees little—he admits—that can be gained by protracted periods of study and meditation. Still, what other channels are open to him in life? He has also learned with age to accept his fate and is reconciled to the fact that he will die close to the hexagon in which he was born. Humility, then, which comes with a more balanced notion of one's place in the cosmos, makes its appearance more readily in the second phase of life. The narrator no longer believes, as he had when he was young, that he will be able to dominate fate and possess infinite knowledge.

As a senex figure, the narrator is but one of the infinite collection of parcels that is being recycled eternally. His body, he now understands, will be cast across the railings of the hexagons after his demise, to be transformed into disparate entities, scattered particles in an endlessly active cosmos. In this capacity he will play his part in a giant game—nurture what might otherwise have become arid.

The senex figure in religious and philosophical tracts, and in myths and legends as well, represents age-old wisdom, a kind of *pater familias* type, reminiscent of the role played by kings, priests, ministers, rabbis, doctors, and the like. This archetypal image, psychologically speaking, is invested with special powers, unusual prestige—a mana personality. It is the narrator, as a senex and psychopomp, who believes he will clarify what has grown murky, explain what is abstruse, disperse what has become impacted, enabling the young and inexperienced to further their course in the life process—but with their eyes open! Or is this a further illusion? Can youth be taught? Or must each individual experience the trials and tribulations of the life process to reach a deeper and broader understanding of his role and goal in the world?

As a senex figure, the narrator explains various approaches to existence. The idealists argue, he says, that "the hexagonal rooms are a necessary form of absolute space or, at least, of our intuition of space" (p. 52). George Berkeley, the eighteenth-century idealist, whom Borges quotes extensively in his essay "A New Refutation of Time," was convinced that the apparently objective world exists in the consciousness of individuals: *esse est percipi*. Berkeley stated:

> . . . neither our thoughts, nor passions, nor ideas formed by the imagination, exist without the mind. . . . And it seems no less evident that the various sensations or ideas imprinted on the lenses, however blended or combined together (that is, whatever objects they compose) cannot exist otherwise than in a mind perceiving them. . . . The table I write on, I say, exists, that is, I see and feel it; and if I were out of my study I should say it existed, meaning thereby that if I was in my study I might perceive it, or that some other spirit actually does perceive it.[14]

The narrator pursues his cerebral philosophical and religious speculations and refers to certain mystics who "claim that their ecstasy reveals to them a circular chamber containing a great circular book," and that this "cylical book is God" (p. 52). Rather than giving value judgments that would commit him to favoring one point of view over another, he quotes classical statements concerning the universe. "The library is a sphere whose exact center is any one of its hexagons and whose circumference is inaccessible" (p. 52). Such a statement is not original. We learn in other Borgesian writings that Pascal wrote in the seventeenth century that "nature is an infinite sphere whose center is everywhere, whose circumference is nowhere"; that Giordano Bruno, a century earlier, stated that "we can assert with certainty that the universe is all center, or that the center of the universe is everywhere and its circumference is nowhere." Perhaps he took this idea from the twelfth-century theologian Alain de Lille, who might have found it in the third-century *Corpus Hermeticum,* which contended that "God is an intelligible sphere whose center is everywhere and whose circumference is nowhere."[15] Such ratiocinations remind one of Cornell's endless boxes and of Nevelson's eternal squares; each paralleling and replicating the other. So, too, are truisms handed down from century to century, like homiletic games, ready to be refuted, challenged by would-be winners.

Despite his age, the narrator pursues his mathematical computations, driven to do so by an inner urge, an inexplicable fire. As he goes on, so does Borges's closely knit story: it teems with numerological information that tantalizes and beguiles both the narrator and the reader. Each is invited to plunge into numerical symbols and decode their mysteries. In that numbers and letters exist in both the manifest and nonmanifest world, they are composites of opposites, each flowing into the other. As suggested in the *Sefer Yetsirah,* they represent the "solvent" activity of God. So, too, do mortals exist in both limited and transpersonal dimensions. The narrator feels, perhaps, that like Enoch, who was called upon to talk with God (Gen. 5:24) and transformed into the angel Metraton, he may one day be wafted up by Him into supernal realms.[16]

The narrator, therefore, pursues his studies. Each of the five shelves in the hexagons contains thirty-five books of uniform format; each book is 410 pages in length, each page has forty lines, each line, some eighty black-colored letters.

The number thirty-five, a combination of three and five, is a spiritually active number that implies completion at some future time. Three, a highly significant number in Buddhism, Judaism, and Christianity, as we know, is also identified with the triangle: half of the archetypal images in Borges's hexagons. As such, it needs double the amount to represent fulfillment. The number five, as previously noted, may be associated with equilibrium, but not stasis, as attested to by Shiva, whose number is five: he is the god who creates and destroys the world. Thirty-five, then, in Borges's work, may lead to completion, but needs one more digit to round out the five and add up to six—those interlocking triangles, the number associated with the universe that is "sealed on all sides with the six permutations of the name YHWH."

As for the numbers 410, forty, and eighty, all have four in them or are multiples of this number. Plato suggested that four represented the realization of an idea; three symbolized the idea as an abstraction or an ideal. Since four is looked upon as the concretization of an amorphous content, it represents the living out of a notion in the workaday world, the manifestation of an archetypal image buried within one's collective unconscious. So powerful a force can this visualization sometimes become that it may even direct an individual's existence. The four, in this regard, is of utmost significance in religious literature: the forty years the Hebrews spent in the desert after their exodus from Egypt; the forty days of the flood; the forty months Jesus preached; the forty days during which he appeared to his disciples prior to his ascension (Acts 1:3); the forty days of his temptation (Matt. 4:2); the forty hours of his entombment.[17] Four, then, serves as the accomplishment or fulfillment of values or processes; it indicates the beginning and end of earthly existence.

The number 10, as in 410, when identified with the Sefiroth in Kabbalah, indicates the end as a new beginning and the beginning as an end: the potential that exists in existence; the cyclical process. The 8, made up of two connected zeros, is also identified with eternity. In 410, 80, and 40 we are faced with infinite circularity, perpetually recurring patterns of life, each a fragment of the *unum mundus*.

Borges's mathematically deductive and reductive reasoning processes, so cleverly nuanced in his tale, introduce yet another notion: the chance factor. "The perfect Librarian," he writes, may be the product of chance or of a "malevolent demiurge" (p. 51). The notion of chance is as complex as that of infinity. Indeed, it represents all that is uncontrollable and unknowable in the cosmos. It is antifate, as is the zero, the nought: elements that are continuously present in the eternal cosmic flux. Chance stands for the world of possibilities from which the creation of the book, the poem, the human being, the animal, and all other manifest forces emerges. For the Kabbalist, the world of chance may allude to the *Ein-Sof* (the *deus absconditus*, or God without limits, the Hidden God): that is, "a sphere where nothing can be predicted yet must be postulated."[18] It is this world of chance that Prometheus battled against, that Orpheus attempted to transcend. It stands as a constant reminder of humankind's subservience to the laws of probability. The world of chance, then, spells disorder and multiplicity for mortals since it is outside of their understanding. Psychologically, it transcends the ego, representing as it does the collective unconscious. The narrator, who attempts to rework, reorder, and recreate his world—in keeping with his understanding and his patterns of behavior—in a single, all-encompassing conjunction of conjunctions, will find himself at a loss.

Pinning down chance, as when throwing dice, resolves a quandary, but by the same token destroys the possibility of experiencing or knowing the absolute—the ideal/idea. Nevertheless, to throw dice, to write, to number may be regarded as an affirmation of one's individual will and identity, since it marks out a future course. It is, then, one person's struggle against the ineffable: *being and nothingness.* By throwing dice one fixes chance in the number or the idea the upturned faces of the dice represent. Still, doubt subsists in the mind of the dice-thrower or author: Is it he who is acting (throwing the dice)? Is it he who is writing the literary work? Or is it the chance factor—the collective will—exteriorizing itself within the individual in the dice or the written document, thus obeying, unconsciously, the laws of cosmic causality?

The word "chance" (from the Spanish *azar,* the French *hasard,* the Arabic *az-zarh,* or dice game) symbolizes humanity's rejection of the law of probability. Since time immemorial people have been attempting to break divinity's power by means of hermetic letters and numerical symbols, to mention only a few of the ways. Even the narrator, though he knows better, still seeks to understand the infinite ramifications of the chance factor, and in so doing attempts in his way to control his destiny and the creative process. We have said that as a senex figure he understands, intellectually, the limitations imposed upon the mortal by divinity (the universe); still, emotionally, such barriers have not yet been integrated in his psyche. Is he, then, attempting to divest himself of the human condition each time he takes pen in hand to write a word, letter or number? Is he trying to stabilize chance? To concretize the amorphous? And in so doing, is he trying to control phenomena as did the magicians of old, the architects who filled space with their archetypal geometrical constructs? And who is the "malevolent demiurge" mentioned by Borges?

According to Gnostic tradition, the demiurge is the creator god, and because he separates what had been unified—God and humanity—he is considered evil. This creator god, or demiurge, must not be confused with the supreme divine being: the hidden god, invisible and ineffable, whose presence throughout the universe can be known only in glimpses, through gnosis, illumination, recognition. The Kabbalists also believe in a Hidden God, the *Ein-Sof* previously mentioned: a transpersonal Divinity about whom nothing can be known except through moments of heightened consciousness or mystical ecstasy. For the Kabbalists, however, there is no demiurge: *God is One.* He makes his presence known through the ten Sefiroth. God, the creator, then, is only one of the aspects of his ineffable essence, that aspect of him that can be made accessible to mortal being. He is the "Root of all Roots," that which is limitless and without end.[19]

Now that the narrator has introduced the concept of chance and of the demiurge into his tale, so too do dualistic notions enter into the picture: God and his mortal creation, the rational and the irrational sphere, the ego and the collective unconscious, good and evil. Questions about such dualities certainly cannot be resolved. They can, however, be speculated upon. The narrator continues to do so for his enjoyment as well as to increase his understanding of the world.

When referring to the distance existing between the divine and the human worlds, the narrator compares his handwriting, "on the cover of a book, with the organic letters inside: punctual, delicate, perfectly black, inimitably symmetrical" (p. 53). That the narrator should remark on their blackness brings a point to mind. The Torah was believed by Hebrew mystics to have existed prior to creation in the form of "black fire on white fire," which burned in this nonmaterial condition before God. The written Torah became manifest only through the power of the oral Torah, which Moses heard on Mount Sinai. The "white fire is the written Torah, in which the form of the letters is not yet explicit."[20] Since the letters on the scrolls or books in "The Library of Babel" are described by the narrator as "perfectly black" and endowed with other attributes ("punctual, delicate, inimitably symmetrical"), they may be looked upon as manifestations of primordial and amorphous words: their true meanings may still be concealed in the white and black light, in forms and shapes not yet brought into being on paper, still unstructured, awaiting a hand to guide them. Yet this hand—if it be of mortal origin—will never understand the essence of the words inscribed, since they exist in a transpersonal dimension, inaccessible to humankind's rational mind.

As the narrator pursues his speculations, he arouses feelings of malaise in himself and the reader, and he returns, to steady himself, to the security offered him by numerical postulations and orthographical symbols that *are twenty-five in number* (p. 53). The number twenty-five is made up of the twenty-two letters of the Hebrew alphabet, a comma, a period, and the space surrounding these imprints. To give further credence to his speculations, the narrator blends historical with legendary notions, offering the reader "a general theory of the Library" (universe, Self), which his father had subsumed "in a hexagon on circuit fifteen ninety-four" (p. 53). At this juncture, he introduces three mystical letters that lie at the heart of his tale: MCV.

M = *mille*, C = *centum*, V = *quinque* (1105). As such, these are both numbers and letters for the Kabbalists and for Borges: active, sensuous, colorful, rhythmic, living forces, imposing their presences on other numbers, letters, commas, periods, and empty spaces surrounding them. Archetypal in dimension, they are energetic forces activating both the visible and invisible glyphs with which they come into contact. Sometimes the narrator refers to the noises emanating from this mélange as "cacophanies, verbal jumbles and incoherencies"

(p. 53). Yet there are moments when this incomprehensible and confused mass does take on meaning: "This dictum, we shall see, is not entirely fallacious" (p. 53).

MCV may bring to mind the tetragrammaton. For the Kabbalists, the tetragrammaton refers to the four letters of God (YHWH) or the "fourfoldedness of the letters of God's name," which are "woven in a secret indirect way, but also directly as a kind of leitmotif" into the very texture of the Torah.[21] YHWH, for the Hebrew mystic, is a living, engendering force that goes through permutations and combinations, in keeping with certain secret formulas appearing in sentence form in the printed Torah as it now exists. God's name, and its holiness, however, are not only never pronounced by the pious, but the original pronunciation is unknown today, for the name of God is absolute and therefore inconceivable to mortals. It is read as *Adonai*. The four letters are also to be viewed as four paths, four mental states or feeling functions, four sensory images (letters or numbers, as previously identified with the number six), which are progressively effaced as one penetrates more deeply into the four arcane letters. The initiate who studies and meditates upon these glyphs re-forms and recombines them, thus energizing what is already in a state of flux. In so doing, he may believe he is reconstructing the primordial *textus*, or text (*textus* defined as that which is woven closely, as knotted cloth or words; texture), that is, the name, but he will never achieve his goal, since the finite cannot understand the infinite; yet he can blend within its totality.[22]

In Borges's tale we are given not four but three letter/numbers: MCV, a celestial digit, active but incomplete. "All this I repeat," says the narrator, "is true, but four hundred and ten pages of inalterable MCV's cannot correspond to any language, no matter how dialectical or rudimentary it may be" (p. 53).

MCV may or may not have mystical significance. It may simply be part of Borgesian homiletic play, a way of satirizing and ironizing the entire approach to the godhead, life, literature, and learning. On the other hand, since Borges uses such ideograms in this and other tales, it stands to reason that he is fascinated, mesmerized—and haunted—by them. They must represent some need within him, some energetic power which seeks extrapolation. That his narrator cannot understand the language to which the MCV alludes brings to mind the notion of Pythagorean and Orphic philosophers, who believed that in the beginning there was only one language, an idea implicit, of course, in the biblical Tower of Babel myth. The narrator refers to some of the librarians he had met who spoke of languages different from the ones spoken today, also of a unique language. Now, however, dialects, vocabularies, grammars, pronunciations heap confusion upon confusion. The narrator refers to languages ninety floors above the hexagon upon which he is now standing, which he considers completely incomprehensible. Ninety, as a multiple of the Trinity, brings another order into being: a different spiritual pattern that synthesizes plurality—the three becoming one. But the zero of the ninety also represents infinity: the concept of perpetual and continuous death and renewal. For the Kabbalists, it stands for the origin, or the center, indicating the eternal nature of the cosmic mystery. Moses de Leon, the author of parts of the *Zohar,* considered the origin and its center "the sum total of all subsequent mirrors, that is, of all external aspects related to this one degree." It is the point of mystery, the total and the disparate. Like the hole in the center of the Chinese jade disk, referred to as *Pi,* the mystic's "unvarying mean" is representative of the *prima materia,* a central force, a single unitary entity in a monistic universe, thereby solving the basic contradictions of the duality introduced in the concept of the mobile and the imobile. It is that force which integrates the Gnostic demiurge with the belief in the *Deus absconditus:* the dual and the one.

In sequences of superb Borgesian metaphors, we learn about further discoveries made by the chief of an upper hexagon in terms of language and numerical combinations: the struggles, wars, inquisitions, killings, and bigotry that resulted from the decoding of these emblems by prophets, messiahs, apologists—"the greedy abandoned their sweet native hexagons and rushed up the stairway" (p. 55). Here Borges seems to be poking fun at all revealed religions and their absolute certainty concerning the righteousness of their beliefs. Despite the ravages perpetrated by those who considered themselves God's gift to humankind—prophets, messiahs, and the like—still the narrator hopes that one day searchers will not exhaust themselves with peripheral matters but will find direct access to that "total book" (p. 56) which might be hidden on some shelf in the library. But then the narrator suggests that this, too, may be a superstition! Or is it?

In an interview, Borges was asked his opinion concerning his religious credo. He does not believe in a personal God, he stated unequivocally. But,

If you think of God as an ethical purpose, as an intellectual purpose, as what Matthew Arnold called "the something not ourselves that makes for righteousness," in that case I believe in God. Perhaps there is a moral purpose or intellectual purpose to the universe; however, I know nothing about that. I know that I am attempting in my own tiny way to further that purpose by writing quite unimportant short stories.[23]

Borges's library is infinite, unlimited, and cyclical. If a librarian crosses a hexagon any which way, "after centuries he would see that the same volumes were repeated in the same disorder (which, thus repeated, would be an order: the Order)" (p. 58). What Borges suggests here, through his narrator, is that there is continuity in the chance factor: it exists within what we call a world of improbabilities. Though we do not understand its functioning, it represents a constant, an asymmetrical/symmetrical arrangement, an order within the space/time continuum as envisaged in Borges's archetypal hexagons. As Borges suggested:

> I tend to be always thinking of time, not of space. When I hear the words "time" and "space" used together, I feel as Nietzsche felt when he heard people talking about Goethe and Schiller—a kind of blasphemy. I think that the central riddle, the central problem of metaphysics—let us call it thinking—is time, not space. Space is one of the many things to be found inside time—as you find, for example, color or shape or sizes or feelings. But I think the real problem, the problem we have to grapple with, and of course the problem whose solution we'll never find, is the problem of time, of successive time, and therein, the problem of personal identity, which is but a part of the problem of time.[24]

It is with the architectural archetype that Borges, like Descartes, feels most at home, and he is able, therefore, to use it to give credence to his philosophical and psychological tale. Within the paradoxically limitless boundaries of the hexagonal library, a metaphor for the universe and the Self, Borges experiences freedom, fun, and play—as well as dread. The riddle he poses, the puzzle he sets forth, the homiletic conundrum he postulates for the reader in his mathematical and verbal construct, are embedded in both ordinary life and in dimensionless spheres. They follow an order—their own—creating, in so doing, fresh arrangements, classifications, codifications, and categories that the reader must decipher at his own pace, using the great Kabbalistic writings as a framework.

"The Library of Babel" is drama; it is poignant and meaningful. It is *methectic* rather than *mimetic*, for it allows all those approaching it to participate in mental calculations, cerebral speculations, emotional leaps into personal and impersonal dimensions. Hence readers may be swept up by endless hexagonal spheres, shelves, books, hallways, closets, spiral stairs, and dangerous air shafts, trying all the while to center themselves, to stabilize what is forever off-balance, to still the flow as they attempt to make ORDER in what they consider to be the DISORDER of transpersonal dimensions existing within Borges's stunning archetypal hexagonal galleries.

EIGHT

Fuentes: "In a Flemish Garden"
A Parapsychological Happening in an Architectural Construct

A nineteenth-century French baroque mansion in Mexico City is the site for the parapsychological experience dramatized in Carlos Fuentes's haunting tale "In a Flemish Garden" (1954). Eerie and vacant, this architectural construct is a repository for earthly and celestial forces, a sacred space where the manifest and unmanifest assume equal power. A wizened old lady is the high priestess or anima figure in Fuentes's tale; it is she who directs the dramatic events, who lures the narrator, her votary, deep into her darkened domain—a fourth dimension where time is reversible and the invisible takes on shape and contour. The sensate world, acting as a catalyst, animates tactile feelings, enkindles aromatic perfumes that emanate from the garden in the back of the mansion, creating a panoply of nuanced luminosities and shadowy sequences.

More than simply a locale for a personal drama, Funtes's mansion takes on mythical configurations: that of an ancient Mexican pyramidal temple, a *teocalli*, or house of God, where a religious ritual is lived out, where solar and lunar forces vie for dominion. A cultural struggle is also at stake, between European and Mexican ways, Christian religious views and those promulgated by indigenous deities such as Quetzalcoatl, Huitzilopochtli, Tezcatlipoca, Xochipilli, and Coatlicue. The energy concentrated in the sacred inner space that is the mansion paves the way for the unitive experience undergone by the protagonist: it consolidates rather than disperses libido, thereby activating unconscious contents, transforming what had been a seemingly rational and ordered outlook into an irrational and traumatic experience. "In a Flemish Garden" may be viewed as a psychological, existential, and cosmic encounter.

Born in Mexico City (1928), Carlos Fuentes, the son of a diplomat, spent his early years traveling from Washington, D.C., to Santiago,

Buenos Aires, and Geneva. His exposure to many cultures, races, and religions accounts for the cosmopolitan nature of his creative work. After completing a degree at Catholic University of America in Washington, D.C., he went to law school at the National University in Mexico, then became a member of the Mexican delegation to the International Labor Organization and cultural attaché to the embassy in Geneva. He was following in his father's footsteps, preparing himself for the career of an international diplomat.

The year 1954 was a crucial one for Fuentes. Not only did it see the publication of *The Masked Days*, which includes the short story "In a Flemish Garden," but it was the year Fuentes decided to break with his past and become a writer. In opting for such a career, he rejected not only his parents and what they stood for, but his heritage, his entire middle-class upbringing. It must be noted that two years before his decision to carve out his own future, he had joined the Communist Party, hoping, as did so many idealists at the time, that in so doing he would help his country economically.

No longer able to lead the facile and carefree existence that his father's connections had offered him until now, Fuentes set to work writing articles for magazines, exploring both theoretical and ideological views. He also began composing short stories and novels: *The Air is Clear* (1958), *Aura* and *The Death of Artemio Cruz* (1962), and many more. By 1962 he had withdrawn from the Communist Party, believing that its political restrictions denied him the freedom vital to an artist.

An international and mythical flavor exists in many of Fuentes's short stories and novels, particularly in "In a Flemish Garden." Such an all-encompassing vision permits him to juxtapose European and Mexican cultures, primitive and industrialized societies, protagonists whose inner tensions are such that a schism, a break in their psyches, comes to pass unless the problems are resolved. In "In a Flemish Garden," nostalgia accompanies an increasing sense of terror, an inability to see clearly into the crossroads that lie ahead. Like Edgar Allan Poe, whom he so admires, Fuentes is a master at sustaining a mood of suspense and indulging in metaphysical and symbolistic probings. Inspired also by the fantasy world of H. G. Wells and the depiction of charming exterior domains by Henry James, Fuentes's spine-tingling mystery entices the reader to follow his protagonist into his sacred space—his mansion—to worship the high priestess, to come under the spell of her secret, unknown, and inexplicable power.

Written in diary form to give the impression of greater veracity, Fuentes's tale concerns a mansion located on Puente de Alvarado, one of the most populated and busiest streets in Mexico City. A lawyer who has just bought this magnificent home, which dates back to the French intervention in Mexico (1865–67), believes that its charm and historicity, as well as its elegance and the romance associated with it, will be appreciated by his North American business associates. Only one problem exists. The mansion lacks "human warmth." To remedy this situation, he asks a young friend of his, the protagonist of Fuentes's story, to move into the mansion for a while. The lawyer assures him that he will have no worries concerning the building's maintenance, since its tapestried walls, ceiling, murals, baroque columns, polished brass, intricately carved woodwork, and spotless floors have been meticulously cared for by a caretaker couple living on the top floor. The protagonist agrees, packs his suitcase, and moves in.

That the young man of our story is asked to live in a mansion that has remained uninhabited since 1910, so as to bring it "warmth," would suggest that its new owner believes him to have a catalytic personality—one filled with flame and energy. The house, however, is virtually empty and cold, perhaps revealing quite another condition. For Poe and Balzac, furniture, draperies, carpeting, and other household amenities are metaphors for spiritual and psychological attitudes. In "The Philosophy of Furniture," Poe tells us that "the soul of the apartment is the carpet," and the colors it sheds throughout the room determine the emotions of the moment. So, too, does Balzac write at length about the furnishings in his novels; for him they also take on metaphysical value, each object mirroring the inner landscape of the characters involved. The vacant mansion in Fuentes's tale replicates the protagonist's own unlived, listless, and destitute inner condition. To be sure, he possesses psychic energy, but it is devoid of focus. He has no center of gravity. Undeveloped and unfulfilled, his psyche, we soon learn, is fragmented, atomized, and certainly in need of some outer force to redirect it. The pull and tug of daily existence no longer answers his needs. A period of indwelling, then, is in order: the mansion—this unoccupied yet contained space, this *teocalli*, into which libido will be decanted—will become the recipient for the parapsychological transformation ritual to occur. Far from the light of consciousness, the protagonist, when penetrating the mansion, will be returning to a more primitive level within his subliminal world; it is there that he will encounter archetypal forces that may or may not heal him. A microcosm reminiscent of the *teocalli* of Tenochtitlán of pre-Columbian days, where Aztecs performed their religious rituals, Fuentes's sacred space discloses an attitude—and as the events are lived out, the various folds within the protagonist's unconscious will be laid bare.

No sooner does the young man enter the mansion than feelings of nostalgia erupt within him: a romantic past is constellated, intellectually and tactilely. His state of wonderment encourages him to visually caress the Ionic capitals and caryatids; the murals on the vaulted ceilings painted by disciples of Francesco Guardi all seem to burst into life and fill him with inexplicable excitement. As for the "gleaming fragrant floors" and the walls "stained by spectral rectangles where paintings once hung,"[1] they usher in a world of fantasy, infiltrating the past into a present reality, tapping a seemingly limitless source of marvel and mystery.

We learn that Maximilian, the ruler of Mexico, and his wife, Carlotta, had once lived in the mansion. Let us recall that when Napoleon III was Emperor of France (1852–70), he placed Maximilian, the brother of an Austrian archduke Ferdinand, on the Mexican throne, believing European influence would predominate in this area. Commander-in-chief of the Austrian fleet and governor-general of Lombardo-Venetia, Maximilian had visions of liberal reforms when he arrived in Mexico in 1864 with his wife. He failed in effecting the innovations he had in mind, alienating both liberals and conservatives from the very outset and even annoying the Americans by violating the Monroe Doctrine. As long as Napoleon III was able to provide Maximilian with the troops necessary to maintain his power, all went well. By 1866, however, the emperor of France felt impelled to recall his military forces from Mexico for political reasons. Maximilian's situation grew dangerous. He considered abdication. His wife, however, the daughter of Leopold I of Belgium, decided to go to Europe and request aid from the pope and European rulers. Her mission failed. In desperation, as an alternative to leaving the country, Maximilian assumed personal command of the military. A year later, he was captured and shot. After her husband's demise, Carlotta spent the many years left to her in loneliness and sorrow. She died insane in 1927. The mansion in Fuentes's tale may be viewed as a paradigm for the dwelling place Maximilian and Carlotta enjoyed during their stay in Mexico: the sacred space in which they experienced their love, the failure of their political goals, and the rage and violence they aroused in others.

The narrator's entry in his journal (on September 19) informs us that soon after entering the mansion for the first time, he walked toward the western part of the building and spent much time looking through the glass doors that separate the library from the garden. An outsider, since he cannot yet communicate viscerally with the garden area—he can see it only from behind a concrete object—he can nevertheless smell the aroma that emanates from the world of nature and longs to immerse himself in what he believes will be a most nutritive element. Until he finds the key that will open the French doors, he will be forced to stare at the objects of his desire from within, ardently, almost passionately. The red and white *siemprevivas* (the Spanish version of forget-me-nots), which shine and glisten beneath the drizzle, attract him most particularly. For some unknown reason he feels ineluctably drawn to them. They trigger in him a panoply of sensations. He has the impression of being transported to Belgium, a land known for its richly tinctured gardens, its multitude of flowers, as well as its gray and mournful climatic tones. Lines from a poem by Georges Rodenbach (1855–98) flow into his mind; their subtle music, swelling rhythms, bell-like resonances, and muted colorations replicate the liquid images that are so much part of Belgian landscape. The darkness of the visualizations depicted by Rodenbach in his verbal recollections draws the protagonist and reader alike into the heart of the *feeling* world—far from the brash and harsh light of consciousness. A nocturnal mood of tenderness, as well as clusters of languishing modulations and undulations, impress themselves upon the narrator as he observes, concomitantly, a mist rising from the garden floor, then hovering about. Strange shapes, specters of a world long since dead, take on contour for him, filling the fog-laden scene. A sense of regret for a once-great love takes hold of him and spreads throughout his entire being.

The narrator, spellbound and stupefied at the sight of the garden and its *siemprevivas,* cannot tear himself away from the vision. Still cut off by the window/door, as eyes separate the soul from the world outside, he remains a voyeur, unable to communicate with the strange silhouettes that appear and vanish before him. He stands transfixed. Glass is a paradoxical entity: though it permits light to shine through it and visibility to occur, it is nevertheless concrete and therefore a barrier—a wall of sorts. Like the ancient acolyte proceeding in his rite of passage through the *teocalli,* circumventing obstacle upon obstacle, so Fuentes's protagonist must also reach out visually, perceptibly, intuitively, and also physically into the garden beyond, penetrating that other reality—fertile, shiny, but shadowy.

As the narrator looks out into the garden, amid its discernible forms and multiple levels of mist and haze, he distinguishes two pupils, two orbs, black circular observing presences. To whom do they belong? Where do they come from? Are they reflections of his own eyes in the glass?

"I haven't yet found the keys to the doors," the narrator writes, implying that he has not as yet unraveled the mystery of the mansion (p. 16). Keys are important factors in religions and in literary works: St.

Peter holds the keys to paradise for the Christian; Janus opened the sky at daybreak and closed it at sunset for the Romans; Mephistopheles possessed the keys needed for Faust's redemption, and so forth. Keys allow hierophants to unlock the doors leading to their inner spheres, thus doing away with obstacles impeding their access to deeper levels of consciousness. Not everyone succeeds in finding the key to that outer or inner world which will help them to evaluate elements encountered in their life's trajectory. Even the people holding the key to their problem may not be master of their destiny and responsible for their future. Although the protagonist in Fuentes's tale finds the key and opens the door leading to the garden where the mystery is embedded, one wonders whether he is sufficiently objective to apply the thinking function and judgmental perceptions necessary to further the initiatory process.

What does the garden represent that its penetration should be one of the goals of the acolyte/protagonist in Fuentes's tale? Unlike the forest, where nature is in its wildest and most primitive condition, the garden is ordered, subdued, and enclosed. Gardens were significant for Europeans, Belgians in particular, because their brilliant colors enlivened an otherwise mournful landscape, and their fragrance injected subtle sensations and springlike feelings into what was perhaps a melancholy outlook. For Aztecs, gardens were important mystically as well as aesthetically. The palace of King Nezaualcoyotl at Texcoco could boast of elegant and exquisitely appealing gardens planted in orchestrated hues and gradations of aromatic plants. Columns and floors were made of jasper and other precious stones that were carved and sculpted in floral forms, adorning the homes of such eminent rulers as Motecuhzoma. The floating gardens of Tenochtitlán as well as the hanging gardens situated on the white porticos of Mexican palaces were known for their appeal. Even the poorest homes during the Aztec period had their plantings, dazzling both the earth and heavens with their unforgettable mosaics of flowers.[2] Statuettes of the deities Huitzilopochtli and Tezcatlipoca were adorned with sweet-smelling flowers, wreathed in multicolored garlands or displayed singly.

A historical and psychological dimension is also implicit in the garden image of Fuentes's tale. The red and white *siemprevivas*, for example, imply that nothing is to be forgotten, for memory remains forever. These flowers, given to Emperor Maximilian by the Indians as a token of their affection and admiration for their new master, disclosed touching devotion on their part. Not many years later, however, this warmth and tenderness was transformed into rage and murder—and for Carlotta, into insanity.[3] *Siemprevivas*, then, may be looked upon as a paradigm of nature's volatility and also as a mirror image of humankind's fickle nature: the polarities, antagonisms, and harmonies that exist inchoate within it.

Colors have their emotional equivalents. The red of the *siemprevivas* is linked with fire and warmth, but when the brilliant tones fade, icy coldness permeates the atmosphere. Red is also identified with blood: a nourishing and life-giving principle. When representative of the blood of Christ in Holy Communion, it allows initiates to bathe in a transpersonal force, to attain immortality. Red may also stand for raw instinct, uncontrolled inner urges, passion, war. Red is also reminiscent of the feathers worn on the arms and legs of Aztec brides before their marriage ceremony. In this regard, it stands for the feminine principle, a world immersed in heart and feeling.[4] Fuentes's use of this coloration is mysterious and ambiguous. Veiled at first, hidden, remaining untouchable outside of the mansion, in the world beyond the glass doors, its blazing energy emerges slowly at first, in the form of ductile sensations, then more powerfully in convoluted patterns of psychic activity.

Each culture has its blood sacrifices, its sacred purification rituals. So-called civilized lands sacrifice their young in wars, in inquisitions, in extermination camps, in all types of torture, and the like. For the ancient Mexicans, however, blood sacrifice was implicit in the cosmological process. It was believed that when a child is born the sun is divested of those sparks of light it has placed within the new infant, and hence its own *scintillae* are depleted. If the sun's blood supply or energetic particles are not renewed, this solar force will die, and the tribe, the nation, the earth will be clothed in darkness, ice, and death. Each human being who sacrifices himself to the sun, to Tezcatlipoca, does so to insure the continuity of his people.[5] As his heart is cut out and offered to this primal force, reminiscent of one who has been flayed, he restores what has been depleted. Flaying intimates a splitting open of that which encloses life, a liberation of a seed that can grow and enkindle new beings. Like blood sacrifice, war among the Aztecs was not waged for political or economic reasons, as it was in other lands; rather, it consummated a religious ritual—a holy struggle.[6]

White, which indicates the absence of color, also represents the sum total of all colors. As such, it is a paradigm of the diurnal and nocturnal worlds, the moment of transition between death and life, the visible and the invisible. Like a birth or death passage, it stands for a period of mutation, announcing the coming of a lunar female or solar male world. White, as in dawn, is rich in potential. But it also represents that which precedes death: a livid, vampiric sphere, where specters, apparitions, and ghosts enshroud the atmosphere. For the Aztec, the west is white; it stands for deadly hues, allowing one to enter the invisible world of vanishing consciousness.

Since life for the Aztecs is conditioned by the sun, the west, into which this solar force disappears nightly, is called the house of mist. But once the sun is out of sight, its future course is uncertain; the gray hour becomes the time of sacrifice. It is then that the warrior's soul ascends to the Father Sun, praying and hoping that this life-giving and life-taking force will reenter the world. Warriors, immolating themselves daily to insure regeneration of the sun, adorn themselves with crowns of white down. They also cover their sandals with similarly colored feathers, thus further isolating themselves and preventing their feet from touching the earth. Such rituals must be accomplished, they reason, since they are no longer really of this world but already partaking of the next.[7]

A paradigm for purity, virginity, a world divested of sensuality, white stands for both the sacrificial element in humankind and the as yet unlived: the postulant who has not been initiated into the life/ death process, the being who is at the crossroads. Such is the case of our narrator. He has neither stepped out into the workaday world, consciously, vigorously, and positively, nor has he been able to deal in a fecundating manner with the forces of his unconscious. There is no fluid relationship between these two powers within him. He is at a halfway point in his life, so to speak, experiencing the *white* condition, not knowing whether to turn inward or outward in his existential journey.

As the narrator continues to note his reactions to the mansion in his diary, he realizes that he is becoming increasingly removed from the everyday world, the land of the living, and is being "invaded by a kind of lucid languor, a sense of imminence." He has allowed himself to become permeated and subjugated by the perfumes of memory and the odors of anterior existences. So, too, has his vision modified. Things have grown unclear, mist-ridden, inhabiting a kind of white zone. Forms and silhouettes rise up before him, swell, expand, flow forward. A sense of motility fills his being now; his emotions take on greater fluidity and volatility.

What is happening, psychologically speaking, that the protagonist should experience such permutations of feelings? That reversibility in space/time factors should also becloud his senses? His libido is being driven inward during this period of introversion and not outward, as is usually the case when it is involved in the hustle and bustle of daily existence. Contents within his unconscious are therefore being stirred up; archetypal images erupt into consciousness; forms and shapes of all types take on consistency, energy. He mentions in his diary the advent of the equinox when the sun crosses the equator and night and day take on equal duration (September 23). So, too, has he, as we have already mentioned, reached the midpoint: the rational and irrational spheres still balance each other out. His ego is functioning as it should, adapting to both inner and outer worlds. But it is also at this point that anxiety intrudes in the form of an approaching autumn, a darkened world as replicated in the deep green of the garden's vegetation, now in sharp contrast with the red and white *siemprevivas*. The premonitory images of the cold winter, the dying leaves, a stark landscape of mournful and remote tonal values, all leave the acolyte with feelings of deep distress and loneliness.

"A gray veil is descending," he notes (p.17); the soil in the garden is bathed in water. The Aztec god Tlaloc comes to mind—the deity of rain that nourishes the land by heaping cottony clouds in the heavens. His abode is Tlalocán, where all is well watered, the terrestrial paradise for the Aztecs. The narrator feels renewed in this pure essence falling from celestial spheres and permeating the foliage in the garden, but the heavy clouds permitting this change of focus and psychological condition also veil reality, hide truth behind a shroud of mystery. The narrator/acolyte seems unable to pursue his rite of passage; he now realizes, unconsciously, that a veil stands before him and the object of his search, dispersing, annihilating the very essence of the garden experience. One senses that an anima figure is concealed behind this dark, moist, shadowy world—denying the acolyte the full illumination he seeks.

That the veil is gray is of consequence to both European and Mexican. In the Middle Ages, Christ was depicted in paintings and sculptures in gray mantle when presiding over the Last Judgment; in religious tracts, be they Jewish, Christian, Muslim, or Buddhist, gray is the color of ash, fog, semi-mourning, melancholia, and ennui. Gray also replicates the deathly tinctures of a wintry Nordic landscape, like those in Belgium, when blustery winds blow thick cloud formations into the sky, blocking out the warmth and luminosities of the sun's rays. But, as the protagonist notes, though "the smoke of autumn hovers over the garden," and with it feelings of departure and extinction that seem to encapsulate him in Mexico City, "we don't notice the season" because "one fades into another with no change in pace" (p.17). Clearly, we are living in two worlds, clinging to two cultures, two religious principles, two visions of the life/death process. Which one—if any—will release its hold upon the narrator's psyche? Or will both maintain their dominion over it?

Strange auditory and tactile elements of unknown origin now enter the picture. As the narrator stands amid the hazy, darkened, rain-soaked garden, he hears "heavy" and "deep breathing," which he likens to "slow foot-steps among the fallen leaves" (p.18). The notion of breath brings to mind a spiritual presence, God breathing into Adam's nostrils, thus transforming inert matter into a living soul; it also conjures up ghostlike figures for the primitive, associations with the dead. Psychologists view these emanations as personifications of unconscious contents in the living world. As for the walking heard by the narrator, this motile factor calls the rhythms of life into play. Both the breathing and the resounding of footsteps parallel the production and resorption of the universe, the inhaling and exhaling of vital cadences, pulsations, laying the groundwork for a return to a primordial state: to the mother, the unconscious, dissolution.

A *nigredo* condition, which alchemists identify with the *prima materia,* is being experienced: night preceding the restoration of light, death prior to rebirth. The breathing and the slow footsteps in their ineluctable march are composites of earth forces and abstract essences, each containing a past, present, and future—each a living memento of the death/life experience.

As for the liquidity that permeates the entire garden sequence and is personified as "imperceptible and tenacious," it may be said to act as a dissolving agent, in the psychological sense. Just as water decomposes and disperses matter that is fixed, so its psychological equivalent may alter an attitude, a point of view. Rainwater is a transitional force for Fuentes's narrator: it plays the role of mediating factor, linking him with life and death, with conscious and unconscious factors, as we shall see.

Water is the source of life. But when identified with Ophelia, this same nourishing and fecundating force becomes fatal; when linked with Chiron, who carried the shades across the River Styx, it also leads to death. For the narrator, the water diffused in the glistening plantings is reminiscent of the uterine fluid that protects the fetus. In this fertile, dank, and perhaps dismal sphere, the narrator strolls through the glimmering shrubs, the brilliantly colored *siemprevivas,* and notes his senses heightening, his nervousness reaching an inordinate pitch. "Silhouettes of memory" flood his mind's eye; visions of bygone eras now move him deeply; frightening shadows form and re-form on his path, studding the outer landscape with all sorts of nightmarish yet tantalizing phantasmagorias.

The narrator has yielded to subliminal powers. No longer in contact with the sun-drenched domain, with industrial life and consciousness, which have heretofore dictated his thoughts and actions, he has become deeply involved in a frightening mystery—that of matter. What are these visions he keeps seeing? These forms that have taken on consistency and potency? Let us recall that Democritus, the pre-Socratic atomist, referred to unsubstantial images or phantoms as *eidola* (sing. *eidolon*), or lower souls. Reality for Democritus was made up of "invisible" atoms, which he called *eidola* in their materialized form. Dreams and hallucinations, which Fuentes's protagonist experiences, may be said to be made up of individual atoms grouped together under certain forms and shapes, attracted to each other by atmospheric or energetic conditions. These *eidola,* or visual perceptions, may also be considered as thought perceptions. In either case, they can influence and are influenced by those who project upon them. Such *eidola* as the protagonist encounters in the garden are so powerful, energetically speaking, that they redirect his libido. As he confronts these potent surges of forms, which take on depth and consistency, his body rhythms are affected by these particles, creating within him a condition of malaise[8] (see chapter 3).

Overwhelmed by the spectral shapes he has just seen, the narrator closes his eyes just a bit, as if attempting to block out still further the workaday world, consciousness, forcing libido to pursue its actively inward course. In so doing, he induces clusters of sensations to form: Javanese tobacco, wet sidewalks, sounds, smells of all types, each permeating his being like visitations from other spheres. He suddenly feels as if he were circling about. Such activity cuts him off still further from rational existence, the world of actuality, and buries him more deeply in the abysmal waters of subliminal domains. Like the ancient Aztecs who conjured up visions and hallucinations after imbibing peyotl or the "sacred fungus" *teonanacatl,*[9] the narrator allows himself the luxury of blending European and Mexican cultures in nuanced and oscillating pulsations.

Circles, in myths, frequently represent *temeni,* sacred or protected areas in which evil is held in check. So, too, in medicine, are disinfectants spread in circular fashion over an infected area, thus preventing the spread of microbes. Exorcists paint circles to drive out contaminated or tainted souls. What remains within the circle is that inner empty space where the transformation ritual is to take place (where the embryo develops in the womb), where the idea cooks and ferments, feelings incubate, metals alter, and insolubles become soluble.

As the protagonist undergoes circular vibrations and undulations, he feels himself liberated from the servitude of the workaday world, linear time, rational thought processes, with which he had, evidently, found himself at odds. By absorbing "the totality of this quadrangle of vague light" (p. 18), he is incorporating the four of the quadrangle, which represents an earthly condition—with the circle, a paradigm for eternal values. The combinations of the square and the circle, discussed in previous chapters, is reminiscent of the mandala, one of the oldest thought patterns known to humankind. The mandala, as we know, is used in a traditional Hindu meditative technique that aids in transcending material and space/time factors and also brings about certain harmonious mental and psychological conditions by rooting out disruptive foreign psychic elements. The ego, in this manner, is allowed to center itself, to isolate itself from the collective psyche and experience renewal and increased strength. Such a mandala image helps our narrator to concentrate on the garden and contemplate its flowers, tonal nuances, vibratory cadences. In so doing, his spirit or energy packets seem to move forward to a central point, an inner order, which exists, paradoxically, within the diversity of the garden. A new balance comes into being as he (his ego) unites with a nontemporal sphere (the collective unconscious), transforming what had formerly been his contradictory nature into a harmonious whole, the irregularities of his personality into a smooth, flowing course.

As the acolyte/narrator looks about in the garden, the mandala formation gains in impetus; every living entity not directly encapsulated by this archetypal image seems to grow vaguer and dimmer in his mind's eye, darkening in hue, blending increasingly into the moist and verdant contours of the image. The entire vision is compared by the protagonist to the canvases of the fifteenth-century Flemish painter Memling. Some of his great works, *The Betrothal of St. Catherine* and *The Legend of St. Ursula,* for example, housed in Bruges, bring the religious question to mind: the Virgin, a sublimated anima figure, is sensed. An airy, ideal, and unreal vision comes to the fore. Is it art/artifice or an illusion that he is now seeing? he wonders. Is the garden experience "fictitious, an invented landscape?" (p. 18). Is it a Mexican garden? A Flemish one?

The narrator cannot answer his own questions. Inexplicably, he is overcome with such terror that he runs back into the house, through the hallways, to the other side, the living room, and there looks out of the window to Avenida Puente de Alvarado. The sun glares, jukeboxes pound away, streetcars are deafening. Reality, the present, the workaday world is now encountered. What are his reactions to the "Sun God without shading or effigies in its way, a stationary Sun Stone, a sun of shortened centuries" (p. 19)? He feels comforted by its presence. He can relate to this brilliant body, understand it consciously, rationally. For the Mexican, as we know, the sun was the most important of all factors. Let us recall that they were called the "People of the Sun."[10]

It is on the east side of the house, identified with the sun god Tezcatlipoca, to whom humanity's welfare was entrusted, that life, activity, noise, brilliance is enjoyed. In ancient days, it was in the east that the Aztec priests held the bloodied hearts of their sacrificial victims up to their lord. Life was made out of death as day of night.[11]

Since the sun is identified with consciousness and the terrified protagonist rushes to the east side of the mansion, he indicates a deep-seated need for establishing contact with the workaday world: allowing his ego to reemerge into the light of consciousness. This mood, however, is quickly dispelled as he hastens back once again to the west side of the mansion. That he keeps going back and forth, as he does several times in the story, discloses an inability to experience harmony of being. A need to rectify an imbalance within the psyche is evident. Neither the garden experience (death of consciousness) nor the living room sphere (an overly conscious and frenetic existence identified with modern industrialized life) seems to answer his needs.

For the Aztecs the west was linked with darkness, disaster, cataclysms. It was an area where monstrous divinities leaped into being and wizards of all types performed their veiled, vicious, and venomous feats of magic. The Aztecs believed that every fifty-two years when the sun set, it might never rise again. Would this be their last day of earthly life?[12] In Fuentes's story, the rain-soaked, murky, and tenebrous garden area is also associated with death and, psychologically, with an oncoming eclipse of the ego, of consciousness. Again the acolyte/narrator observes the flowers and vines as they shed their summer colorations for autumnal tonalities. He seems increasingly bound to this mysterious realm, to these livid, mesmerizing, haunting, ineluctable powers. He quivers slightly as he hears rhythmic breathing and senses spectral presences about him.

Hours pass. The narrator focuses on one object after another in a kind of hypnotic interchange. His rational world grows dimmer, attenuated, as the swelling waters of his unconscious increase in tenacity, sweeping away, pulverizing, atomizing those factors which might bind him to the world of the living. He jumps back abruptly as if struck by a face moving about in a tenebrous area of the garden. He stares at this face, which "never varied in its gaze, impenetrable in the deep shadows beneath its brows" (p. 19). Now a figure stands before him; then it turns away. Its "small body, black and hunched," makes such inroads on the narrator's psyche that he covers his eyes with his hands, veiling the object from view, cutting from him the outside world, a replica of an inner climate—fearsome, tremulous.

What has he seen that his reactions should be so immediate and so intense? He does not know. He thinks about phoning a friend. But there is no phone in the house. If he really wants to escape from his fear, his dilemma, he will go out into the street or return to his own home. But some ineluctable power keeps him from leaving this strange mansion. What is it that so fascinates him? As he mulls over the vision he has just seen, he begins to doze in an armchair in the library. He awakens with a start; the aroma of *siemprevivas* fills his nostrils. The garden seems to have come alive again, to beckon him. He again penetrates this mysterious space, attempting to get to the heart of the matter. The archetypal image he had observed so briefly before now takes on contour, depth, materiality. He sees a little old woman about eighty years of age, picking some flowers. How did she enter the garden? Such logical questions when dealing with a para-psychological event seem to be misplaced.

The acolyte/protagonist continues to search out this slim form draped in black. "Her skirts brushed the ground, collecting dew and clover; the cloth sagged with the weight, an airy weight, a Caravaggio texture" (p. 19). To compare this apparition to the works of the seven-teenth-century baroque painter, with his restless dispositions of light and shadow, may indicate a similar drama occurring in the pro-tagonist's psyche. Let us recall Caravaggio's *Calling of St. Matthew* or *Conversion of Paul,* and the emphasis placed on light and shadow in these canvases, creating acute binary opposition and conflict. Fuentes's metaphor fuses feeling and visualization and continues to do so as he pursues his description of the old lady's face, "shadowed by a black lace coif which covered tangled white hair," materializing a non-material image with bloodless lips, livid skin tones, an "arched and sad" mouth. Rent from the world of the living, wearing that "eternal smile devoid of any motivation," she is beyond recall, outside the pale, a phantasmagoria; but for the narrator she is alive, vital, powerful.

Who is this figure of such affecting numinosity? This wizened old lady gathering the moist flowers placed with such artistry all about the garden is certainly an anima figure: an inner image of woman that the protagonist has carried within his unconscious. An autonomous psy-chic content in the male personality, the anima establishes for man the kind of emotional and sexual relationship he will have with the op-posite sex. When a man falls in love, for example, he projects his an-ima onto a flesh and blood woman. In the case of the narrator, he has come under the spell of an ancient force, a ghost, which he experi-ences as an *idée fixe,* a fantasy—and she dominates his world. Anima figures, which have been portrayed in every form and guise, from virgin to harlot, since time immemorial, represent eros, love, passion, relatedness. But unless an anima figure can be brought to con-sciousness, danger may lie in store for that person who projects this archetypal being too deeply upon the external world. For some writ-ers, such as Dante with his Beatrice or Petrarch with his Laura, su-prapersonal visions provide harmony of being and the deepest kind of inspirational force.

In Fuentes's story the narrator reveals a condition of psychological passivity by not leaving the house and striking out in the sun-drenched world. Nor does he have the strength to reject the inroads made by his fantasy figure. Helpless, in need of a positive, comforting, and motherly force within his life, he yields to his longing to discover the identity of this presence to whom he is drawn and describes her as follows:

> She looked up; her eyes were not eyes . . . what seemed to emerge from beneath the wrinkled lids was a pathway, a nocturnal landscape, leading toward an infinite inward journey. This ancient woman bent down to pluck a red bud; in profile, her hawk-like features, her sunken cheeks, reflected like the vibrating planes of the reaper's scythe. Then she walked away. (P. 20)

The anima figure vanishes as suddenly as it had appeared, vaporizing or sinking into the ground, dispersing into the heavens. The dematerialization is followed by renewed deep breathing, rain pouring down, then quietude.

We might suggest that the protagonist, whose world exists beyond the Newtonian and Euclidean empirical sphere of cause and effect, is experiencing a condition of *hyperesthesia:* an extreme exaltation of perceptive faculties that frequently occurs during hypnotic states, thereby increasing the potency of the senses. The slightest suggestion offered by the unconscious under such conditions, in the form of an image, word, glance, touch, breath, or fleeting thought, is felt so intensely that it is immediately communicated to some obscure stratum of the unconscious, to an intuitive or other subtle level of the subliminal world that consciousness cannot reach. In the case of our acolyte/narrator, the anima image of the wizened old lady taps energy patterns beyond those of human intelligence and endows him with a keener sense of reality. Under such conditions, he is able to understand and relate to the parapsychological experience that has brought him the vision and the endopsychic perception.

The eyes the protagonist saw in a previous image might have been instrumental in bringing on the hypnotic trance: those eyes he thought belonged to the old lady, which were in fact reflections of his own in the glass doors. They were not normal orbs, capable of clarifying a person's vision and understanding, but rather two voids, maws, endless abysses, where forbidding blackness had taken over; where the irrational, like tumultuous waves, pounded out its energetic pulsations as its fluid particles flowed ever more deeply into primeval spheres. What he had been peering into was the space/time continuum: the fourth dimension, which encapsulates the very mystery of life—the heart of a world that was eluding him.

This anima figure with her "hawk-like features" and "sunken cheeks," divested of the color of life, floats ghostlike in and out of his field of vision—real yet unreal. That she is associated with a scythe,

the cutting and shearing instrument used by Saturn, the god of time, links her with death. When identified with Attis and Cybele, this instrument takes on the contours of a self-mutilating and castrating force.

Alarmed, lest this archetypal image wreak havoc in his world, the acolyte/narrator writes in his diary (on September 23) that he has withdrawn into his room and barricaded the door. Deep down, he realizes that no barrier can protect him against this creature, this infectious force that has already spread her noxious fumes throughout the mansion. He knows intuitively that as a split-off who lies buried so deeply within him, she will govern his fate, grasp at his flesh as she does at the flowers in the garden. This primitive being, alive in those dark and secret realms within his unconscious, enjoys her dominion over him—her numinosity.

Witches, with whom we may identify this old woman, represent the shadow world, noctural emanations, terrors of the night, fleeting memories that arise from nearby tombs or *teocalli*. They are, in Goya's world, for example, thoughts and feelings personified in spectral form. Reminiscent of the ancient Lamias, Liliths, Circes, Medeas, and other famous she-demons, these succubi who come to men at night and copulate with them act outside the conscious sphere, destroying the ego, the center of consciousness. No longer does the protagonist's ego stand as a mediating force between inner and outer worlds as it had at the outset of the story. It has been divested of its power, been atomized, diffused, castrated.

In his bedroom, tomb or womb, the acolyte/narrator attempts to harness those material powers at his disposal which he hopes will help him remain afloat. But soon he realizes that such efforts are to no avail. He cannot fight off the inroads made by unconscious contents in the form of archetypal images. He now hears "the faintest rustle outside the door, then the whisper of something passed beneath the door" (p. 20). He turns on the light and sees the corner of an envelope outlined on the floor. He grabs hold of it. In "spidery and large, erect letters, the message consisted of one word: TLACTOCATZINE" (p. 21). In Nahautl, the Aztec language, *Tlactocatzine* signifies "lord" or "master." It was this word that the Indians pronounced, handing their new rulers the red and white *siemprevivas*, when Maximilian and Carlotta arrived in Mexico.

The narrator's dread is momentarily assuaged, for in Hispanic folklore the image of this kind of old woman usually acts as a spiritual power, representative of bygone memories—a mana personality, able and willing to feed those with whom she comes into contact. When she becomes a comforting and nurturing being, he seems to long for her presence even more desperately than before and thus becomes increasingly alienated from the sun-filled world. No longer does he straddle two attitudes—sun and moon, day and night, present and past. He has slipped into that nether region, that dim and haunting sphere, where moistness and darkness have obliterated all luminosities. As if reliving an Orphic mystery, we may say, he has gone down to Hades to consult the dead, to seek out *manteia,* the divining power.

A clock strikes six, a kind of backdrop for the tenebrous, leaden atmosphere that prevails. The narrator, snatched out of his lethargy, goes down to the living room. He is astounded by the waltzes he hears emanating from an old Pleyel piano. As he draws nearer to the instrument, the object and sound vanish. Silence. The world of shadows and dematerialized forms and shapes, once limited to the library and garden area, has now taken precedence over the living room. The anima figure, like an oceanic force, but conducting her convolutions in the most nuanced and subtle of ways, has inundated the house: she is high priestess of the *teocalli.*

In the library again, the acolyte/narrator is startled to see her reappear, this time skipping about, miming "a little girl playing with her hoop" (p. 21). Moments later, as he stands in the garden, its heavy and lugubrious atmosphere weighing him down still further, a condition of stasis reigns: "the air became motionless, fathomless, and all sound was suspended" (p. 21). The old woman is wearing the same unequivocal smile as before; her eyes are "lost in the depths of the world; her mouth open[s], her lips mov[e]"—the entire vision chilling him, icing him. Fire, equated with life, now fosters its opposite: the icy frigidity of death.

After having locked the garden door and then returned to his bedroom, where he feels safe and out of reach of this phantasmagoria, he is overcome by the fragrance of *siemprevivas* that invades his room—a second sign of this enchantress who lives in remote regions, in anterior worlds. In the silent emptiness of the mansion at eleven o'clock at night, he senses the "dull light of the garden" and hears "her starched skirts outside his door" (p. 21). A letter awaits him. "My beloved. The moon has risen and I hear it singing; everything is indescribably beautiful" (p. 22).

We are in the heart of the lunar world now, the unconscious. Let us recall in this connection the etymology of the name Mexico: the root of the word is *metzli,* meaning "the moon" in Nahautl, the *sictli,* "navel" or "center,"[13] thus reaffirming the importance of this force. Unlike the sun, viewed as a male principle, representative of spirit, order, illumination, and the highest of thinking processes, the moon is identified with the feminine world: cold, dark, vacillating, enigmatic, and therefore frequently dangerous. The moon, as powerful regulator of storms, floods, tides, and nature's growth, is in command of life's forces, as is the anima figure in Fuentes's story. Since the moon changes its contours and, by extension, its personality (its invisible phase corresponding for some primitive peoples to the death of humankind), it incorporates both celestial and infernal domains, linear and cyclical time. The woman is Carlotta: young, middle-aged, old— and all in one—who was and is and will always be in love with her husband. Although both are long since dead, they are more powerful existing as they do in a remote sublunar sphere within the acolyte/ narrator's unconscious than they had ever been when walking the earth.

No longer related to the world of the living, the narrator's identity has been diffused, and he functions as a kind of medium. It is the autonomous anima figure who dictates his feelings and sensations; it is she who is the recipient and dispenser of moon power, who generates chaos within him, who ushers in eerie light, luminscent darkened circular ways—as well as the comforting love experience. Like the ancient moon goddesses, Cybele and Hecate, Fuentes's anima figure is the promulgator of nocturnal visions, an inflammatory force that will ignite insights that carry the narrator to the most archaic region in his psyche.

Returning again to the library, he observes this wizened old lady in yet another posture, sitting on the garden bench, veiled, bathed in a kind of soft spectral aura. As he walks toward her, "the same air, void of any sound, enveloped her" (p. 22). The old woman takes his hands and kisses them. He feels overcome with sensations of well-being. Then he looks at her more closely, peering deeply into that essence before him, and realizes at this very moment that he is touching "nothing but wind—heavy, cold wind" (p. 22). An orchestration of threnody-like musicalities intermingles with the aroma of the *siemprevivas:* death and life are one as visual and aural sensations amplify. He hears a voice, an echo "of spilled blood copulating still with the earth" (p. 22), and everything about him fluidifies, burgeons, as the *siemprevivas* again emerge, as if from a tomb, out of the "spectral hands of an ancient woman." Without warning he hears the word KAPUZINERGRUFT repeated: it refers to the magnificent graves, kept up by the Capucin monks, in which the Hapsburgs are buried in Vienna. People to this very day bring flowers to honor the dead, thereby restoring life to what otherwise would be an inactive mausoleum, stirring memories of past beauty, bringing into existence what has been inhumed but lives still in the sensate world.

The narrator frees himself from the grasp of the invisible hands and runs back to the front door of the mansion, which he tries unsuccessfully to open. Drained, he sinks to the floor and in so doing chances to look at the door more closely. "It is sealed with thick red lacquer," and in its center there shines a coat of arms: "a crowned double eagle, the old woman's profile, signaling the icy intensity of permanent confinement" (p. 22). The acolyte/narrator, now congealed with cold, understands that he, identifying with Maximilian, has been incarcerated in the Hapsburg tombs, existing in the old world and the new, deeply embedded within the Great Earth Mother.

The Hapsburg dynasty, which reigned in Austria from 1278 to 1918, stood for continuity of power; at various times its enormous empire included Germany, the Low Countries, Spain, Austria, and Mexico. But for the acolyte/narrator, the Hapsburgs exist in only two people, Maximilian and Carlotta, and for him, the family represents love. The energy incorporated in the archetypal image of the reigning couple is so formidable as to have displaced everything else in the conscious sphere. The mansion in Fuentes's tale is a *teocalli*, a sacred space, as is the *Kapuzinergruft* in Vienna; both are strewn with red and white flowers, those *siemprevivas*, potent forces whose memories are eternal.

The eagle in the Hapsburg coat of arms represents power for both Europeans and Mexicans. Associated with enormous speed as it flies through the brilliant daylight, this bird is the only one able to stare directly into the sun, and for this reason it has been adopted by monarchs as a warlike emblem; by men of religion (St. Jerome) as representative of ascension; by gods (Tezcatlipoca) as a sun force. As a source of light and energy, its feathers were worn around the necks of the Aztecs as they performed their ritual dances to the sun. Indeed, Aztec soldiers who fought and died in battle were frequently referred to as Knights of the Eagle, their livers being consecrated to this celestial force.[14] The anima figure in Fuentes's story is also aquiline: her eyes are luminous, powerful, flamelike, as are those of the eagle; it is she who sees through veils and other obstacles that impede others from truth and life. Like the powerful and fearless bird, she transcends matter and space, peers directly into the life-death unity.

The "crown of gold" in the coat of arms indicates a superior force at work. Because it rests on the head, a crown represents preeminence, cyclicality; it rules the domain of instinct. A circular representation, it unifies what is multiple. Its crescent form, however, reminiscent of the lunar body, implies a remote, hidden, and feminine domain, linking it with the wizened old lady of Fuentes's tale.

That the door upon which this coat of arms has been placed is sealed in red emphasizes the bloodiness associated with Maximilian and Carlotta's rulership, as well as the religious rituals of Roman Catholic Communion and Aztec sacrificial immolation.

In a world of blood and death, in a sphere where the unconscious holds dominion, the acolyte/narrator confesses that he now knows he is being held captive—he is growing increasingly iced. To be chilled during psychotic episodes indicates an inability to cope with something in one's daily existence. In the case of Fuentes's narrator, he yields to the invasion from the unconscious. His ego, frail and weakly structured, grows increasingly grim and despondent. He longs for freedom but is too passive to struggle for it. Slowly he yields to the powers of the anima figure—that autonomous image existing so formidably in his unconscious.

A man possessed is a man imprisoned, a soul that has died. No communication is possible now, as it was at the outset of the story, between east and west, life and death, the rational and irrational. The entire *teocalli*/mansion is buried in blackness, entombed in shadowy, silent shapes that utter their inaudible tonalities, move about in slow or rapid invisible gyrations. The narrator has regressed to a preformal state, playing out his role as Maximilian, Carlotta's beloved.

Like those ancient Aztec priestesses, those goddesses of the maize, whose religious celebrations were of such import in seeing to the well-being of the tribe, the specter of Carlotta remains for the acolyte/narrator a guardian force, offering him the incense, the nourishment he needs, the love and understanding that not only comfort him but empower him to pursue his underworld life. Like the *Kapuzinergruft* in Vienna, the *teocalli*/mansion is kept alive with the radiantly colorful and aromatic flowers she picks from an eternally burgeoning and moist garden. "They're the same flowers the Indians brought you when we arrived here: you, the Tlactocatzine," she tells him, her voice seemingly issuing from the very earth itself. Only now does he understand that he has entered her world, completely and irrevocably; that he has always been wedded to her and will remain wedded forever, like the two eagles on the coat of arms, in an archetypal embrace.

How may this parapsychological experience be explained? Jung believed that a factor mediates between the apparent incommensurability of body and psyche and that it is this element that endows matter with a kind of "psychic" faculty and psyche with a sort of "materiality." As such, each is able to influence the other: "living matter has a psychic aspect, and the psyche a physical aspect." It may be stated, then, that reality in general is "grounded on an as yet unknown substrate possessing material and at the same time psychic qualities."

There are causal correspondences that link psychic and physical events, thus fusing two seemingly disparate spheres.[15]

Initiatory or precognitive dreams or telepathic or parapsychological experiences, as Fuentes has described in "In a Flemish Garden," cannot be explained in the normal rational manner, in keeping with Newton's established theory of causality, which leads one to believe that everything within the universe has a causal explanation. If, as we have said above, physical and psychic matter are linked, then acausal correspondences link psychic and physical events.[16]

Parapsychological experiences cannot be explained by the time/space factor, since each one of them breaches those dimensions. The psyche travels in "a variable space-time concept," a dimension governed by its own laws and incomprehensible to us. One may posit that acausal phenomena, such as an extrasensory perception, have an energy relationship, but if the event occurred in some remote past, how does energy apply? Our concept of time and space, like our belief in causality, is an abstract intellectual theory. The psyche functions in another sphere, according to its own governing principles. Certain patterns of behavior may be deduced as archetypes giving off a specific effect, or a "specific charge," but they cannot be explained.[17] When the unconscious wells up into consciousness, as is the case for Fuentes's narrator, it brings subliminal intuitions and perceptions with it—forgotten memory images. These images that emerge may be acausal; that is, the person experiencing them cannot make any connection between what actually happened and what occurred in the dream. Therefore the images that came into consciousness have no rational or causal relationship with the objective situation as far as one knows.

The parapsychological experience depicted in Fuentes's tale may be considered a projection of the psyche and looked upon as an entity made of the same basic energy as visible matter, but differing from it by its "infinitely high frequency or intensity." Since projection emanates from the psyche's innermost being and exceeds the speed of light (according to the above definition), it is therefore not observable in the normal way. Jung wrote:

It might be that psyche should be understood as *unextended intensity* and not as a body moving with time. One might assume the psyche gradually rising from minute extensity to infinite intensity, transcending for instance the velocity of light and thus irrealizing the body. In the light of this view the brain might be a transformer station, in which the relative infinite tension or intensity of the psyche proper is transformed into perceptible frequencies or "extensions." Conversely, the fading of introspective perception of the body explains itself as due to a gradual "psychification," i.e., intensification at the expense of extension. Psyche-light intensity in the smallest space.[18]

Only should its frequency slacken to the speed of light, or less, would the psychological projection be observed by the human eye. The brain "tunes down the intensity of the psyche until it becomes bound to lower frequencies," which are then interpreted according to one's empirical understanding.[19] According to this definition, what may be considered an impossibility (a parapsychological experience) becomes realizable in another domain that transcends empirical logic. Under such circumstances the mind is considered a mediating force: a kind of computer that transforms high-frequency-energy intensity into lower levels, which the brain can then translate into an understandable language.

That Fuentes's protagonist, a *puer*, is swept under by the anima image, that he dies, psychologically speaking, as do the sons of the Great Mother, is not surprising. It is the maternal force that once gave birth to him that swallows him up again, to live with her in her damp, dismal womb. Frequently around the ages of thirty or forty, when inner development becomes stunted, as is the case with Fuentes's narrator, outer conscious attitudes no longer seem to be in tune with inner needs: one works against the other and thus suffers a kind of death/rebirth as its focus alters. If the ego cannot give up an attitude, it must be sacrificed. When the unconscious and conscious are enemies, when east and west, light and darkness, present and past are at odds, one surrenders to the other.

Fuentes himself has explained that the memory-image of Carlotta, the aristocratic figure born of two worlds, took hold of him when he was only a child.

> . . . this obsession was born in me when I was seven years old and, after visiting the castle of Chapultepec and seeing the portrait of the young Charlotte of Belgium, I found in the Casasola Archives the photograph of this same woman, now old, dead, placed inside her cushioned, iron coffin, dressed in the nightcap of a little girl; the Charlotte who died insane in a castle the same year I was born. . . . Perhaps Charlotte never found out that she was growing old. Until the very end she wrote love letters to Maximilian. A correspondence between ghosts.[20]

The *teocalli*/mansion was the sacred space where someone—perhaps Fuentes himself through projection—experienced a death/rebirth ritual; where a parapsychological experience breathed a living soul into a powerful priestess/princess—a poignant and tragic avatar of the Eternal Feminine.

NINE

Wang Shih-fu: *The Romance of the Western Chamber*

The Architectonic Archetype

The architectonic archetype is at the root of *The Romance of the Western Chamber*, by the thirteenth-century dramatist Wang Shih-fu. Every aspect of the play is designed to work in harmony with the others: song, speech, costume, dance, musical accompaniment, makeup, gesture, movement, scenery, lighting, form a cohesive whole—a single and integrated pattern of expression. As in the work of a master builder, no part of the spectacle is sacrificed or omitted in an effort to enhance another aspect of the ritual. All is mathematically conceived and ordered; nothing is left to chance or impulse. There is no room for deviation. The play follows a specific blueprint modeled upon a design completed according to precisely structured and measured rules and conventions. Reminiscent of a pagoda, the monument/play maintains a delicate balance; its intrinsic beauty stands out strikingly, its line, form, and mass remaining indelibly vital in the mind's eye.

An archetype, defined as an inborn motivating dynamism (which is to the psyche what an instinct is to the biological sphere), determines the behavioral, visual, and psychological motifs in *The Romance of the Western Chamber*. That the architectonic archetype should be operational in Wang Shih-fu's play accounts for its measured pace, its methodological and reasoned nature. The architectonic archetype is the outcome of a mode of psychic functioning inherent in the makeup of the Chinese people and resulting from centuries of spiritual disciplines based on Taoism, Confucianism, and Buddhism.

Taoism, evolved by Lao-tze (c. 604–531 B.C.) in the text attributed to him, the *Tao Te Ching*, posits an Absolute, or *Tao*, which is indescribable and which precedes everything in the created and noncreated universe. It emphasizes a transpersonal world of the spirit and introduces the concepts of the "Great Whole," the "Great Emptiness," and the "Endless Circle": unifying forces that are structured on dis-

parity—the *yin* and *yang*—but that are absorbed in oneness, or *Tao.*
The supernatural sphere, with its spirit worship, is also a factor in
Taoism and symbolizes the interrelationships between the visible and
invisible world: form and formlessness, existence and nonexistence,
which cohabit in the all-embracing matrix that underlies all and is
everything. "Tao is like a dream: invisible, intangible, obscure. It is
invisible yet there is form to it. It is intangible yet there is a feel to it. It
is obscure yet there is method to it. The method is true and so there
are signs of it."[1]

The vision of life introduced by Confucius (551–479 B.C.) was more
paternalistic and existentialist than Taoism. Neither Confucius nor
Lao-tze, however, believed in a personal god. Heaven represented a
moral order, and it was incumbent upon each person to create his own
life to be lived according to prescribed standards. Born into a feudal
society where everything was hierarchical, each class dependent upon
the one above, Confucius based his canon on a system of ethics and
moral principles in which ancestor worship and filial duty played a
significant role. The Great Man (the noblest and highest in China and
the world being the emperor) sets the example and "invites others to
follow it."[2] Humanity and morality are uppermost in Confucius's system of values, as attested to by such sayings as: "Do not do to others
what you would not desire yourself."[3] Dignity, piety, and social graces
are likewise required, accounting in part for the complex rituals and
rules of etiquette implicit in Chinese society.

Buddhism, introduced into China in the first century B.C., lived in
harmony with Taoism and Confucianism. The chief concern of Buddha, who lived in the fifth century B.C., was to relieve human suffering, which he believed to be implicit in earthly existence. Only by
maintaining a detached attitude in life—which meant abandoning desire (personal ambition, craving, longing, selfishness)—can one overcome pain and frustration. In his "Sermon of the Turning of the
Wheel of the Law," Buddha spoke of the four noble truths: Pain is due
to the "birth sin," the result of actions committed in previous existences; pain terminates only by experiencing Nirvana, thus putting an
end to one's *karma,* or incarnations, a condition one may achieve if one
follows the Eightfold Path: right faith, right judgment, right language, right purpose, right practice, right obedience, right memory,
right meditation.

Contemplative by nature, the Chinese blended the tenets of Taoism,
Confucianism, and Buddhism into their spiritual and physical life.
Meditation, which the three philosophies encouraged, allowed them
to absorb cosmic energy from the exterior world into their own inner

beings. During moments of intense perception, for example, the meditator feels fed, enriched, and experiences at times what is termed enlightenment or illumination. At this instant, the superfluous, or the garment of an object, is sheared off, and its essence, or simplicity—its *li*—is penetrated. For the Chinese, the *li* corresponds to the eternal principle that transcends time and space: it is immaterial, indestructible, and supersensible. The *li* is the profoundest spiritual force within an object (building, temple, tree, bird, flower, wall)—within every aspect of existence, be it concrete or abstract. Just as the *li* exists within an object, so it is operational within a human being throughout nature—everywhere—in one single reality. It is that factor which orders an entity from within; that force which makes a phenomenon what it is not; *li* is "is-ness" or "such-ness" in Buddhist terms.[4] Its manifestation in the thing—that element which gives the thing its independent quality, its separateness—is also, paradoxically, the very force that allows the thing to experience its original unity, its relatedness with the Great Whole.

In keeping with the *li* tradition and with Taoist, Confucian, and Buddhist philosophies, the monastery complex where *The Romance of the Western Chamber* takes place is not visible. Yet it exists powerfully as a concrete entity. That it is not present onstage is understandable, since Chinese theater most frequently calls for a virtually bare stage. What is unique in Chinese theater and Oriental theater in general is the energy implicit in invisible stage accessories and objects. Buildings, windows, doors, a room, a wall, a tree, a flower, are described in detail in the dialogue and singing interludes—they exist architectonically. Thus their very spirit, the feel of the object depicted emerges in the verbal images which pepper the script. Its *li* then flows forth, becomes operational, and reaches deeply into the hearts and minds of those involved. As a result, each object, whether animate or not, takes on dimension and force and reverberates with its own life spirit.

Inhabiting both a linear and transpersonal space and time scheme, invisible and visible objects exist as energy centers embedded within the conscious and unconscious psyche. Because of the spectacle's architectonic substructure, it follows specific and subtle patterns of behavior regulated by an inner system of coordinates, correspondences, and philosophical and numerical schemes. It is no wonder that the emotions and actions of the protagonists in Wang Shih-fu's play are disciplined, their speech suitable to their status, their gestures stylized, their dance steps and singing interludes conducted according to traditional conventions.

Although the Peking-born Wang Shih-fu was one of the most popular dramatists of his time, little is known about his life. Of the fourteen plays he wrote, only three are extant. Nor can one call *The Romance of the Western Chamber* an original work. Custom in China frequently called for a playwright to base his work on a previously written poem, story, or theatrical piece. Wang Shih-fu refashioned *The Romance of the Western Chamber* according to his own vision but based it largely on a ninth-century narrative by Yuan Chen, who wrote of the love between the student Mr. Chang and the beautiful Ying-ying, and concluded with their painful separation. Tung Chieh-yuan's poem, composed in the twelfth century and based on Yuan Chen's work, also served as a source for Wang Shih-fu's play, written a century later. Both Tung and Wang reunited the lovers at the end. Scholars consider *The Romance of the Western Chamber* to be a Chinese version of Romeo and Juliet.

The plot of Wang Shih-fu's play is uncomplicated. Madame Ts'ui's husband, a prime minister who died before the play opens, has been temporarily buried in the P'u Chiu Monastery. For political reasons, the family cannot reach Po-ling, where official burial is to take place, and has taken up residence at this monastery. According to Confucian doctrine, careful attention must be focused on burial rites and offerings for the dead. Mme. Ts'ui's family (consisting of the beautiful nineteen-year-old Ying-ying; Hung Niang, her maidservant; and Juan Lang, a young adopted son) and the monks in the monastery therefore feel a sense of respect and propriety, an obligation to obey the social codes. "If there is careful attention to burial rites, if the offerings are made to the dead," Confucius wrote, "the people, I promise you, will turn fully to Excellence."[5] In keeping with Confucian, Taoist, and Buddhist tradition, sobriety, control, and reverence are maintained in Wang Shih-fu's play; respect is granted to parents, and standards are adhered to without exceptions or adjustments.

The architectonic archetype becomes evident from the very outset of *The Romance of the Western Chamber:* in the cosmic quietude that descends upon the ordered happenings that follow age-old traditions, in the meditative approach of the protagonists, who maintain whatever degree of measure and harmony is required by their roles. Each individual is motivated by a singleness of purpose, a determination to find his or her way—*li,* or essence—and therefore the ultimate end of all things. That the monastery complex, even though it is not visible onstage, is the point of convergence in the play reveals the functioning of a spatiotemporal order: a need to experience a center of gravity. Such focus on balance results from the power vested in the architectonic archetype. Chaos and turbulence must either be blocked or absorbed into the cohesive whole so that an ordered and measured outlook, inherent in traditional Chinese culture, may prevail.

The architectonic archetype, which sees to the maintenance of inner/exterior harmony, existed, as we have suggested, preconsciously in the traditional Chinese psyche. It was apparent in the people's attitude, for example, toward their country (considered the center of the world), their capital city (the center of their nation), and the emperor's palace (the center of the capital city). The circle, representing heaven, and the square, a symbol for the earth, were implicit in architectural constructs and in city planning in traditional China. As a primordial image, the square and the circle joined in one motif may be looked upon as a mandala. The geometric diagrams implicit in the mandala were used as meditative devices by the Chinese: the image allowed them to contemplate and concentrate on a single central point, thereby unifying what was differentiated in the psyche, harmonizing what was discordant.

In keeping with such a spiritually ordered system, it is not surprising to learn that Buddhist monasteries and traditional Chinese houses (the *Ming-t'ang*) were built according to specific mathematical and geomantic rules: the microcosm (the building) was linked to the macrocosm (the Great Whole). The roof, for example, of the square *Ming-t'ang* has a hole in it, which allows smoke to be expelled and, at the same time, water to be gathered and conserved. This central axis, which traverses the entire house, symbolically joins heaven, earth, and the underworld, unifying what is disparate. Each of the corners of the *Ming-t'ang* faces a cardinal point that corresponds to a season and to an element. In keeping with this cosmic and numerical system, the four sides of a house have three doors each: twelve in all, representing the months of the year and the signs of the zodiac. For the Taoist, whose philosophy is built on interrelationships of polarities, the various parts of a house correspond to subtle centers within the human body, and the ascensional or descensional movements within the building correspond to psychic or spiritual evolution or devolution. Important, too, is the fact that each edifice in the monastery complex is surrounded by a circle, either a ring of jade, a ring of trees, or a round garden. A pagoda stands next to the monastery complex in *The Romance of the Western Chamber* as well, the circles and the pagoda accentuating in this manner the mandala design: the square and the circle.

The mandala, implicit in the monastery complex, includes duality and bipartition: polarities that will blend or flow into one another, forming a conjunction of opposites during the play. That the phenomenological object or line is not considered static by the Chinese, but active, reflects Taoist and Buddhist views of life: all is in a state of flux, nothing is absolute or permanent. Hence anything may be stimulated to grow, be completed, disintegrate, and be reborn, since each individual (or object) plays a role in a never-ending cyclical pattern. It is in flux that potential may be manifested, find fulfillment, and decline, only to begin a new existence. So, too, may intangible content be transformed into a tangible reality, the unconscious image into the conscious shape.

The monastery complex and the other phenomenological objects that play their part in *The Romance of the Western Chamber* (door, window, wall, tree, table, and so on) exist concretely, but paradoxically, in an abstract sphere—the dialogue. Psychologically speaking, they inhabit the conscious and unconscious realms. As manifestations of the architectonic archetype, these concretions may be looked upon as centers of energy, as mobile forces infused with weight, speed, and density. Each works upon the protagonists in its own special way, arousing a whole affective dimension, which, as the case may be, brings the individual spiritual or psychic order or disorder.

That the play opens in late spring is significant for the Taoist, whose relationship with nature is so intimate. The season is also an expression of the architectonic archetype: the ordering factor in the human sphere. Both these viewpoints are at work in the play. When, for example, the protagonists inhale or exhale the cool pure air during the play, they are taking the natural world into themselves and, in so doing, experiencing universal rhythms that add serenity to what might be a troubled heartbeat, thereby ordering and balancing what could lead to disarray.

Time is also a factor in *The Romance of the Western Chamber,* a steadying force and another example of the architectonic archetype. Unlike the Westerner, whose existence is based on the scientific notion of causality, which divides, sifts, classifies, weighs, and isolates life into days, hours, minutes, and seconds, the traditionally oriented Chinese lives within the moment: cyclically, atemporally. Each instant belongs to itself and is also, paradoxically, linked to the whole. Time and space are experienced, therefore, as emanating from being itself, as implicit in the circle of events that is *Tao.* The sense of time and timelessness is, therefore, evident in the change of seasons, an aspect of a life cycle, a space/time continuum. Seasons represent differences, perhaps nature's own contradictions, which finally resolve themselves by realigning the conflicting forces into a harmonious whole.[6]

Madame Ts'ui suggests that late spring is a time for weariness, a period she experiences with "tears and blood."[7] The winter, which saw her husband's death, was long and painful. Emptiness and powerlessness have overtaken her—a prelude to the living out of every moment in the cosmic wheel, which also sees to a *renovatio* with spring in its eternal rebirth and recycling of all.

Since there is no one in the courtyard, Madame Ts'ui permits her daughter to come out of the house. Ying-ying appears; her head is slightly lowered, signifying deference as well as timidity. During the period when the play was written, young girls of good Chinese families were kept at home under strict surveillance. Their chief occupations were needlework and learning how to run a house.[8] Ying-ying's existence may be described as reclusive and repressed. She is, to say the least, fertile field for outside influences, for chaotic situations that will surely undermine the ruling architectonic archetype.

Sadness inhabits Ying-ying's countenance; depression, her gestures and movements. Certainly this mood is the result of her bereavement and is reflected in her attitude toward nature. As is implicit in Taoist and Buddhist philosophies, trees, flowers, rocks, and mountains are metaphors of an inner climate. In Ying-ying's case, the fallen flowers around her are likened to "innumerable sorrows I bear in silence" (p. 5). The east wind is also personified. She considers it cruel and heartless, since it has scattered and blown the flowers away. Wind is representative, usually, of the spiritual male principle, and Ying-ying views the wind as a destructive force. In this case, it may be considered a premonitory image. The young woman has led such a protected existence that it stands to reason she may be cut down by adversity in the form of a masculine/spiritual attitude or force.

She sees her walled-in existence also in terms of a phenomenological object: "Gate after gate of the lonely monastery is firmly barred" (p. 5). A structured image is used to express her feelings of isolation and disenchantment. Barred, cut off from normal relationships, forced to live according to prescribed standards, social laws, and circumscribed regimens, whatever spontaneity or authentic feeling she might have had has been repressed. Her actions, therefore, are controlled, restrained; such a psychological condition is manifest in the traditional tiny footsteps she takes as she moves about the stage and the manner in which she manipulates her two-foot-long sleeve and cuff, which she waves about gracefully in descending circular movements as she makes her way into her house.

The twenty-three-year-old scholar-hero, Mr. Chang, arrives on stage. His bearing is noble. He wears no makeup, as is customary according to the very rigid conventions of Chinese theatrical arts. He informs the audience that he is from a good family. That his page carries his lute is not surprising. Music was one of the six arts in ancient China, and scholars, who were accorded a very high place in society, were expected to be fine musicians. Since the sixth century, the lute had been considered to be one of the most noble instruments, sonorous and beguiling; Mr. Chang's lute is gracefully shaped, like a pear, with a redwood neck topped by an ornate scroll.

Music was based on the relationships between number, note, and the cosmos. For the Taoist, then, it ensured a harmony of opposites: heaven and earth, *yang* and *yin,* and so forth. The fundamental note (drawn from the five notes based on a twelve-note system) had a mystical character. When sounded, it reflected an aspect of the eternal principle within the entire universe; it was also the basis for an individual's well-being, that of the state, and that of the earth. It is not surprising that each dynasty had its own fundamental note: a pitch determined by an involved theory and standardized by the Imperial office of Music, which had been established in the first century B.C.[9]

Mr. Chang, the prototype of the scholar, wants to stay at the monastery on his way to the capital to take the highest examination in the land. What was virtually unique in the old Chinese system was the set of competitive examinations a young scholar had to pass if he sought to enter government service. According to the Confucian canon, such an occupation was considered to be one of the most respected and important of careers. Mr. Chang's goal is just that: to serve the government and advance within its ranks. When he will actually proceed to the capital, he does not know. He first wants to see his old friend and "sworn brother," General Tu, who has, after having won first place in his competitive examinations, embarked on a military career. Appointed Generalissimo, General Tu commands a force of one hundred thousand men and is military guardian of the P'u Pass.

That Mr. Chang has traveled prior to his arrival at the Buddhist monastery and will pursue his travels to the capital whenever the time is deemed ripe is significant. According to Taoist and Buddhist doctrine, when the time spent in achieving one's purpose is directed toward a certain goal—a Way—it may be fruitful and broadening; it also endows life with a certain continuity and harmony. In Mr. Chang's case, however, his movements at this point in his life, he confesses, are as "undirected as those of a leaf in the wind" (p. 6). He is, then, searching, perhaps for his own spiritual center, questing for his groundbed, his house, his balance.

Since Chinese theater is a combination of poetry, drama, song, dance, and mime, it is not surprising that Mr. Chang both recites and sings his feelings. Specific musical modes are repeated throughout the musical interlude, emphasizing certain images that may be associated, both rhythmically and visually, with waves, clouds floating about, and the sea. As the images take on density and liquidity, they reveal themselves as sinuosities, paving the way for the transmutation process: Mr. Chang's discovery of his potential and its fulfillment. Thus far in life, we learn, Mr. Chang has emphasized cerebral matters—the *yang* way—and in so doing, has been obliterating the *yin* factor. Such a one-sided view has left him vulnerable, a prey to the feeling world, imponderables, changeable emotional patterns, thus altering the dominion of the architectonic archetype. Imbalance, therefore, seems to rule what had formerly been a stable and ordered way. Chaos, the great divide, is imagistically described in the following sequence:

> The foam of the waves, white as snow, reaches the heavens,
> And looks like the autumn clouds that roll in the sky.
> The floating bridges, kept together by robes of bamboo,
> Look like black dragons crouching on the waves.

(P. 7)

The assistant at the monastery comes to greet Mr. Chang, as he would any distinguished guest requesting hospitality. He offers the visitor serenity and tranquility in the worship of Buddha. There follows, interestingly enough, an architectonic description of the Hall of Buddha, part of the monastery complex.

> The quarters of the priests below,
> The kitchen to the west,
> The hall for expounding the law of Buddha to the north,
> And the bell-tower in front.

(P. 10)

Such mathematical and directional details are usual in Taoist tradition, where form arises from the formless, and something from nothingness.

The lengthy description of the monastery links the tangible with the intangible world in one spatial composition. So, too, are the senses (feeling, touch, sight, smell, taste) knit together, inhabiting a space/time continuum. The objects enumerated during the discussion (hall, bell-tower, pagoda, passage, residence, and so forth) are considered neither as separate entities nor as static objects. These architectonic devices participate directly and actively in the accelerating or slackening of the play's action. As such, line, plane, mass, and surface form patterns of energy, matrices that radiate sensation, affective charges that then flow toward the protagonists. They reflect to some extent, and are responsible for, the depth or superficiality of the emotional relationships.

Organic form, as envisaged in the descriptive architectural terms, plays its role in the newly emerging world of feeling. As Mr. Chang looks at the building to the west, for example, he indicates, symbolically, a deep-seated need for the feminine principle. For the Chinese, the west represents the land of blackness, old age. Astrologically, the sun disappears in its own house, and its descent preludes the emergence of the moon, which is associated with the woman. The moon, or *yin*, element is cold, misty, mysterious; a covered and inward domain, it stands for the passive, nonmanifested force—the unknown, and therefore the feared. Bathed in darkness and shadows, it lives only when the sun's rays shine upon it; it has no life of its own. Yet the world of shadows and darkness within which the moon exists has positive attributes: conception and germination occur in darkness, wetness, humidity. It is in the west that gardens are set out in China, one of which will play a significant role in *The Romance of the Western Chamber.*

Ying-ying enters the garden area with Hung Niang, her servant. Mr. Chang is stunned by her beauty. In accordance with Buddhist and Confucian traditions, however, he explains that his powerful emotional reaction is due to the fact that he must have known this girl in a previous incarnation, perhaps five hundred years ago. But whereas the Buddhist credo calls for detachment, Mr. Chang is visibly shaken by the experience. Feelings grow rarefied and sublimated as Mr. Chang sees her fondling the flowers. He compares her eyebrows to "the crescent of the new moon," her lips to "red cherries," her teeth to "white jade," her voice to that of "the oriole singing amidst the flowers" (p. 11). The aroma emanating from the images themselves—a truly synesthetic experience—is wafted his way, causing him to see her as a breeze, a willow, blossoms. "She leaves the slight imprint of her steps on the fragrant dust," he exclaims, thereby sensualizing objective reality. Clusters of energy patterns arise from his visualizations, setting off multiple rhythmic charges.

That Mr. Chang compares Ying-ying to flowers, the moon, cherries, and jade indicates his affinity for nature's rhythms and organizational patterns. As a flower, she dwells in the *yin* fold: ephemeral, fragrant, beautiful, and soft to touch. As jade, however, a mineral that is hard, durable, strong, and virile, she stands for *yang*. The combination of flower and jade transforms Ying-ying into a complex of opposites, giving her wholeness and substance.

Jade in Chinese tradition, it must be mentioned, is significant. It expresses both purity and beauty and is associated with solar, imperial, and indestructible qualities. It assures the Taoist immortality, since he believes that if one places it on a corpse it prevents decomposition. In that it is considered perfect, it is related to transcendence. It is sonorous when touched by other objects, be they jade or stone, echoing cosmic harmonies, which then radiate throughout the atmosphere.

Mr. Chang's joy, however, is short-lived. Ying-ying disappears into her house. But her timing is controlled; her reactions studied. Nothing is left to impulse. For the first time he realizes the great obstacles set in his path with regard to Ying-ying. She shuts "the gate of the remote courtyard where flourish the blossoms of the pear tree" (p. 14).

A white wall "as high as the blue sky" (p. 14) separates his dwelling from hers. This concrete object, juxtaposed with the abstract image of the heavens, underscores both the interrelatedness of these entities and their divisiveness. Immense energy is needed to cross from one domain to the other, to unite earthly to celestial spheres—man to woman. To reveal the difficulty of the task and the pain involved, Mr. Chang breaks into song, recalling the "fragrance" of his previous— and virtually hallucinatory—experience. He sees her again in his mind's eye: a metaphor of the lily, musk, hibiscus, and the aroma of these natural forces lingers in his nostrils; he can feel them, touch them. He hears the "tinkling sound" made by her jade ornaments, and it haunts him, envelops his very being. Slowly the architectonic archetype is being depleted of its power. In one final glance, Mr. Chang looks at the pagoda, which "throws a round shadow" about the area (p. 15), thus endowing him with some semblance of balance as he blends the squareness of the earth factor, represented by the monastery, with the circularity of eternal spheres—re-creating the mandala image. In this way he attempts to balance what has been virtually overturned and to return to his once seemingly measured, rational, and hierarchic comportment.

Yet, Mr. Chang feels that something has ignited within him. He turns to the superior of the monastery, as if propelled by some inner mysterious force. He asks him for a room "near the Western Chamber," where "the main passage runs by the anteroom" (p. 21). He knows that from this vantage point he will be able to gaze on Ying-ying. His request is honored.

Meanwhile Hung Niang enters the stage. She is making final preparations for the service to honor Madame Ts'ui's late husband—in the Buddha Hall. One of the most interesting characters in the play, Hung Niang has a personality and temperament of her own; she displays wit, ingenuity, and fire. She will be the go-between for the lovers and will pave the way for the suspenseful happenings to come. Speaking in metaphoric language to Mr. Chang, she warns of the dangers awaiting him if his advances should be aggressive. Comportment and obedience to Confucian dicta are of vital importance.

> Words, like arrows,
> Must not be uttered at random;
> For once they enter the human ear,
> They cannot be forcibly removed!

(P. 25)

Mr. Chang does not heed Hung Niang's advice and asks her impertinent questions concerning Ying-ying's character. She is offended and shows her displeasure by quoting Confucius: "Speak not what is contrary to propriety, and make no movement which is contrary to propriety!" (p. 26). Order reigns in Madame Ts'ui's household, she iterates. She rules her family "strictly and sternly, and is cold as ice and frost" (p. 26). No one dares enter her chamber, situated in the center of the house, unless asked to do so. That Madame Ts'ui lives in the "middle" chamber indicates the centering role she plays within the family unit, the balancing effect of her personality. The architectonic archetype is operational in Madam Ts'ui's world and her mind dictates her acts. Hung Niang is aware of this ordered and restrained approach to life and rebukes Mr. Chang for his offensive ways and his "love-sickness" (p. 26).

Later Hung Niang repeats the conversation she had with Mr. Chang to Ying-ying, who is distraught by the tenor of the words. She must not inform her mother of Mr. Chang's attitude. As Ying-ying makes her way to the garden to burn incense, she holds her right palm inward, then sweeps her right cuff downward to her knees, flinging it backward with a twist of the wrist, suggesting the depth of her disquietude.[10] She sings of her feelings in slow and mellifluous sonorities. Her breathing is abdominal, a difficult feat for a performer, who masters this technique only after years of training. She compares her feelings to fire, to the moon.

> Oh! How unexpected love affects my heart,
> When I, leaning against the brazier, am purposelessly watching the moon!

(P. 32)

That Ying-ying identifies with the moon, that mysterious constellation known for its changeable, fickle nature, indicates nascent desires within her, an alteration of inner rhythms within her being, as her heartbeat grows excited, frightening. Since she is no longer in complete command of her emotions, the architectonic archetype is no longer fully operational within her psyche. Forces beyond her control have leaped into her being, overturning the controlled and regulated inner climate. Like the moon, which symbolizes indirect knowledge and passivity and shines only when illuminated by the sun's rays, Ying-ying responds to Mr. Chang's catalytic energy patterns. Without his fire—the sun principle—she will remain cold, remote, restrained, living in a solitary and tenebrous lunar realm.

Mr. Chang observes her carefully as he stands hidden behind the garden wall in the corner, near some rocks. It is from this vantage point that he feasts his eye on her and then on the moon, evoking both in a love song. The wall, protective and imprisoning, limits his activities. Yet, as exemplified in the Great Wall of China, this powerful structure is invested with overt and covert powers. An archetypal symbol, the wall that encloses, as does the uterus, delays action and so allows for a period of gestation in order to encourage growing feelings and desires to deepen. What Mr. Chang views beyond the wall is bathed in mystery and "wrapped in silence," engendering sparks of excitement, triggering volatility.

Ying-ying places the incense-burner on a table; the wind carries "the delicate fragrance" of her white raiment to Mr. Chang. "She outvies in the beauty of her carriage, the goddess of the Moon" (p. 34), he states. An important metaphor here, since Chinese women traditionally held a feast for the Moon Goddess (Heng-ugo) on the fifteenth day of the month during the full moon of the autumn equinox. To endow a mortal with divine attributes as the young man does indicates the power of the anima image that prevails in his unconscious. This night vision, this dream, this sublimated entity exists now as vapor, mist, lending an eerie quality to the entire scene, as her image floats in and about the smoke rising from the burning incense—everything ascending heavenward, illuminated by the subtle, silvery moon beams. The metal silver, identified by Chinese alchemists with the moon, represents the *yin* element, underscoring still further the feminine aspect of Mr. Ching's visionary experience.

Ying-ying is captivated by the poem Mr. Chang now chants. "What a pure fresh poem!" she remarks. "I will compose one to rhyme with his," she tells Hung Niang (p. 37). Describing her solitude, the passing of youth, she wonders whether the author of the poem will take pity on her. Moments later, Hung Niang brings the poem to Mr. Chang, who is delighted by her rapid response to his emotional outburst. The architectonic archetype seems to rule at this time, since he reflects upon the poem's wisdom and Ying-ying's literary talents. The poem is written, he remarks, in good Confucian tradition; it reveals the order of her thoughts, her measured personality.

Every word has revealed her feelings,
And is pleasant to hear.
Soft are her words,
And pure are her rhymes.

(P. 37)

He must find a way of crossing the wall: she is so close and yet so distant from him. Solitude again prevails as Ying-ying and Hung Niang return into the house. Now Mr. Chang's lamentations spin out his yearnings in images associated with the moon: dew, pure green moss, coldness, brilliant moonlight as it sifts its way through the flowers (p. 38). The wind has risen again, and before returning to his room, Mr. Chang pauses to look at the "branches of bamboo" hurtled about by the gusts of air.

Bamboo for the Chinese is a plant of good omen, and hence it became an important element in landscape paintings of the thirteenth century and in poetry. For the Buddhist, bamboo represents rectitude and is frequently used for meditative purposes: it transports the individual from an earthly and personal frame of reference to a heavenly and cosmic experience. Bamboo possesses a language of its own, which may be understood or perceived through intuition. During such moments of enlightenment, space seems to open up, recede, conjuring up both an earthly and a spiritual dimension—life in its totality encapsulated by this one stunning visualization. Bamboo in the play also mirrors Mr. Chang's loneliness, since each branch stands out starkly as pure line and mass in an infinite distance.

Act I concludes with a religious ceremony. The sound of "the sacred drums and brazen cymbals" sings out in rhythm with the priests— their hieratic gestures and the lines and circles they form as they move about, illuminated by the flickering candlelight in the giant hall. Mr. Chang, however, rather than experiencing the wholeness and serenity of the meditative way, has become obsessed with his love for Ying-ying. Gone is the Taoist, Buddhist, and Confucian rectitude and poise—the ruling architectonic archetype. As he burns incense in honor of the Buddha, it is to ask him to accord his aid in arranging for a "secret assignation" (p. 43) with his beloved.

The service is over. Mr. Chang stands alone in the center of the deserted place of worship. Stillness is evoked by the emptiness of the image: the Great Void dictates its feelings, since it is the ultimate source of everything. As the *Tao Te Ching* states: "Great space has no corners; great ability takes time to mature; great music is soft and mellow; great form is shapeless and contourless."[11]

The serenity of the monastic atmosphere, already interrupted covertly by the tempestuous nature of Mr. Chang's new love, is overtly shattered as five thousand bandit soldiers surround it. Their leader, the Flying Tiger, wants to kidnap Ying-ying and make her his wife.

Madame Ts'ui is understandably agitated. As for Ying-ying, she has thoughts for Mr. Chang and expresses them in yet another poem, which mirrors her perception of impending calamity. Nature has turned destructive as "thousands of petals" are being "twirled in the wind" and the "pear tree blossoms are being scattered by the rain" (p. 51). She hears only loneliness as she inhales deeply of the lily and musk, repeating the very images Mr. Chang used in his song of despair. Yet, despite her turmoil, the architectonic archetype seems to take over again. She measures her thoughts, orders her feelings, rationalizes her actions as she attempts to deal with the dangerous problem facing her and her family. She must yield to the Flying Tiger, she informs her mother, and gives three reasons for her decision: to save her mother, the monastery and its priests, and her adopted brother; to ensure her father's proper burial; and to make certain of the continuation of her clan (p. 55). Her mother, however, the central force in her world, is opposed to her resolution. To accept such a marriage would be "an indelible disgrace in the history of our clan," she tells her daughter (p. 55). Instead, she has decided to offer her daughter in marriage to the man who will induce the Flying Tiger to withdraw his claim.

Mr. Chang is overjoyed. He has a plan: he will send a letter to General Tu, his "blood brother," informing him of the situation and the dangers involved. Let us recall that such a course is significant in Confucian doctrine: proper performance of filial and fraternal duty earns "Manhood at-its-best."[12] Reliability in friendship and loyalty to family, tradition, and parents are the goals of each individual who strives for excellence, accomplishment, perfection, and virtue.

Mr. Chang asks the superior of the monastery to ask the Flying Tiger to wait for three days before he takes Ying-ying as his wife. The family is still in mourning and the ceremony necessary to comply with religious tradition cannot be completed until three days have elapsed. Tension is provoked. Will the superior convince the Flying Tiger to wait? Will the letter be delivered to General Tu? Or will it be intercepted by the enemy?

General Tu arrives at the crucial moment and forces the enemy to surrender. Everyone's gratitude is infinite. After the general's departure, Madame Ts'ui invites Mr. Chang to stay in her home—in the library, the Western Chamber. The library, to be sure, is well suited to the intellectual proclivities of the poet-scholar. It is a sphere where the mind may be expanded, thus assuring success in this area. Madame Ts'ui invites him to a feast celebrating his move, which the lovers interpret as a celebration of their marriage—promised Mr. Chang as a reward for having saved the situation.

Mr. Chang dresses up in his graduate's robe of pure white and dons a brilliant gilded buckle for the feast. Events, however, do not go as planned. Madame Ts'ui has withdrawn her promise to give her daughter to Mr. Chang. Years ago, she explains, she had promised Ying-ying to her nephew, Cheng Heng, and has now written him to this effect. She seeks an advantageous marriage for her daughter and suggests Mr. Chang do likewise for himself. Annoyed and hurt, the poet-scholar informs Madame Ts'ui that he is surprised that money, prestige, and class considerations should be the motivating factor in her decision—a deception since it broke a promise.

Ying-ying sings out her grief. Her eyes, "once brilliant as stars," have now "lost their sparkle," and her "fragrant breath is now consumed in sighs" (p. 86). She can bear her sorrow no longer; her loss is mirrored in the empty landscape conjured up in her song. As for the Western Chamber, where she thought she would be consummating her nuptials—a prelude to a new life orientation—it has "become an empty dream!" (p. 87). Tears fill her eyes, and she is also filled with anger at her mother's trickery.

Although Ying-ying is ordered to her bedchamber, Hung Niang speaks out her dismay in cold and reserved terms. "One good deed deserves another," she says. Now more than ever, she realizes that she must intervene. She asks Mr. Chang to take out his lute and sing his feelings to Ying-ying, who will soon repair to the garden to fulfill another incense-burning ceremony.

The lute is now called upon to express his powerful feeling world. Tones and rhythms, following a mathematically set order, replicate both the individual's and nature's cadences: the fleeting and flowing patterns that are the source of a never-failing life force. For the Taoist, music is composed of a web of unbroken lines, movement, and change; it fills the atmosphere with vibrant modulations, ripples, waves, energy patterns. Perhaps better than other artistic media, music endows feeling with a sense of permanence, ephemerality with a sense of concretion. Like clouds, however, music streams forth, forever wandering, forming and re-forming its sonorities, and hence symbolizing the impermanence of all that lives. Mr. Chang's tones infiltrate the atmosphere, filling the void with substance, feeling, eros. Music nourishes what is starving, and in so doing creates a new psychic state: a cosmic existence that preludes plenitude of being.[13]

In this exquisite scene, Mr. Chang makes his lute companion to his sorrow, conveying his love in sequences of visual images, both liquid and solid, but always smooth and touchable. On the other side of the stage, as Ying-ying sings out her pain and disappointment, the moon is invoked once again, as are the wind-swept blossoms, the red flowers—all of which underscore the turbulence of her feelings. Then she ceases her song, remains in place, enraptured as she listens to the sounds emanating from the Western Chamber, powerful and vibrant as "sabres and spears of the mailed horsemen" (p. 102). Just as Mr. Chang had clearly assessed her poetic talents, so the architectonic archetype takes over in her as she evaluates his vocal propensities in logical, judicious, and discriminating terms.

> From beginning to end, there is a great variety of notes;
> His song is neither like the sound of a bell in the silent night,
> Nor like that of the weeping of Confucius at the sight of the unicorn,
> Nor of the song about the unfortunate phoenix.
>
> (P. 104)

Ying-ying has a sudden change of heart when she learns that Hung Niang has gone to the Western Chamber to inform Mr. Chang of her love. She discovers Mr. Chang's letter, carefully placed in her vanity case by Hung Niang, and becomes angry. The daughter of a prime minister cannot behave in such a common manner, she tells Hung Niang. Nevertheless, her attitude changes and she expresses her willingness to meet Mr. Chang in the garden that very night.

> Await in the moonlight at the Western Chamber,
> Where the door stands half opened by the breeze,
> While the shadows of the flowers move on the wall,
> The Precious One may be coming!
>
> (P. 134)

A Taoist, Mr. Chang explains the meaning of the symbols used by Ying-ying. The first line tells him to await his beloved when the moon is about to rise; then she will open the door for him; after that he must climb over the wall and she will be there to receive him (p. 135).

A complex personality, Ying-ying again acts slyly and coyly. Even though she has sent Mr. Chang the poem, she indicates to Hung Niang that she may decide not to meet him after all; she refuses to give the maid a straightforward answer. In fact, when Mr. Chang does climb over the wall and finds Ying-ying burning incense, she grows annoyed. His behavior is improper, she states, and she orders her maid to drag him off at once or she will inform her mother. Hung

Niang, well versed in the writings of Confucius, which call for people to deal honestly with each other, cannot account for Ying-ying's deceptive ways.

Ying-ying soon has another change of heart. She sends Mr. Chang another poem assuring him that she will come to his room this very night. Tension is acute. Will she change her mind? Is this another ruse? Mr. Chang can hardly bear the anguish.

> I stand on the silent steps.
> The night is far advanced and a fragrant vapour is spread
>   throughout this golden space.
> Solitary is the library,
> And sad unto death is the student.

(P. 167)

Mr. Chang waits, bathed in the light of the moon that floods the pavilion. He listens carefully to the wind as it sounds in the bamboo branches.

Ying-ying does arrive with her coverlet and pillow, thereby indicating her willingness to be his body and soul. In keeping with the architectonic archetype, her movements are demure, measured, graceful. Her feet are close to the ground as she walks in tiny, even steps; her hands, though encumbered, are elegantly poised. The love ritual takes place in the library: a secret, enclosed area of learning. Here Ying-ying will sacrifice her maidenhood and be initiated into womanhood. Mr. Chang—in ritual stance—kneels before her and embraces her. Overwhelmed with timidity, Ying-ying refuses to raise her head. Her disarray is outward now: "Her golden hair-pins seem to be falling from her locks" (p. 173). The greater her turmoil, the more beautiful she appears to Mr. Chang. Slowly, he unbuttons "her robe and unties her silk girdle" (p. 173).

Every aspect of the love ritual is described by Mr. Chang in song: he clasps her swelling breasts, which he compares to jade, but softer, more fragrant, supple, warmer. He sings of the "stained spot of delicate red" after the lovemaking, and the eroticism of the lines indicating the loss of Ying-ying's virginity is flagrant. No longer is he the poor student, the lonely traveler, consumed with sorrow, sick with love, but a man who knows the meaning of bliss. He holds Ying-ying's hand, looks at her deeply, "her face, like an apricot, and her cheeks, like peaches," as "the bright moonlight" shines upon her (p. 176).

In the days to come Madame Ts'ui grows suspicious. She notes Ying-ying's change of countenance, mood, and speech. She is "most unusually wrapped in thought," she tells Hung Niang (p. 178). Annoyed because she feels Madame Ts'ui has mistreated her, Hung

Niang tells her that the couple have been keeping company for a month. She blames Madame Ts'ui for this situation—she acted in bad faith.

When mother and daughter confront each other, Ying-ying holds her sleeve in front of her eyes but never touching her face, her elbow extended outward a bit, thus symbolically expressing her fear, despair, and shame. Madame Ts'ui does not blame herself for the state of affairs. In accordance with Buddhist doctrine, it was brought about by sins committed in another existence. Madame Ts'ui does not mince words. She calls Mr. Chang into the room and informs him that he must leave at once for the capital, that he must prepare for and pass his examinations. Only when he becomes a government official will he be worthy of marrying her daughter.[14] For three generations, Madame Ts'ui tells him, her family has never been allied to anyone without official rank (p. 188).

The lovers are disconsolate but yield to tradition, order, and law—reasoning that just as the universe is governed by rules and regulations, so individuals and society must also adhere to certain standards of propriety. Nevertheless, Ying-ying cannot help but sing out her pain: the west wind rises with great force, autumn has set in, the sun has grown dim—her plaintive, confused, stressful song discloses the intricate network of feelings involved.

In an exquisite love duet, Mr. Chang promises to study hard, to pass his examinations, and return. As for Ying-ying,

> My red sleeves are soaked with my tears of love,
> But well I know that your blue gown is more soaked still.

> (P. 197)

Colors mirror passion. The blood that flowed forth when she gave herself to Mr. Chang has depleted her energies, creating a new landscape blanketed in grayness, mist, cold: autumnal hues that mirror mystery, evanescence, an amorphous and vaporous quality—as if she were to linger on as a memory or shadow, a vestige of what had once been a beautiful living being.

Mr. Chang and his servant leave. They walk along meadows and climb mountains, Mr. Chang singing of the lonely monastery he has just left. Melancholia permeates his world, which is compared to faded leaves and chill autumn winds. They stop at the Bridge Inn, where they take a room for the night. Mr. Chang's sleep is restless; he dreams of his beloved. She has followed him and he sees her clearly before him, reliving his tumultuous passion. Bright frost, white dew, cover the images flowing forth from his unconscious. In keeping with

Taoist belief in the livingness of the invisible world, the images now buried in whiteness seem paradoxically to open space up to him as temporal and atemporal existences merge in the unfolding dream. At this very instant, Ying-ying again appears to Mr. Chang. She has opened the door and he takes her by the hand. The deeply moving stage sequences pave the way for the dimensionless universe to come into existence. As Lao-tze wrote in the *Tao Te Ching*, "Even if we try to see the Way, it cannot be seen," but it may be described in terms of dimly merging shadow figures.

Six months have passed. Mr. Chang has passed his examinations and is third on the list. He sends Ying-ying a poem announcing his return. Before his arrival, however, he is feted in the capital as Compiler of National History in the Imperial College of Literature.

Ying-ying responds to Mr. Chang's poem with one of her own. She also sends him certain objects, for he will understand, she is sure, the symbolic significance of each of them: an undergarment, so that it "will be as if he and I were together"; a belt, which "will encircle him in front and behind and protect him"; a stocking, which "will secure him from wandering astray"; a lute, which brought about their union; a jade hairpin, which will prevent him from putting her at the back of his mind now that he has attained such honors (a hairpin is worn at the back of the head); a spotted bamboo pen, which reminds her of the bank of the Hsiang River, where bamboo grows wild—a place stained with her tears (pp. 228–29).

Mr. Chang receives Ying-ying's gifts and comments on their meaning, their measured and thoughtful associations; he also mentions the beauty of her calligraphy and her literary talent, which is unsurpassed. "My Ying-ying is second to none in the world," he states (p. 235). Not only is her beauty incomparable, but her poetic gifts are equally unique: "I will regard it [her poem] as a sacred book / And use it as a charm" (p. 235).

All, however, is not well. Cheng Heng arrives at Ying-ying's home before Mr. Chang's return. He wants to claim his bride. Nothing will change his mind, despite the fact that Hung Niang tells him Mr. Chang is a philosopher of the Confucian school, a poet, a prose writer, a moralist who knows and behaves according to the highest principles of conduct and who is good and kind (p. 246). In order to gain his prize, Cheng Heng resorts to deceit and informs Madame Ts'ui that Mr. Chang is already married. Ying-ying is not to be his second wife, Madame Ts'ui cries out in dismay. Events move swiftly toward their climax when Mr. Chang arrives and is shocked by the accusation.

> If I have a bride elsewhere
> May I die on the spot!

(P. 257)

Never could anyone take Ying-ying's place in his heart, Mr. Chang asserts. General Tu arrives, accuses Cheng Heng of his villainy, and threatens to kill him for his cowardice. Forced to confess the truth, Cheng Heng takes his own life.

The marriage decree is sanctioned, and in good Taoist, Buddhist, and Confucian tradition, the couple

> . . . will live together undivided for ever until old age,
> And will be together for eternity.

(P. 269)

Wang Shih-fu's drama is lived out within the monastery complex that includes the Western Chamber. Conventions, laws, and intricate organizational patterns rule the characters, the scenes, the gestures, the choreography, and the music. The inborn affinities of the human participants for patterns, numbers, and structures evident in *The Romance of the Western Chamber* endow both performers and audience with a sense of spatial orientation, a predisposition toward an inner and outer temporal and atemporal order. The basic architectonic archetypal image, whose components emerge in the dialogue and musical sequences (squares, circles, planes, diagonals, perpendiculars, matrices, lines, and so on) are experienced by the protagonists not only quantitatively but qualitatively as well, according to feeling tones that link, bind, affect, and coordinate their lives into a cohesive whole. It is by means of these objects—both concrete and abstract—that the *li,* or eternal principle, is apprehended.

The Chinese view of the world is built on a substructure: a modality based on introversion, meditation, a system of checks and balances—the architectonic archetype. The Western way, in contrast, is most frequently the result of spontaneous exteriorization of feeling. The controlled and ordered directives implicit in *The Romance of the Western Chamber*, with its metered networks of rituals and etiquette, are the criteria used for measuring anguish, passion, love, hate—feeling forces or units of psychic energy. In this way, restraints are placed on instincts; organization orders emotional states; form and design structure action. Existence is experienced according to a deeply embedded blueprint implicit in Taoism, Buddhism, and Confucianism—spiritual attitudes that have dominated Chinese civilization, and therefore its art, for centuries and centuries.

TEN

Mishima: *The Temple of the Golden Pavilion*

An Archetypal Feminine Sun and an Archetypal Masculine Moon

The edifice referred to in Yukio Mishima's novel *The Temple of the Golden Pavilion* (1956) was an ancient Zen Buddhist temple in Kyoto, considered so perfect and beautiful as to be declared a national monument. In Mishima's work the Golden Temple plays such an important role in the spinning out of the events that it takes on the dimensions, psychologically speaking, of an archetypal image composed of both sun and moon forces and those people and things associated with them. What is unusual in Mishima's scheme, however, is that the sun is feminine and the moon is masculine, whereas the reverse is true in Western lands. According to Shinto belief, the sun goddess Amaterasu (Heavenly-Shining Goddess) is the authority figure, the great regulator and progenitrix, who sheds her golden glow, her spiritual and fecundating intensity, over the world in daylight hours. Her counterpart, Tsuki-Yomi (Counter of the Month), the moon god, who is passive, fickle, secretive, and mysterious, inhabits the night world. The difference in archetypal emphasis created a cultural and religious ambiguity and conflict in Mishima, who was deeply Japanese and yet greatly influenced by Western thought. As a result, the numinosity of the Golden Temple in his novel fosters a complex system of reactions and attitudes that determine the protagonist's inner structure and lifestyle. It also paves the way for increased tension and friction, which reach incandescent power, cutting, jarring, and castrating the protagonist, who is possessed by this archetypal force—driving him to extremes in both his fantasy world and his behavioral patterns.

Yukio Mishima (1925–70) was born in Tokyo into a samurai family. After spending the war years working in an aircraft factory, Mishima was graduated from the University of Tokyo (1947), took a position for a short time in the finance ministry, then traveled extensively in Europe and North America, after which he decided to devote his time to writing. Mishima's output was enormous: twenty novels, over thirty plays (No, Kabuki, Bunraku), travel pieces, literary criticism, newspaper articles, translations, filmscripts, musical comedy, nightclub acts. He also appeared onstage in some of his plays and wrote songs for his female impersonator friend, Maruyama Akihiro.

Mishima was particularly fascinated by the beauty and power of the male body, as is evident in all his writings. For the Shintoist and Zen Buddhist, physical prowess, discipline, self-reliance, self-denial, and purity of being are closely linked to the philosophy of the samurai: *Bushido* (the Way of the Warrior). Health is primordial; physical flaws, ailments, and deformities are considered signs of pollution, to be washed away and so sanctified. In Mishima's introduction to *Taido— The Way of the Body* (1967), a volume of photographs in which he described the cult of the body, he idealized the male form in Greece as depicted in sculptures during that country's heroic age. In fact, so taken was he by these sculptures that he had a statue of Apollo placed in his garden in Tokyo. One can readily understand why Mishima should have written *My Friend Hitler* (1968), in which he disclosed his admiration for the virile beauty of the male warrior—in life and in death. A splendid melancholy force, the male body for Mishima was as lyrical as poetry. Because of its ability to harmonize body and spirit, it was also an embodiment of wisdom. When samurai ethics reigned in Japan, Mishima believed, there existed an intimate connection between physical prowess and ethics. Since the end of World War II, however, this association had vanished, and Mishima set to work to retrieve it in the personal army he created for himself in 1968: the *Tate No Kai* (Shield Society).[1]

To worship the hero archetype—the male body—was to allow this primordial image to gain increasing autonomy over his psyche. Unlike the Zen Buddhists, who called for detachment in worldly and spiritual matters, Mishima projected Apollonian values onto the archetypal samurai, and his identification with these powers became so strong that he lost his objectivity in the process, as did his protagonist in *The Temple of the Golden Pavilion*. So important did this image of the splendid male torso become in his subliminal sphere that it was instrumental in his decision to commit *seppuku* (ritual suicide) in 1970. Death by one's own hand represented for him a *summum bonum*: it was an act of courage and a mark of freedom—the ultimate realization of the glory of the male, who ends his existence in the prime of life and in

"Beauty." To conclude one's earthly trajectory ritualistically has another advantage: it fuses life and death into a transpersonal event, and as such, into the work of art.

The Temple of the Golden Pavilion is based on an actual incident. A Zen Buddhist acolyte was in training at the ancient Kinkakuji temple in Kyoto. His father, a Zen priest, had wanted his son to follow a religious career, and, at the outset of his studies, his outward behavior seemed to warrant such a decision. In time, however, his actions grew erratic: he gambled, stole, cut classes, went to geisha houses. In 1950, the young acolyte burned down the Golden Temple. Ugly and a stammerer since childhood, he was seemingly envious of the beauty of this extraordinary monument that attracted so many visitors to its portals. He had planned to commit suicide after burning down the temple but at the last moment had a change of heart. "I hate myself, my evil, ugly, stammering self," he said during his trial. Never, however, did he voice any kind of regret for his deed. The psychiatrist in charge of his case diagnosed him as a "psychopath of the schizoid type."[2]

Mishima's in-depth study of the spiritual and psychological evolution of his protagonist, Mizoguchi, follows the general lines of the real case. What remains formidable and unique in Mishima's work is the dramatic role played by the ever-present, active, anthropomorphized Golden Temple. Not merely an architectural wonder overlooking a pond, this building takes on the dimension of a living, vital personalized entity: a sun/moon force. As an archetype it is a potent and energic principle, acting upon and reacting to the protagonist's psyche in accordance with the depth of his projection. Everything Mizoguchi feels, thinks, senses, longs for, is valorized in terms of the Golden Temple: when describing a person, for example, he uses similes such as "lovely as the Golden Temple" (p. 22). His life is lived for and within this solar (feminine) and lunar (masculine) image, so possessed is he by its dominion. The Golden Temple may also be considered a fetish: an object that compensates for his loveless childhood and acts, so he believes, as a bridge toward relatedness. In time, however, we realize that just as his stuttering and ugliness have prevented him from communicating with the outside world, spiritually and viscerally, so the Golden Temple, in its capacity as a sun and feminine principle, has cut him off from the community, incarcerating him within its aura—holding him spellbound in the inner sacred space over which it reigns. Alienated from the world of reality and from his inner self, Mizoguchi grows increasingly introverted, yielding ground to the power of the Golden Temple within his inner world, allowing it to become a depotentiating force. In Mizoguchi's fantasy world, the temple is personified as a castrating, burning, bruising, incandescent woman, who has to be destroyed so that masculine lunar power can prevail.[3]

The temple, as representative of a condition of celestial beatitude and unity as well as of worldly conflict and diversity, plays an important role in Japanese culture. Its situation, construction, and plan are, in fact, a crystallization of both an individual and transpersonal scheme of things. Each quadrangle, square, and circle—and the shadows cast by the various parts of the edifice, altering continuously as they do during daylight and night hours—reflects temporal and atemporal attitudes, a linear and space/time continuum. As a sanctum, the temple is an earthly manifestation of the mystical "center" and may be looked upon as space in the process of completing itself and as a paradox of emptiness in fullness.

At the outset of *The Temple of the Golden Pavilion*, Mizoguchi has only heard his father, a Zen Buddhist priest, say of this national treasure that "there is nothing on this earth so beautiful as the Golden Temple" (p. 21). He has also been told that it once served as a retreat for the famous fourteenth-century Shogun Ashikaga Yoshimitsu, who, after a successful life and years of unremitting warfare, abdicated, took the tonsure, and lived at the Kinkakuji temple, where he experienced the serenity and peace he so longed for. Mizoguchi himself has never seen the "real" temple; he knows it only through photographs. He tells us that as a young man he spent many long hours sitting in his room, gazing out at the distant hills, dreaming of this three-storied Zen Buddhist sanctuary with its sloping roof made of fine-grained wood, its lecture halls, sanctuaries, and meditation areas, its elegance and harmony, which were born from a happy fusion of Japanese landscaping and Buddhist architecture.

In his fantasy world, Mizoguchi likens the Golden Temple to the sun, and thus it becomes a paradigm of beauty and power, acting as a compensation for the despair and worthlessness—the self-image—he carries in his heart. In Mizoguchi's mind's eye, this glorious structure is endowed with magical qualities able to rectify an inadequate life experience: it stands for all goodness, all perfection, all beauty.

> The rays of the sinking sun shone on the young leaves that covered the hillside and it looked as though a golden screen had been set up in the midst of the fields. When I saw this, the Golden Temple sprang into my mind. . . .

> When I saw the surface of the distant fields glittering in the sun, I felt
> sure that this was a golden shadow cast by the invisible temple. . . . I used
> to see the Golden Temple soaring up into the morning sky amidst the
> rays of the sun as it rose from the folds of those eastern hills. (P. 4)

As a sun force, the Golden Temple is female: nutritive, fertile, engendering a whole sexual universe. Its fire, its energy, the passion its
presence arouses in Mizoguchi's universe, are so extreme that they
blind him, psychologically speaking, and stunt all possibility of emotional growth. He is unable to experience a middle ground, a pause, a
no-man's land where differentiation and evaluation can be ushered
into existence to counterbalance extremes. In his solitary world he
experiences what has been defined as a state of *enantiodromia*: the
transformation of one superlative into its opposite. Extreme light, or a
sun factor, will bring about extreme darkness, or a moon dominant.

Let us recall that according to Shinto doctrine—Zen Buddhism incorporated this animistic religious view into its philosophy—the sun
goddess, Amaterasu, was the progenitrix not only of the Yamato clan
(from which the first emperors came) but of the entire Japanese people. The cult of this deity in Japan (the chief shrine is at Ise) is so great
that worshipers still salute this luminescent and warming body daily,
welcoming her into the world every morning by clapping their
hands.[4] It was Amaterasu who was the guardian of agriculture and
who gave the Yamato clan (fifth century A.D.) the three insignias (the
mirror, the sword, and the jewel) that symbolized their power and
that of future Japanese emperors. Two of these objects, the sword and
the mirror, figure importantly in Mishima's novel as hierophanies intimately connected with the Golden Temple. They also possess psychological significance in Mishima's work: the sword is both a phallus and
a castrating implement; the mirror symbolizes the spirit of the sun
goddess and, as such, is an object of worship; it also reflects a condition of narcissism.

Mizoguchi identifies the Golden Temple with the moon force: the
mysterious world of the man, within which are indulged secret and
shadow practices.

> Like a moon that hangs in the night sky, the Golden Temple had been
> built as a symbol of the dark ages. Therefore it was necessary for the
> Golden Temple of my dreams to have darkness bearing down on it from
> all sides. In this darkness, the beautiful, slender pillars of the building
> rested quietly and steadily, emitting a faint light from inside. Whatever
> words people might speak to the Golden Temple, it must continue to
> stand there silently, displaying its delicate structure to the eyes of the
> world and enduring the darkness that surrounded it. (P. 20)

The moon god, Tsuki-Yomi, reproduced in various sanctuaries in Japan (including Ise) as a white disc with a hare in the center, ushers in the shadow world. As a symbol of procreation and fertility, the hare is particularly apt in describing the psychological situation: it reveals iconographically the inroads that the world of darkness will make into Mizoguchi's psyche during the course of the narrative. That the hare is also associated with augury indicates its premonitory powers. The shadow, psychologically speaking, represents those factors within a personality which the ego considers negative; it contains inferior characteristics and weaknesses that the individual cannot allow himself to recognize as his own.

Mizoguchi's sense of inferiority, evident during the hours of moon glow, arouses resentment within him, an inner rage at the thought that he is missing out on life, that he is cut off from normal intellectual and sexual intercourse. What Mizoguchi does not realize is that his anger is not really in collision with the established moral order as exemplified by Zen Buddhism, a collective religious credo and thus arbitrary in nature; rather, he is suffering a deeply personal and human conflict resulting from what he considers to be his physical faults: his ugliness and his stutter. Mizoguchi, psychologically, has not been able to come to terms with his shadow; he has not succeeded in assimilating what his ego considers to be negative factors within his personality. Rejected, forced to live underground in dank and dismal domains, these unconscious contents grow in strength and thus stunt any semblance of spiritual and sexual evolution. Darkness does fecundate the seed, but if the sun cannot penetrate later, nothing will grow.

Other factors are also at work in Mizoguchi's world: his eye is caught by the copper-gold phoenix that crowns the roof of the Golden Temple. Birds, let us recall, were sacred to the sun goddess Amaterasu. In fact, in ancient days Yata-Garasu, the many-footed crow, was worshiped as Amaterasu's messenger.[5] The copper-gold phoenix represents the core of mystery, because it never crows at the break of dawn, never flaps its wings, yet flies about in airy spheres and "through time on its shining wings." Reminiscent of the mythical phoenix—which, when it knew that death was imminent, made a nest of sweet-smelling wood and resin and allowed the sun to beat down upon it until the flame reduced it to ash, whereupon it rose again from the marrow of its bones—this spot of gold in the form of a bird is archetypal in dimension, occupying a sacred transpersonal dominion.

Living in close relationship with the sun and moon, the copper-gold phoenix may be considered, because of its paradoxically stable and fluid nature, as an archetype of transformation. It corresponds in Mizoguchi's psyche to solar elements—fire, the color red, aggressiveness, the rebirth implicit during summer months—as well as to lunar qualities—snow and iciness, blackness, passivity, and death. Like the Golden Temple, it transcends the workaday world of ideas, of rational intelligence, and lives in supernal spheres, where differentiation is no longer an issue nor a possibility.

The inroads made by the archetypal Golden Temple and the phoenix on Mizoguchi's psyche are halted momentarily when his father finally takes him to the Zen Buddhist sanctuary. The exaggerated value that he has projected onto the temple and the bird prior to his arrival—subject and object having already become one—pave the way for the disappointment he experiences upon his first encounter with these hierophanies. "The Golden Temple cast a perfect shadow on the surface of the pond, where the duckweed and the leaves from water plants were floating. The shadow was more beautiful than the building itself" (p. 24). The image of the duckweed ushers in a dark and ominous note. This flowering plant, which floats on fresh water like green scum, is a mirror image of Mizoguchi's own polluted subliminal world. The purity of his early feelings toward the archetypal sun/temple force as envisaged in the early sequences of the novel has now been vitiated by the appearance of the real sanctuary: illusion versus reality has created tension and friction within him. Not only does Mizoguchi no longer consider the Golden Temple as an object of beauty, but its very presence fills him with "a sense of disharmony and restlessness" (p. 25).

In the past, what is now irreconcilable—illusion and reality insofar as the Golden Temple and the phoenix are concerned—coalesced and operated as a single force in Mizoguchi's psyche. When he viewed the Golden Temple in his mind's eye, this anima figure during her sunlit hours endowed him with a sense of wonderment, bedazzling him, injecting him with joy and pleasure. These moments of heightened excitement were all the more pleasurable because, as libido took over, his ugliness seemed to vanish, his stuttering disappeared, linking him, he believed, to the world at large and permitting him to relate to what had previously been his fragmented psyche.

As a sacred power, the Golden Temple was experienced as a mandala: a composite of opposites upon which Mizoguchi concentrated his energy and from which his spirit moved forward to abstract worlds, from differentiated spheres to unified ones, from his own imperfection and disorder to a condition of perfection and harmony. The energy of the archetypal golden Temple allowed him to rise above his constitutional weaknesses, not because he accepted them or assimilated what they represented into his psyche, but simply because the temple image blocked them out, as fire obliterates everything when it rages. The fact that he was the butt of ridicule, that he was poor, ugly, and a virtual pariah in school, no longer mattered. He lived within the orbit of the Golden Temple and under the dominion of its solar and feminine power, cut off from the workaday world, unable to differentiate or evaluate his reactions but content in this *participation mystique*, this paradisiac state of the adolescent, the *puer*.

Life is not static; what is considered perfect alters in dimension, in focus, in action and reaction. The solar goddess Amaterasu, as manifested in the archetypal Golden Temple, becomes more demanding as she acquires greater power. She seeks a son/lover, a mortal who will fulfill her spiritual and sexual needs—a votary. Mizoguchi, to be sure, will never be able to satisfy these needs. The sun goddess demands a perfectly formed physical specimen, which Mishima offers his readers in the form of a young hero, "brilliant like the light reflected from the cluster of leaves" (p. 7). A former student at the middle school that Mizoguchi attended before his enrollment in the Zen Buddhist monastery, this gorgeous young man, now a student at the Maizuru Naval Engineering School, returns to his alma mater for a brief visit. Mizoguchi looks at his sunburned face, his black visored cap, his sparkling gold braid, the sword that hangs from his waist—an instrument of pride and beauty for the samurai. Even the smell of the young man's "sweat-moistened skin" arouses Mizoguchi's excitement (p. 8). Important as well is the association Mizoguchi makes between physical prowess and beauty and May flowers: tulips, sweet peas, anemones, daisies—exquisite because of their form and color, but also because they are ephemeral. Such an identification brings to mind the young flower gods of antiquity, Hyacinth and Narcissus, who also died young.[6] This young naval student, representing the power principle, will fulfill his mythological mission in Mizoguchi's subliminal sphere as the sun's son/lover.

This young solar hero incorporates in himself all those qualities Mizoguchi lacks. The objects associated with him, therefore, are endowed by Mishima's protagonist with magical powers, as are fetishes in general. The young man's spirit is as much alive in the sword as it is in his beautiful body, and the sensations catalyzed by both excite Mizoguchi spiritually and sexually. A concomitant reaction also occurs: the greater Mizoguchi's adulation for this hero type, the more pronounced seem his own ugliness and deformity—or, to put it another way, the more brilliant the sun, the blacker the shadow. Hence his suffering and solitude increase to such an extent that Mizoguchi can no longer repress his reactions: his shadow can no longer be hidden. It must be expressed overtly, as it is when Mizoguchi takes out his rusty little penknife and engraves "several ugly cuts" on the back of

the beautiful black scabbard of the sword (p. 9). No one sees him perpetrate this deed, since he works in secret.

The mutilation of the young man's scabbard is Mizoguchi's first aggressive act: it is his way of hurting the feminine principle. The scabbard, the sword's cover or sheath, protects its contents from harm and
in this connection may be compared to the uterus, which sees to the
well-being of the fetus. By cutting the outer object, which, as a container, may also be looked upon as an imprisoning device, Mizoguchi
can get to the sword: the phallus, which until now has been incarcerated, rendered powerless by the all-powerful anima figure: the scabbard, the Golden Temple, the sun principle.

The sword as a cutting and maiming object may also be considered
in its castrating quality. According to the Shinto and Zen Buddhist
ideologies, as has already been mentioned, the sword was given to the
Yamato clan by Amaterasu and thus became a hierophany, representative of authority and enlightenment. Since ancient times a
numinous quality has been bound up with the sword in Japan: when
in the process of making one, the swordsmith always prayed to the
guardian god to bring the steel to life. For the Zen Buddhist, the
sword represented the hero; it signified the physical prowess and rectitude of the soldier. In fact, in past times the sword was looked upon
as "the soul of the samurai."[7] But aside from its symbolic value in
terms of the martial arts, it also contained spiritual import. Like the
mind, which moves about in all directions, unhindered in its intuitive
forays, the sword could flash through matter instantly and completely.
It could cut, sever, destroy the acolyte's greed, anger, and folly; psychologically, it killed an individual's ego, thus preparing him for transcendence, or the egoless condition that is the goal of Zen Buddhist
meditation. To accomplish this end, the sword had to be directed toward self and not toward an outer object. To blemish the young man's
sword, as Mizoguchi has done, encourages him to think of himself as
being endowed with the heroic strength of the samurai and the ascetic
discipline of the Zen Buddhist. Unlike these powerful beings, however, who work in the light of consciousness, Mizoguchi works within
darkness and in secret, merely repressing still further his mangled
self-image. Nor is he motivated by any high purpose, in contrast to the
samurai and the Zen Buddhist. Mizoguchi does not "have the slightest
feeling of wanting to accomplish something," he says.

That Zen Buddhism was associated with Bushido—that is, with samurai ethics and martial arts in general—sheds light on our analysis.
Zen Buddhism was introduced to Japan from China by the Buddhist
priest Eisai (1141–1215). *Zen* means "meditation," a condition when the
mind becomes vacant and differentiation is thereby transcended: life

and death may be approached objectively, in a detached manner—undisturbed. Zen Buddhism is antirational and antischolastic. It preaches harmony and oneness with the cosmos through the intuitive experience rather than through book learning or logical thought. A Zen master, for example, will pose a problem (a *koan,* or kind of riddle) to an acolyte that might be considered unimportant or irrational by a Westerner but that, for the practitioner of Zen, is the one path leading to the transpersonal sphere of deeper reality. A master might ask his student to describe the nature of the sound caused by one hand clapping. After meditating upon this *koan,* the student may experience a sudden flash of insight concerning the Buddha, or unity with the universe, or other notions that lead to expanded consciousness. To understand the intuitive mode of functioning requires spiritual and psychological education in this system of proceeding, as well as long years devoted to rigorous physical discipline. Such a Spartan procedure answered a need in the samurai, who was always attempting to strengthen his inner fiber, his character; it also gave him a philosophical basis for his life and contributed to a great extent to the powerful position acquired by this sect in Japan.[8]

The immediate aesthetic and spiritual perception of reality or truth revealed to the Zen Buddhist in the intuitive or telepathic experience appealed to the samurai because he was interested not in philosophical speculation but rather in discovering a simple and direct way of attaining a deeper reality that would help him cope with his dangerous daily existence. The discipline required of the Zen Buddhist and of the warrior released him from entertaining a fear of death: he forced himself into an egoless experience and learned to sacrifice his ego, or individual existence, to the Self, or collective world. Just as in the physical sphere the notion of sacrifice entails the giving up of what is most precious and sacred—a human life—so in the spiritual sphere, the rational world must be set aside so that the irrational and intuitive mode of experience may be known. Such a step requires going *mad:* the releasing of subliminal powers. At this point the samurai can face the thought of death and can experience, at the same time, a sense of liberation. So, too, does the Zen Buddhist achieve his goal of detachment. When one has made up one's mind to die—to give up the things of the earth—one is free from the gnawing, grasping terror accompanying a worldly life.

Mizoguchi is no ascetic; nor does he have the capacity to meditate for protracted periods of time on any subject. He does dream, however, and fantasize. But this does not lead to a condition of detachment; rather, it leaves him vulnerable to archetypal forces. Such an emotionally deformed condition, which might also be described as perverse, in that it disturbs the emotional maturation process, is making deep inroads on his psyche. An incident Mizoguchi relates before his admission as an acolyte in the Golden Temple attests to a regressive emotional condition; an inability to relate to the feminine principle arouses anxiety in Mizoguchi, which he tried to expel through retribution, in this case a death wish. For some time, Mizoguchi tells us, he had been sexually attracted to Uiko, a good-looking young nurse who bicycled to work daily before dawn. He finally decided to walk to the spot where he knew she would be passing on her bicycle. When she arrived, he stood firm in front of her bicycle as it screeched to a halt. He felt strong, powerful, possessed of stone-like qualities at this moment; as if his "I" had been cut from the "Thou"; detached for a split second, understanding the "meaninglessness" of existence. "What an extraordinary thing to do," Uiko said, annoyed. "And you only a stutterer!" (p. 12). She bicycled around him and left. Later Mizoguchi expelled his rage inwardly by wishing her dead. His anger took on such dimension that he included the whole of humankind in his death wish. "Other people must all be destroyed. In order that I might truly face the sun, the world itself must be destroyed . . ." (p. 13).

Two months later Mizoguchi learned that Uiko was pregnant, that she had betrayed her country by helping her lover, a deserter. She fled from her home when government soldiers attempted to arrest her and tried to join her lover in hiding at the Kongo temple. Mizoguchi followed the crowd that was pursuing her. As she ran up the 105 moss-covered steps of the sanctuary, then walked along its top gallery, he gazed up at her silhouette, reacting to the interplay of light and darkness: "The lower part of the stone steps was wrapped in shadows but higher up they were bathed in moonlight" (p. 16). A man suddenly appeared, said something to Uiko, then pointed his revolver at her and fired. The soldiers on the ground returned the fire immediately as Uiko fell dead; the man put the muzzle of the revolver to his temple and shot himself.

That this episode is played out in the night and early dawn hours, when the moon world takes over, may indicate the inroads being made by the shadow sphere on Mizoguchi's world. Darkness, equated with unconscious and destructive feelings, is being opposed to the light of the solar hero who visited Mizoguchi's school. During the entire episode of the chase to and over the temple, Mizoguchi's emotions alter. At first his libido is aroused by the erroneous thought that Uiko has deceived her lover by leading the soldiers to his hideout. He identifies with this anima figure now: both she and he are hated and reviled by those they love. "Now she belongs to me!" (p. 17), he thinks, interweaving his own mangled fantasy images into the event. He is "intoxicated by the pellucid beauty of Uiko's treachery" (p. 17). When he realizes that her lover shot her and himself because of his deep feelings toward her, she becomes "a woman who has given herself over to one man alone," and in so doing, has betrayed him, not the soldier or society.[9]

Just as the young solar hero has to be destroyed (and is, symbolically, when Mizoguchi carves those mutilating lines on his scabbard), so it is necessary to punish Uiko fatally for her rejection of him. Rather than trying to relate to what Uiko represents in his psyche and understand the power the anima wields over him, thereby discovering the inoperative elements within his inner world, he again tries to eliminate them by killing her. His inner rage has taken on such authority in his subliminal sphere that it blocks out any and all differentiation.

When Mizoguchi enters the Zen Buddhist monastery of the Golden Temple as an acolyte, he brings along with him all his projections. A new male figure, representing light, health, and beauty, is to play an important role in his life: Tsurukawa, a fellow student. From an affluent Tokyo family, this handsome young man, with his "fast, cheerful manner of speech," radiates joy (p. 38). Mizoguchi understands the dichotomies involved in their relationship. Tsurukawa is the solar force and, as such, a feminine principle; he, the lunar, masculine counterpart, is deeply embedded in his insalubrious, dark world. Each is rooted in his own extremes: "I knew instinctively that this boy would not love the Golden Temple as I did. For my attachment to the temple was entirely rooted in my own ugliness" (p. 39).

Mizoguchi's description of Tsurukawa as a sun figure is arresting: "Each of his eyebrows was glittering gold in the sunlight and his nostrils were dilated from the sultry heat" (p. 43). He is described in terms of light, fire, and burnished gold: "His future was so concealed that he was burning. The wick of his future was floating in cool, clear oil" (p. 69). Tsurukawa is libido, fire, passion, excitement: an archetypal force that Mizoguchi associates with the Golden Temple in its anima aspect.

Whether he is projecting onto the architectural monument or onto Tsurukawa, both archetypal images prevent Mizoguchi from finding fulfillment and experiencing any kind of joy. He lives within the orbit of these dazzlingly beautiful feminine forces, which stultify any semblance of independence within him. Whereas the Zen practitioner believes in freedom and fluidity of the mind, divesting it of intellectual deliberations and affective disturbances, Mizoguchi's psyche has become increasingly confined, incarcerated in the archetypal imagery of the Golden Temple and the complex associations he projects upon it.

The Zen Buddhist doctrine of no-mind, or egolessness, of non-hindrance, requires a dissociation from sensation, feeling, and thinking functions, for these prevent spiritual and visceral objectivity. The mind must be able to flow in freedom while, paradoxically, experiencing its own unmovable center. Mizoguchi has no such stability; he can experience only extremes. Such a one-sided or distorted orientation will only increase his identification with objects and people, thereby destroying any kind of equilibrium he might enjoy. To be free from the opposites, essential to Zen Buddhist dicta, obliges an individual to cut those ties which strangle him, those bonds which crush him. Such an attitude implies not a withdrawal from life, however, but rather a turning toward life—as a deeper experience. Because Mizoguchi suffers from *enantiodromia*, the energic charges emanating from the temple create an inner turbulence that forces powerful sun rays or equally dominating lunar rays to overcome him: feminine, then masculine; good, then evil.

Rather than experiencing reality by means of intuitive flashes, thus leading him on to transpersonal spheres and paving the way for an increase in consciousness, Mizoguchi limps along, becoming increasingly enmeshed in and dominated by a world of polarities: burning sun or chilled blackness. These extremes tear him apart, increase his sense of worthlessness, his solitude, his rage and passion, and his need to expel these powerful forces within him in destructive ways. The greater the numinosity of the archetypal image, the more his world is dictated by this energic force. In time, Mizoguchi comes to believe that if the Golden Temple were to be destroyed by American incendiary bombs, as much of Tokyo has been (World War II is still going on), he would be liberated from its power. What has been considered eternal by society—and sublimely beautiful—would take on mortality and hence resemble him, its power over him diminishing as a result.

That Mizoguchi chooses the firebomb as a fantasized means for the Golden Temple's destruction is reasonable, to be sure, since a war is going on, but other reasons also enter into his decision. Fire, for the Shintoist, is of extreme significance not only because of its association with the sun but in its origin as a separate deity: Kagu-Zuchi. This god, who caused his mother's death by being born and was killed by his father in revenge, is comparable, psychologically speaking, to Mizoguchi. Although the acolyte's mother is still alive, he despises her and wishes her dead. As for his father, who died from tuberculosis shortly after Mizoguchi became an acolyte, he virtually killed Mizoguchi by forcing him to become a Zen priest. It is the wrong vocation for him; as we have seen, he is not sufficiently balanced to experience the deeper meaning of the Zen Buddhist experience.

Fire spells excitement and increased libido for Mizoguchi because it is in itself a terrifying element for the Japanese; a great many houses and temples are built of wood. In traditional Japan, incantations to the god of fire were repeated frequently in an attempt to protect the people from this destructive force. In fact, on New Year's Day the faithful in Kyoto would make their way to the temple of Gion to receive pure fire from the priest's hands, which they then took home and used to light the fire on their own hearth, convinced that this ritual would protect them against the annihilating power of the fire god throughout the year.

To burn, for Mizoguchi, means to protect, purify, beautify, but also to destroy. Burning will heal what is diseased, he feels, will befriend what has been buried in loneliness.

> Existing under the same curse, under the same ill-omened fiery destiny, the temple and I had come to inhabit worlds of the same dimension. Just like my own frail, ugly body, the temple's body, hard though it was, consisted of combustible carbon. At times I felt that it would be possible for me to flee this place, taking along the temple concealed in my flesh, in my system—just as a thief swallows a precious jewel when making his escape. (P. 469)

The friction, warmth, and fecundating power associated with fire also provoke sexual fantasies in Mizoguchi: ". . . something like a huge heavenly compressor that would bring down disasters, cataclysms and superhuman tragedies, that would crush beneath it all human beings and all objects, irrespective of their ugliness or their beauty" (p. 74). Like the sun, fire sublimates, transcends the concrete world, and, as an archetype of transformation, it alters, symbolically, the solitary and alienated state in which Mizoguchi finds himself incarcerated. Fire destroys barriers and in so doing smokes out and burns away obstacles: it devours them as does the *vagina dentata,* that aggressive, cutting, terrifying feminine principle. When associating this paradoxically negative and positive situation with striated colors of the flaming building he sees in his mind's eye, he associates these with the burgeoning of day and the nascent feelings of liberation that ensue at dawn, "like the light of the cool blade of some huge axe that was large enough to cover the entire earth" (p. 48). Flame unites; the axe severs.

During this period, when Mizoguchi is expecting the Golden Temple to be burned down by American bombs, he and Tsurukawa visit the Nanzen temple, not far from the sanctuary where they live. Performing their prayers, kneeling before the statue of Sakamuni, they then walk across the garden to the Tenju hermitage, stop in front of a room with a bright scarlet carpet, and witness a tea ceremony in process.

The tea ceremony, important in Zen Buddhism, was also brought from China to Japan by Eisai. An aesthetic and spiritual ritual enacted in slow and formal steps in a beautiful but Spartan setting, the ceremony ushers in an atmosphere of extreme reverence, tranquility, and purity. Spiritual calm is at the heart of the ceremony—a condition designed to pave the way for an orderly life.[10] What is specifically Zen in the tea ceremony is the thought that mundane life is as important as spiritual factors: "It held that in the great relation of things there was no distinction of small and great, an atom possessing equal possibilities with the universe. The seeker for perfection must discover in his own life the reflection of the inner light."[11]

When Mizoguchi looks into the tea room, expecting to experience inner peace, the opposite ensues. A woman dressed in a most gorgeous kimono with flowers painted on a pale blue background, her vermilion sash glittering with radiant golden threads, illuminates the very air of this sanctum "by the brilliance of her costume" (p. 51). The elegance of her posture mirrors the perfection of her body and the beauty of her spirit. Mizoguchi sees her as the perfect anima figure, inspiring him with a sense of awe. In fact, like the Golden Temple of his imagination, she stands for something unreal; she seems to be a doll placed there by some supernal force.

The woman kneels before a man who has just entered, offering him tea in accordance with the ritual. After he speaks a few words to her, she bows to him, then loosens "the collar of her kimono," pulls "the material of her dress from under the stiff sash," and takes "one of her full white breasts in her own hands" (p. 51). The officer

> held out the dark, deep-colored teacup, and knelt before her. The woman rubbed her breast with both hands. . . . the white warm milk gushed forth from her breast into the deep-green tea which foamed inside that cup . . . settled into the liquid, leaving the white drops on the top. . . . the quiet surface of the tea was made turbid and foamy by that white breast. (P. 52)

The man drinks "every drop of that mysterious tea." After it is all over, Mizoguchi realizes that it must have been a "farewell ceremony." He is correct in his assumption, as we later learn: The couple's child has been stillborn, and the officer's request to drink her milk since the child cannot indicates his need for her warmth and nourishing force. The officer is killed a month after the ceremony.

To include milk in the ancient tea ceremony indicates the intrusion of the feminine principle in her healing and fruitful capacity. Yet the woman as milk giver, as representative of the Great Earth Mother archetype, also brings death upon those who emerge from her: in this case, the stillborn child and the soldier who is about to die. The anima, in her heterosexual relationships, discloses both facets of her personality: constructive and destructive. Her unquenchable thirst for blood, power, pain, radiates in her bounties: the one exists in the other. The seeming comfort she offers the soldier in the tea ceremony is, therefore, a deception, a trap. She feeds him spiritually and physically so as to allow him to experience death gloriously but does away with life altogether for the stillborn child. In the case of both Uiko and the woman of the tea ceremony, the fruit of heterosexual union is death, indicating the impossibility of anything good emerging from such cohabitation.

When, after the conclusion of World War II, the Golden Temple remains standing, Mizoguchi grows dejected; life seems to have lost all purpose. He also realizes that his relationship with the temple has changed. Representative, heretofore, of positive forces, as an architectural monument and in the figure of Tsurukawa—all light, beauty, and goodness—it has now become a distiller of poisons, a constant reminder to Mizoguchi of his ugliness and solitude. As he gazes for long periods of time at the Golden Temple, sweat pours from Mizoguchi's forehead, his legs begin to tremble, something musical seems to reverberate from this archetypal force, resounding within him in rhythmical but silent tones. As he stands immovable, the temple's shadow seems to grow and darken, continuously, powerfully. Mizoguchi understands now that he can no longer remain a passive recipient of this beautiful form, buried as he is in utter darkness. To live as he wishes demands a confrontation. He will have to act overtly and aggressively against this sun principle in her feminine guise, the moon power in his masculine guise. Only then, he reasons, will he possess and overturn the dominion of this power within him.

Mizoguchi's change of attitude is to be concretized in an event. A drunken American soldier and a prostitute arrive by jeep at the Golden Temple. Despite the freezing temperature and snow-covered ground, Mizoguchi notes, the woman is wearing no stockings under her high-heeled shoes, and her flaming red overcoat covers a soiled nightgown made of terrycloth. When the soldier asks for information concerning the temple, Mizoguchi begins reading the guidebook. Moments later the couple start quarreling. The prostitute slaps the soldier's cheek, and he in turn pushes her down on the snow and then orders Mizoguchi to step on her. As Mishima describes it: "The bottom of her red coat opened and her bare white thighs were spread out on the snow" (p. 77). Fearful of being beaten by the soldier, Mizoguchi complies. But other factors also provoke his sadistic act. When, for example, he first notices the woman's blood-red finger- and toenails, this blazing color arouses his long-pent-up sexual desire and rage. These erupting instincts are directed against the feminine force. He also identifies with the soldier, and, inspired by his "exceedingly lyrical voice, feels that the woman deserves retribution for having slapped him. He is reliving the Uiko incident, except that this time he will actually be able to hurt the woman. Mizoguchi's foot descends on the prostrate figure over and over again. "My foot descended and I stepped on something as soft as springtime mud. It was the girl's stomach. The girl shut her eyes and groaned" (p. 77). Suddenly, the "sense of discord" which has so plagued the acolyte vanishes, and as he raises his boot to strike, a kind of "bubbling joy" fills his being (p. 77). Her vibrant body, he says, "seemed to flatter me with its resilience, its groans," and he calls it "a crushed flower of flesh that is coming into bloom." Mizoguchi feels such release from the experience that the power of his emotions sends him "reeling"; the "sensation" that passes at that moment, "like some mysterious lightning from the girl's body" into his own, fills him with feelings of unforgettable "sweetness" (p. 85).

Mizoguchi feels no guilt during the weeks to come. In fact, the incident settles upon him "like gold dust," giving off, he says, "a glittering light that constantly pierced my eyes" (p. 86). When the prostitute returns to the monastery some weeks later to complain to the superior about the sadistic action, which has caused her a miscarriage, she is given the money she demands. Mizoguchi, however, remains silent, refusing to admit he had any part in the incident, though he knows everyone at the sanctuary blames him for it since he was the only guide on duty that day. He treasures the incident, musing upon it and the sensations of pleasure it has brought in its wake.

Tsurukawa cannot believe Mizoguchi capable of the deed and accepts his denial of ever having acted in such a cruel manner. As Mizoguchi lies, he again experiences elation—this time at the very thought of betraying a friend. "If Tsurukawa had followed his characteristic method—his method of turning all shadows into light, all night into days, all moonlight into sunlight, all the dampness of the night moss into the daytime rustling of shiny young leaves—then I myself might well have stuttered out a confession" (p. 83). Tsurukawa's power over Mizoguchi has diminished. The blackness of his world has altered his previous orientation, and a new center, a new point of reference, is about to come into being. To perpetrate evil, to incorporate himself in darkness alone, to reject the solar, feminine sphere, will be an invitation to the lunar, masculine principle to dominate Mizoguchi's lifestyle.

To concretize this new focus in Mizoguchi's psyche, another

character is introduced into the narrative: Kashiwagi, a student who mirrors Mizoguchi's distorted and perverse personality. Kashiwagi is severely clubfooted; his walk, Mizoguchi notes, looks like "a sort of exaggerated dance" (p. 91), endowing the image with a strange motility, reflecting the inner change taking place. What is novel, insofar as Mizoguchi is concerned, is Kashiwagi's acceptance of his own physical deformity. "Physically he was a cripple, yet there was an intrepid beauty about him, like that of a lovely woman" (p. 92). Kashiwagi represents both beauty and ugliness, male and female, but these polarities are buried within a world of blackness, depravity, and perversity.

Kashiwagi is all shadow, as Tsurukawa has been all light. "He was a shadow that asserted itself, or rather, he was the existent shadow itself. Certain it was that the sun could never penetrate that hard skin of his" (p. 92). He has created a whole philosophy of life for himself that requires discipline but recompenses him with a sense of self-sufficiency and his own brand of pleasure. Kashiwagi tells Mizoguchi that he lives "on good terms with his clubfeet," that he knows the world about him will not change, and so he must compromise with it. He suggests that the stuttering Mizoguchi should accept his fault, which will enable him to destroy the power this defect has upon his emotional condition.

Mizoguchi, the stutterer, suffers the life of a pariah because he cannot communicate to the world spiritually or intellectually. The clubfooted Kashiwagi suffers, because of his impaired feet, from an imbalance in the earthly sphere; he cannot, therefore, relate normally to the workaday world. But he has attempted to rectify his situation. He tells Mizoguchi that he does not frequent prostitutes in order to win feminine love or experience sexual gratification. They will do anything for money, he says, which means nothing to him. What he wants is to attract a beautiful girl from a very nice family, and in one instance he thought he had succeeded. Such a girl had rejected her many suitors in favor of him. He realized that she loved him because he was different, because of his deformity. To make certain her passion was authentic, however, he told her he did not love her. So desperate did she become that she offered him her "dazzlingly beautiful body"; at the propitious moment, Kashiwagi could not fulfill the sexual act. Sometime later, he tells Mizoguchi, when he was sent to a sixty-year-old widow on the anniversary of her father's death he started reciting the Buddhist sutras, then told the woman that Buddha had appeared to his mother in a dream shortly before his birth and announced to her that the woman who would worship her son's clubfeet would be reborn in paradise. (Let us recall, in this connection, that when the

Buddha was born he strode through the universe taking seven steps in each direction; thus did he become manifest to humanity.) In seconds, the woman, who was reciting her sutras, started to adore Kashiwagi's feet, even as she continued bending and praying, and it was in this posture that he made love to her. The absurdity of the situation pointed up Kashiwagi's hatred for womankind, his revulsion for woman as a sexual object. Laughing inwardly as the sexual act was consummated, he expressed his cutting, jeering feelings in seemingly joyful overtones. "Clubfeet. . . . This monstrous formation of my feet. This condition of utmost ugliness in which I had been placed. The wild farce of it! And to make things even funnier, the old woman's stray locks brushed against the soles of my feet as she bowed time after time in prayer, and tickled me" (p. 101).

Only after this ludicrous and ironic episode does Kashiwagi—and Mizoguchi through projection—realize that love is impossible, and in so doing, he feels a sudden sense of release from the uneasiness that had prevented him from functioning that first time. Later, Kashiwagi's demands upon women grow increasingly authoritarian. When another young and beautiful girl becomes attracted to him, to test her reactions Kashiwagi throws himself into a ditch, and the fall causes some lacerations on his feet, which she bathes with iodine. Then "she put her cheek against his feet and finally began to kiss them," wearing the "expression of a faithful dog" and smiling (p. 121). The anima figure, first powerfully independent in Uiko, then nutritive in the tea ceremony image, has now become subservient, degraded.

Feet in Mishima's novel not only represent a way of relating to the workaday world, i.e., walking on it, but are sexual objects as well: fetishes. The naked foot, when touching the ground, represents the phallus; when wearing a slipper, the foot has come to mean a feminine symbol of containment, symbolizing the completion of the erotic act. In that Kashiwagi is clubfooted and so much emphasis is paid to this part of his body, an androgynous note emerges. Indeed, we recall that Mizoguchi compared him to a "lovely woman" (p. 92). Kashiwagi is an ambivalent figure, arousing both heterosexual and homosexual desires in Mizoguchi.

It is he who encourages Mizoguchi to attempt sexual intercourse with a female friend of his, and when the acolyte fails, the situation is described both overtly and in terms of imagery. The act, Mishima writes, took place "next to some faded, worm-eaten irises" (p. 125), a perfect visualization of Mizoguchi's decayed and dying psyche. As for the event itself, it is depicted as follows: Mizoguchi fondles the girl, then slips his hand under her skirt; something stops him from further activity, however, and we learn that it is the Golden Temple, which appears brilliant, all-powerful in his mind's eye. "The Golden Temple, which sometimes seems to be so utterly different to me and to tower into the air outside myself, had now completely engulfed me and had allowed me to be situated within its structure" (p. 125).

The Golden Temple had crushed Mizoguchi's advances. He realized that he was still under its dominion, no matter what the avatars. "The moment of illusion, in which I had imagined myself being accepted and embraced by the Golden Temple, had passed" (p. 126). Mizoguchi was impotent. Only one love was open to him, that of the Golden Temple. No human counterpart was acceptable as long as the archetypal image radiated its power. The Golden Temple remained the "controlling force," the "regulating force" in Mizoguchi's life, cutting him off still further from any and all relationships.

Mizoguchi refuses to accept his fate. He rejects the Golden Temple's power over him, for it sucks up any and all enjoyment in life. Therefore, Tsurukawa, as an avatar of the Golden Temple, will have to be destroyed to symbolize its diminishing power. It is at this point that Mizoguchi learns that when Tzurukawa went home to visit his parents he became drunk on the sake given him and was knocked down by a truck and killed. Although Mizoguchi did not cry when his own father died, he now weeps bitterly, as one does when one is divested of a projection and, in this case, a beautiful life force. Tsurukawa had been a bridge, he thinks, between himself and the world at large, between light and darkness. "His brightness corresponded so accurately to my darkness," Mizoguchi notes (p. 128). There will no longer be any light to penetrate his bleak, black world.

With Tsurukawa's death, Mizoguchi notes another change in his relationship with the Golden Temple. Something seems to be "fermenting" in his being, something "utterly incompatible with the Golden Temple" (p. 131). This alteration of focus is mirrored in natural phenomena: in the typhoon that strikes the temple area, in the winds that blow fiercely and cruelly, preluding a concomitant spiritual and psychological change. "Did I possess the temple, or was I possessed by it? . . . Or would it not be more correct to say that a strange balance had come into being at that moment, a balance which would allow me to be the Golden Temple and the Golden Temple to be me?" (p. 131). Powerful winds create havoc with trees, flowers, and architectural monuments; in the subliminal realm, too, these forces are temporarily disorienting, their turbulence whipping up heretofore dormant contents. Mizoguchi sees the "clouds stretched out tortuously beyond the hills," and then he remembers how the landscape looked when he saw the hand of the American soldier who ordered him to stamp on the woman's stomach. This premonitory image indicates, psychologically, the perpetration of another aggressive act on Mizoguchi's part.

A pause in Mizoguchi's inward journey is effected by a musical interlude introducing beauty and harmony into a realm of ugliness and perversion. Kashiwagi has become an expert flute player, and the lyrical sounds of his instrument are pleasurable for him because music, like flowers, is transitory. Indeed, music is "a perfect abstraction and creation of life itself" (p. 139). Mizoguchi wants to learn the flute and also make music. Kashiwagi teaches him how, and in appreciation for the lessons, Mizoguchi picks some flowers—an act of thievery (since the acolytes are not allowed to disturb any part of the sanctuary garden), which serves to arouse his excitement.

Like the tea ceremony, the art of flower arrangement, which Kashiwagi has also learned, occupies a very special place in Zen philosophy. The perfect arrangement includes the linking of three spheres (earth, humankind, heaven) in ascending lines; when this is accomplished, one grasps the very essence and spirit of nature itself. Oneness and not fragmentation comes into being; unity in the harmony of the individual; the one as an aspect of the multiple; mortal as figuring in the transpersonal. Flower arrangement is neither an intellectual nor a logical way of appreciating or even approaching nature and therefore requires a religious attitude, a "superworldly" approach to the experiencing of the nonrelative world.

When Kashiwagi completes a flower arrangement, Mizoguchi is deeply impressed by the fluidity of motion and the freedom of expression infused in what he considers to be a work of art. Beauty and balance have been encapsulated in what otherwise could be called a perverse, ugly, and deformed universe. Kashiwagi has been that agent of transformation which works on what is natural and, through a personal perception, lends it a transpersonal dimension: the factor that distinguishes simply a creative work from a work of art.

> The flowers and leaves, which had formerly existed *as they were*, had now to be transformed into flowers and leaves *as they ought to be*. The cattails and the irises were no longer individual, anonymous plants belonging to their respective species, but had become terse, direct manifestations of what might be called the essences of the irises and the cattails. (P. 145)

Despite the beauty of the floral arrangement, Mizoguchi is aware of the intrinsic cruelty embedded in the work of art: the cutting of the stems reminds him of "dripping blood," a premonitory image of the events to come. The dripping of blood indicates a loss of energy, a wounding, libido being spent, sacrificed, injured. In Mizoguchi's case, it is linked to his fear of castration by the feminine principle as exemplified in the Golden Temple and its avatars: Uiko, the woman of the tea ceremony, Kashiwagi's girlfriends. No longer does he believe in a paradisiac relationship with the temple as he had fantasized at the outset of the narrative, for it no longer glows, no longer offers him the magic of sunlight and beauty. It stands in his way, a towering force cutting him off from the world, just as the flowers in Kashiwagi's arrangement have been severed from their roots. Iconographically, the image of cut stems reveals the splintering of the twin solar and lunar forces that have lived until now in a relatively compatible condition in the archetypal image of the Golden Temple. Feminine and masculine forces, considered as bulwarks in Mizoguchi's world, will now fight it out for dominance.

Kashiwagi invites the woman who taught him the art of floral arrangement to visit him. When she arrives, Mizoguchi recognizes her as the one who offered the officer the milk from her breast during the tea ceremony. This synchronistic incident permits Mizoguchi to experience a segment of his past in his present reality, enriching and expanding his present perceptions. However, when Kashiwagi tells the woman he no longer wants her and can learn nothing more from her, her face blanches. Advancing on her knees toward the alcove where the flowers have been placed, she throws them down in one rapid motion. Kashiwagi grabs her wrists and slaps her face, and the woman runs cowering from the room. "Try to console her!" Kashiwagi tells Mizoguchi. When he catches up to the woman she recites a long list of Kashiwagi's misdeeds, cruelties, and betrayals, and the more she complains, the more Mizoguchi grows aroused. When she invites him to her house, he accepts. Moments later, she unfastens her sash buckle and "scoops out her left breast and holds it to the young man," but at this very moment something happens to him—something comes between him and the sex object. "The flesh did not in itself have the power to appeal or to tempt. Exposed there in front of me, and completely cut off from life, it merely served as a proof of the dreariness of existence" (p. 151).

Although Mizoguchi tries to make love to her, he fails. "The Golden Temple once again appeared before me. Or rather, I should say that the breast was transformed into the Golden Temple" (p. 152). No longer able to tolerate the hell of his existence, he feels "absolved from human law," and this matriarchal force, a castrating entity, will now have to be destroyed so that he can live.

One last cutting incident has to be experienced before Mizoguchi will be sufficiently aroused to act. Kashiwagi tells him that in reality Tsurukawa had committed suicide over the love of a girl his parents did not like. Worse still for Mizoguchi is the fact that Tsurukawa had warned him of the dangers involved in his friendship with Kashiwagi, yet he is now informed that his solar hero, his great idol, had used this same clubfooted individual as his confidant and had written him almost daily when he left the sanctuary to visit his parents. The "butchery" of Kashiwagi's statement tears so deeply into Mizoguchi that he experiences a featureless world, an egoless existence, or so he thinks, so benumbed are his senses. He feels himself sinking into a limitless state of nonthought, into the world of nonrelativity, of transcendence, which Zen Buddhists know after years of discipline. Transcendence has obliterated dualities in Mizoguchi's world, but not in accordance with the Zen Buddhist credo. The sun has withdrawn in favor of the moon, ushering in feelings of blackness and not vacancy, subjectivity and not objectivity; Mizoguchi's world is one of decayed and fungal matter, rather than the glow and bloom of aerated spheres, where earth and heaven are united in a harmony of relationships.

Mizoguchi is now ready to proceed to what he erroneously believes will be his liberation. He goes to a brothel and proves to himself that he can achieve sexual satisfaction. After this deed, on July 1, 1950, under a slight drizzle, "I soaked my body into the darkness of the Golden Temple. Then a strange face appeared before me and made me tremble with fear. As I was holding a lighted match, my face was reflected on the glass case that contained the model of the temple" (p. 249).

Mizoguchi takes out a match and strikes it, but it burns out. He pauses, eats ritual food, performs specific purifications, which, in this case, consist of drinking holy water, and says goodbye to the Golden Temple as it stands "dim in the darkness of the rainy night . . . in deep black, as though it were a crystallization of the night itself" (p. 252). Then he sets it aflame, burning out that virulent rage against this archetypal feminine force, this power which has sought to castrate him, to depotentiate him—to force him to experience the life of a pariah. Linked to the energic principle, this demiurge is no longer considered by Mizoguchi to be an enlightening force; it is one that will consume and destroy him. He watches the ancient edifice burn. "All that I could see was the eddying smoke and the great fire that rose in the sky. The flakes from the fire drifted between the trees and the Golden Temple's sky seemed to be strewn with golden sand" (p. 261). Mizoguchi had planned to commit suicide but instead throws the arsenic and knife he had brought along into a ravine. He takes out a package of cigarettes and starts smoking. "I felt like a man who settles down for a smoke after finishing a job of work. I wanted to live" (p. 262).

A loner who lives in a world of extremes, Mizoguchi never understands the middle road as enunciated in Buddha's Noble Eightfold Path; hence he never can experience the profound nature of Zen teaching. A composite of opposites, he is both helpless and aggressive, passive and active, like a flower blown here and there, cut, jarred, torn asunder. Nourishing a thirst for revenge that will heal the sense of hurt and dissatisfaction his outer ugliness and speech impairment have brought him, Mizoguchi identifies with the beauty of the Golden Temple, hoping to be loved by it and its various avatars. Such does not turn out to be the case. Its dominion over his subliminal sphere is a bulwark against fluidity of communication between the acolyte and the world at large. He lives, as a result, incarcerated in its shadow, impaled by its all-engulfing power.

Like Herostratos, who in 356 B.C. burned down the temple of Artemis at Ephesus on the day Alexander the Great was born in order to earn both fame and punishment, Mizoguchi also wants to prove his worth, to commit the grand act that will transform him from a helpless, impotent pawn, an ugly, malformed pariah, into a strong and virile male. His feelings of inadequacy and inferiority, he thinks unconsciously, will be overcome by the Herostratic act, earning him admiration and acceptance.

What Mizoguchi destroys, however, is that gold factor in the Zen Buddhist temple, that valuable and precious substance which could have, had it been properly assimilated into his psyche, helped him attain the fluidity of feeling, the barrierless existence, which Zen Buddhism teaches. Such assimilation would have permitted him to understand and relate to his own culture and heritage. Instead, however, his distorted psyche increases his feelings of alienation to such an extent that at the conclusion of the narrative he has already cut himself off completely from reality. Blackness controls him now; he has truly become a solitary being in a world where conflict is nonexistent—not because he has experienced transcendence, but because he has become psychotic, unknowing, unfeeling, incarcerated in a sublunar sphere of his own manufacture.

Conclusion

The creative artist—architect or writer—ushers into existence mirror images of what lies inchoate within his depths. These he develops, molds, extracts from that limitless oceanic sphere existing dynamically and vitally within him which is referred to as the collective unconscious. As the inner eye sweeps into the hidden layers and secret folds of this world inaccessible to consciousness, it seizes universal motifs and cultural manifestations of all sorts, which have been the common heritage of all beings since time immemorial. It is the artist or architect who provides shape, line, and mass to these amorphous images that have been dredged up from subliminal spheres.

The architectural images gleaned in these suprapersonal climes reveal to the probing eye of the writer unknown motivating dynamisms inherent in the psyche, which have taken on concretion as towers, temples, castles, and houses. Ibsen, Maeterlinck, James, Ansky, Kafka, Lorca, Borges, Fuentes, Wang, and Mishima—each *saw* into his nonindividual collective unconscious; each wrenched from it those constructs which answered a conscious or unconscious need. When the archetypal images were encountered, when the writer faced these transpersonal visualizations, he felt dynamized by their energic powers. It was at this point that a sense of the divine or sacred—to be understood as the experiencing of the suprapersonal power that transcends the ego—took hold and fired him on. The writer felt endowed or injected by some galvanic impulse; an urgency took hold of him, compelling him to articulate what slumbered *in potentia*. The author in question experienced these dynamisms in multiple ways—obsessively or as haunting and fascinating *eidola*—which shaped the destiny of his protagonists. At times he felt depotentiated, losing momentary contact with reality, experiencing that excoriating terror of being cut off from the world around him and from himself as well. The creatures of his fantasy then became alienated. At other moments, he felt fulfilled and warmed by forces that fed him rhythmic and cradling movements, instilling in him a sense of serenity. As the eye of the writer peered into underground caverns and passageways, into halls without beginning or end, into continuous and unbroken rooms, or lifted himself into airy or atomized supergalactic spheres, he knew the dank and dismal as well as the dazzlingly sublime. Infused with the *prima materia* necessary to build his monumental work, the creative spirit cut, "tore away" (*arracher* is the French equivalent—Malraux's word to describe the writing process) what clung together inchoate within his subliminal domain. The writer aggressively transformed his fantastic visions, silhouettes, and three-dimensional configurations into recognizable shapes. The fine line took precedence over the roughly hewn form, as the writer smoothed, sanded, and grated, divesting the word/image of the debris that, like barnacles, clung to it as it leaped from the inner sea onto land and concretion in the poem, novel, essay, or theatrical piece. The mind's eye crystallized the object of its search, closed in on it. Eye and object now lived in close proximity, relationally and experientially. A sycophantic relationship may ensue under some circumstances, but more probably a symbiotic association takes hold as eye and word, two dissimilar entities, live together in a mutually advantageous relationship.

It is such a trajectory that Ibsen took in plumbing the architectural archetype in *The Master Builder;* that Maeterlinck sounded out in *The Intruder* and *Interior;* that James probed in "The Jolly Corner"; Ansky fathomed in "The Tower of Rome"; Kafka determined in *The Castle;* Lorca fleshed out in *The House of Bernarda Alba;* Borges subsumed in "The Library of Babel"; Fuentes dramatized in "In a Flemish Garden"; Wang Shih-fu explored in *The Romance of the Western Chamber;* and Mishima investigated in *The Temple of the Golden Pavilion.* Each writer was galvanized by an architectural archetype that nourished and/or depleted him, devoured and/or fed his visionary world, which he decanted into his work. Whatever the path, the nothingness that existed in the void took on form and became something, definable and electrifying for the writer as well as for the reader, who in turn rests his eye on an architectural archetypal image and undergoes a kinetic reaction according to his own inner projections. Sound, taste, touch, olfaction, thought—and of course the visual realm—catapult readers into their own *prima materia,* where oneness of being and non-being work in complementary patterns as eternal sources of creativity. As Lao-tze wrote:

Thirty spokes unite in one nave,
And because of the part where nothing exists we have the use of a
  carriage wheel.
Clay is molded into vessels,
And because of the space where nothing exists we are able to use them
  as vessels.
Doors and windows are cut out in the walls of a house,
And because they are empty spaces, we are able to use them.
Therefore, on the one hand we have the benefit of existence, and on
  the other of non-existence.[1]

Notes

INTRODUCTION

1. C. G. Jung, *Memories, Dreams, Reflections*, p. 225.
2. Ibid., p. 223.
3. C. G. Jung, *Collected Works*, 11, p. 149.
4. Edward Edinger, "An Outline of Analytical Psychology," p. 5.
5. Jolande Jacobi, *Complex Archetype Symbol in the Psychology of C. G. Jung*, pp. 48, 36.
6. Ibid., pp. 48–49.
7. Ibid., p. 43. From the Introduction to Esther Harding, *Woman's Mysteries*, p. ix.
8. Edinger, p. 6.
9. S. Giedion, *The Beginnings of Architecture. The Eternal Present*, p. 312.
10. Mortimer Wheeler, *Roman Art and Architecture*, p. 26.
11. Ann G. Tyng, "Geometric Extensions of Consciousness," p. 19.
12. Edouard Schuré, *The Great Initiates*, p. 275.
13. Giedion, p. 471.
14. Nikolaus Pevsner, *The Sources of Modern Architecture and Design*, p. 13.
15. Tyng, p. 4. From Henri Focillon, *The Life of Forms in Art*.
16. Will Grohmann, *Paul Klee*, p. 214.
17. Jacobi, p. 66.
18. *The Complete Greek Drama*, I, p. 198. Translated by Paul Elmer More.
19. Ibid., p. 239.
20. Ludovico Ariosto, *Orlando Furioso*, LVIII.
21. Honoré de Balzac, *La Recherche de l'Absolu*, p. 2.

CHAPTER 1. IBSEN: *THE MASTER BUILDER*

1. Hans Heilberg, *Ibsen, A Portrait of the Artist*, p. 261.
2. Henrik Ibsen, *Eleven Plays of Henrik Ibsen*, p. 86.
3. Edward Edinger, "An Outline of Analytical Psychology," p. 7.
4. Marie Louise von Franz, *The Psychological Meaning of Redemption Motifs in Fairy Tales*, p. 40.
5. Edinger, p. 4.

CHAPTER 2. MAETERLINCK: *THE INTRUDER* AND *INTERIOR*

1. Edward Edinger, "An Outline of Analytical Psychology," p. 7.
2. Bettina Knapp, *Maurice Maeterlinck*, p. 20.
3. Ibid., pp. 24–25.
4. C. G. Jung, *The Structure and Dynamics of the Psyche, Collected Works*, 8, pp. 449, 480.
5. Ibid., pp. 480, 434, 436, 515.
6. Maurice Maeterlinck, *Interior*.
7. Jethro Bithell, *Life and Writings of Maurice Maeterlinck*, p. 75.

CHAPTER 3. JAMES: "THE JOLLY CORNER"

1. Edward Edinger, "An Outline of Analytical Psychology," p. 10.
2. Henry James, *The Short Stories of Henry James*, p. 612.
3. G. G. Scholem, *Major Trends in Jewish Mysticism*, p. 218.
4. Marie Louise von Franz, *Number and Time*, pp. 18, 62, 204.

CHAPTER 4. ANSKY: "THE TOWER OF ROME"

1. Joachim Neugroschel, *Yenne Velt* (Another World), I, p. 3. Includes "The Tower of Rome."
2. Raphael Patai, *The Messiah Texts*, p. 174.
3. G. G. Scholem, *Kabbalah*, p. 11.
4. G. G. Scholem, *Major Trends in Jewish Mysticism*, p. 44.
5. R. J. Zwi Werblowsky and Geoffrey Wigoder, eds., *The Encyclopedia of the Jewish Religion*, p. 278.
6. Scholem, *Kabbalah*, p. 169.
7. Ibid.
8. Jolande Jacobi, *Complex Archetype Symbol in the Psychology of C. G. Jung*, p. 166.
9. Marie Louise von Franz, *The Psychological Meaning of Redemption Motifs in Fairy Tales*, p. 15.
10. The *Sefer Yetsirah* was written approximately in the third to the sixth centuries; the *Zohar* is attributed to Simeon bar Yohai (second century) and Moses de Leon, a Spanish Kabbalist of the thirteenth century.
11. Z'ev ben Shimon Halévi, *A Kabbalistic Universe*, p. 11.
12. C. G. Jung, *Collected Works*, 5, p. 86.
13. Scholem, *Major Trends in Jewish Mysticism*, p. 57.
14. G. G. Scholem, *On the Kabbalah and Its Symbolism*, p. 63.
15. Halévi, p. 58.
16. Ibid., p. 76. Angels are considered messengers also of both positive and negative values.
17. Scholem, *Kabbalah*, p. 168.
18. Jung, 5, p. 178.
19. Scholem, *Major Trends*, p. 265.
20. Halévi, p. 191.
21. *Pi* is the hole in the middle of the jade disk for Chinese: an area of nonbeing or the mystic's nothingness. Scholem, *Major Trends*, p. 49.
22. Halévi, p. 75.
23. Ibid., p. 20.
24. According to Buddhist and Tibetan tracts, namely *The Book of Untying Knots*, during one's earthly incarnation, the soul or psyche must be shielded, barriers must be maintained around the worshiper or mediator.

CHAPTER 5. KAFKA: *THE CASTLE*

1. Mimi Lobell, "Spatial Archetypes," pp. 17–20.
2. Franz Kafka, *The Castle*, p. xv.
3. *Columbia Dictionary of Modern European Literature*, p. 417.
4. Lobell, p. 33.
5. C. G. Jung, *Collected Works*, 12, p. 159.

6. Marie Louise von Franz and Emma Jung, *The Grail Legend*.
7. C. G. Jung, *Collected Works*, 9 (Part 1), p. 361.
8. G. G. Scholem, *Major Trends in Jewish Mysticism*, pp. 40–79.

CHAPTER 6. LORCA: *THE HOUSE OF BERNARDA ALBA*

1. Carl W. Cobb, *Federico García Lorca*, p. 117.
2. Esther Harding, *Psychic Energy*, pp. 189, 169.
3. Edwin Honig, *García Lorca*, pp. 152, 193.
4. Federico García Lorca, *Three Tragedies*, p. 197.
5. June Singer, *Androgyny*, pp. 32–34.
6. Marie Louise von Franz, *Psychological Meaning of Redemption Motifs in Fairy Tales*, p. 27.
7. J. J. Bachofen, *Myth, Religion and Mother Right*, p. 203.
8. Franz, p. 25.
9. Bachofen, p. 57.
10. Ibid., p. 101.
11. Franz, p. 55.

CHAPTER 7. BORGES: "THE LIBRARY OF BABEL"

1. J. M. Cohen, *Jorge Luis Borges*, p. 42.
2. Jorge Luis Borges, "The Library of Babel," p. IX.
3. In the New Testament, "And I saw in the right hand of him that sat on the throne a book written within and on the backside, sealed with seven seals" (Rev. 5:1). Books are archetypal in nature. They are symbols of all peoples eternally. For the Egyptians, *The Book of the Dead* held secret formulae and, as such, was placed in the tomb of the dead person, imploring the gods to favor him during his night-sea crossing: from darkness within the casket unto eternal sun and light in the sphere of the gods. In the New Testament, the book is also identified with sacred wisdom, as attested to in the above quote from Revelation. Identified with the Tree of Life, its leaves are like the characters of a book, representative of the created world, but also containing the sum total of divine secrets.
4. G. G. Scholem, *On the Kabbalah and Its Symbolism*, pp. 168–89.
5. Bettina L. Knapp, *Dream and Image*, p. 247.
6. Scholem, *On the Kabbalah and Its Symbolism*, p. 168.
7. Ibid., pp. 168–89.
8. G. G. Scholem, *The Messianic Idea in Judaism*, pp. 257–81.
9. Charles Poncé, *The Nature of the I Ching*, p. 17.
10. *Sefer Yetsirah*. See G. G. Scholem, *Major Trends in Jewish Mysticism*, pp. 77–80.
11. Fred Gettings, *The Book of Tarot*, p. 208.
12. Johan Huizinga, *Homo Ludens*, p. 136.
13. Hermes Trismegistus, *The Kybalion*, p. 28.
14. Quoted in Borges, *Labyrinths*, p. 228.
15. Ibid., p. ix.
16. Scholem, *Major Trends in Jewish Mysticism*, p. 52.
17. See devotion memorials of the forty hours of Christ's entombment. *New Catholic Dictionary* (New York: Universal Knowledge Foundation, 1929).
18. Murray Sperling and Maurice Simon, trans., *The Zohar*, I, p. 287.

19. Scholem, *Major Trends in Jewish Mysticism,* pp. 214–17, 269–73.
20. Scholem, *On the Kabbalah and Its Symbolism,* p. 49.
21. Ibid., pp. 42–43.
22. Ibid., p. 43.
23. Ronald Christ, "Borges at NYU," p. 402.
24. Ibid. p. 401.

CHAPTER 8. FUENTES: "IN A FLEMISH GARDEN"

1. Carlos Fuentes, "In a Flemish Garden," in *Burnt Water.*
2. Jacques Soustelle, *Daily Life of the Aztecs,* pp. 124–26, 128.
3. Gloria Duran, *The Archetypes of Carlos Fuentes,* pp. 201–205.
4. Soustelle, p. 177.
5. Laurette Séjourné, *Burning Water,* p. 148.
6. Soustelle, p. 101.
7. Ibid., p. 98.
8. Marie Louise von Franz, *Number and Time,* p. 68.
9. Soustelle, p. 155.
10. Ibid., pp. 96–102.
11. Séjourné, p. 59.
12. Soustelle, p. 101.
13. Ibid., p. 1.
14. Soustelle, p. 99.
15. Henri F. Ellenberger, *The Discovery of the Unconscious,* pp. 75–78.
16. C. G. Jung, *Collected Works,* 5, p. 281.
17. Ibid., pp. 480, 436.
18. Marie Louise von Franz, "Archetypes Surrounding Death," p. 45.
19. Ibid.
20. Duran, p. 203.

CHAPTER 9. WANG SHIH-FU: *THE ROMANCE OF THE WESTERN CHAMBER*

1. Frank J. MacHovec, trans., *The Book of Tao,* p. 21.
2. James R. Ware, trans., *The Sayings of Confucius,* p. 27.
3. Ibid., p. 76.
4. Toshihiko Izutsu, "Elimination of Colour in the Far East," pp. 190–91.
5. Ware, p. 22.
6. Mircea Eliade, *Histoire des croyances et des idées religieuses,* II, p. 23.
7. Wang Shih-fu, *The Romance of the Western Chamber,* p. 47.
8. Not until the Ch'ing dynasty (1616–1912) were female impersonators used to portray women. During the Yüan period, when *The Romance of the Western Chamber* was written, actresses performed, though they were treated like courtesans.
9. The five notes based on the twelve-note system were associated with the five elements: earth, water, fire, air, and wood; also with the functions in society: prince, minister, common people, etc. Geoffrey Hindley, ed., *The Larousse Encyclopedia of Music,* p. 26.
10. A. C. Scott, *The Classical Theatre of China,* p. 97.
11. MacHovec, p. 10.
12. Ware, p. 11.

13. Scott, p. 99.
14. Izutsu, p. 180.

CHAPTER 10. MISHIMA: *THE TEMPLE OF THE GOLDEN PAVILION*

1. Gwenn Boardman Petersen, *The Moon in the Water,* p. 203.
2. Nancy Wilson Ross, Introduction to *The Temple of the Golden Pavilion,* by Yukio Mishima, p. vii.
3. Mishima, *The Temple of the Golden Pavilion.*
4. William K. Bunce, *Religions in Japan,* p. 126.
5. *New Larousse Encyclopedia of Mythology,* p. 413.
6. The association between flowers and the male body was made by Jean Genet in most of his plays and novels. Flowers symbolize an androgynous being, which represented the homosexual for both Mishima and Genet.
7. Daisetz T. Suzuki, *Zen and Japanese Culture,* pp. 91, 89.
8. Edwin O. Reischauer, *Japan Past and Present,* pp. 60–61.
9. See Genet's *Quarrel of Brest* and *Funeral Rites* for a similar attitude on the part of homosexuals and criminals toward treachery. Bettina L. Knapp, *Jean Genet.*
10. Tea was propagated in Japan by a Zen teacher, Eisai (1141-1215). The ritual of the tea ceremony was introduced to Japan by a Zen monk, Dai-O (1236–1308); it was Ikkyu (1394–1481) who taught the technique and Shuko (1422–1502) who developed and adapted the ceremony to suit Japanese taste. Suzuki, pp. 272–73.
11. Kakuzo Okakura, *The Book of Tea,* p. 28.

CONCLUSION

1. William Barrett, *Irrational Man,* p. 234.

Bibliography

Ariosto, Ludovico. *Orlando Furioso*. Indianapolis: The Bobbs-Merrill Co., 1968.

Bachofen, J. J. *Myth, Religion and Mother Right*. Princeton, New Jersey: Princeton University Press, 1973.

Balzac, Honoré, de. *La Recherche de l'Absolu*. New York: Oxford University Press, 1914.

Barrenechea, Anna Maria. *Borges the Labyrinth Maker*. New York: New York University Press, 1965.

Barrett, William. *Irrational Man*. New York: Doubleday/Anchor, 1962.

Bithell, Jethro. *Life and Writings of Maurice Maeterlinck*. New York: Scribner's, 1913.

Borges, Jorge Luis. "The Library of Babel." In *Labyrinths*. New York: New Directions, 1964.

Bunce, William K. *Religion in Japan*. Tokyo: Charles E. Tuttle, 1970.

Christ, Ronald. "Borges at N.Y.U." In *Prose for Borges*, edited by Charles Newman and Mary Kinzie. Evanston: Northwestern University Press, 1972.

Cobb, W. *Federico García Lorca*. New York: Twayne Publishers, Inc., 1967.

Cohen, J. M. *Jorge Luis Borges*. New York: Barnes and Noble, 1973.

Columbia Dictionary of Modern European Literature. Edited by Jean-Albert Bédé and William Edgerton. Second Edition. New York: Columbia University Press, 1980.

The Complete Greek Drama. I. New York: Random House, 1938.

Duran, Gloria. *The Archetypes of Carlos Fuentes. From Witch to Androgyne*. Hamden, Conn.: Archon Books, 1980.

Edinger, Edward. "An Outline of Analytical Psychology." Unpublished, pp. 1–29.

Eliade, Mircea. *Histoire des croyances et des idées religieuses*. II. Paris: Payot, 1978.

Ellenberger, Henri F. *The Discovery of the Unconscious*. New York: Basic Books, 1970.

Focillon, Henri. *The Life Forms in Art*. New York: George Wittenborn, Inc., 1958.

Franz, Marie Louise von. "Archetypes Surrounding Death." *Quadrant* (Summer 1979): 5–23.

———. *Number and Time*. Evanston: Northwestern University Press, 1974.

———. *The Psychological Meaning of Redemption Motifs in Fairy Tales*. Toronto: Inner City Books, 1980.

Franz, Marie Louise von, and Emma Jung. *The Grail Legend*. New York: G. P. Putnam's Sons, 1970.

Fuentes, Carlos. "In a Flemish Garden." In *Burnt Water*. New York: Farrar, Strauss and Giroux, 1980.

Gettings, Fred. *The Book of Tarot*. London: Triune Books, 1973.

Giedion, S. *The Beginnings of Architecture. The Eternal Present*. New York: Pantheon Books, 1964.

Gray, Ronald. *Franz Kafka*. Cambridge: Cambridge University Press, 1973.

Grohmann, Will. *Paul Klee*. New York: Harry N. Abrams, 1959.

Halévi, Z'ev ben Shimon. *A Kabbalistic Universe*. New York: Samuel Weiser, Inc., 1977.

Harding, Esther. *Psychic Energy*. Princeton: Princeton University Press, 1973.
————. *Woman's Mysteries*. New York: G. P. Putnam's Sons, 1971.
Heilberg, Hans. *Ibsen, A Portrait of the Artist*. London: Allen and Unwin, 1969.
Hindley, Geoffrey, ed. *The Larousse Encyclopedia of Music*. New York: The Hamlyn Publishing Group Limited, 1974.
Holtan, Orley I. *Mythic Patterns in Ibsen's Last Plays*. Minneapolis: The University of Minnesota Press, 1970.
Honig, Edwin. *García Lorca*. New York: New Directions Paperbook, 1963.
Huizinga, Johan. *Homo Ludens*. Boston: The Beacon Press, 1955.
Ibsen, Henrik. *Eleven Plays of Henrik Ibsen*. New York: Modern Library, n.d.
Izutsu, Toshihiko. "Elimination of Colour in the Far East." In *Color Symbolism. Eranos Excerpts*. Zurich: Spring Publications, 1977.
Jacobi, Jolande. *Complex Archetype Symbol in the Psychology of C. J. Jung*. Princeton: Princeton University Press, 1959.
James, Henry. *The Short Stories of Henry James*. Selected and edited by Clifton Fadiman. New York: Random House, 1945.
Jung, C. G. *Collected Works*. Translated by R. F. C. Hull. Vols. 5, 9 (Part 1), 11. New York: Pantheon Books, 1956, 1959, 1963. Vol. 8. Princeton: Princeton University Press, 1969. Vol. 12. London: Routledge and Kegan Paul, 1953. Princeton University Press now publishes Jung's *Collected Works*.
————. *Memories, Dreams, Reflections. Recorded and Edited by Aniela Jaffé*. New York: Pantheon Books, 1963.
Kafka, Franz. *The Castle*. With an Homage by Thomas Mann. New York: Vintage Books, 1974.
Knapp, Bettina L. *Dream and Image*. Troy, N.Y.: The Whitston Press, 1977.
————. *Jean Genet*. New York: St. Martin's Press, 1968.
————. *Maurice Maeterlinck*. Boston: Twayne Publishers, 1975.
Lobell, Mimi. "Spatial Archetypes." *Quadrant* (Winter 1977): 5–43.
Lorca, Federico García. *Three Tragedies*. Translated by Richard L. O'Connell and James Graham-Luján. New York: New Directions, 1956.
MacHovec, Frank J., trans. *The Book of Tao*. Mount Vernon, N.Y.: The Peter Pauper Press, 1962.
Maeterlinck, Maurice. *Interior*. Translated by William Archer. In *Fifteen International One-Act Plays*, edited by John and Mollie Gassner. New York: Washington Square Press, 1969.
Miller, James E., Jr. *Theory of Fiction: Henry James*. Lincoln: University of Nebraska Press, 1972.
Mishima, Yukio. *The Temple of the Golden Pavilion*. Translated by Ivan Morris. New York: Perigee Books, 1980.
Neugroschel, Joachim. *Yenne Velt*. I. New York: The Stonehill Publishing Co., 1976.
New Larousse Encyclopedia of Mythology. Hong-Kong: Prometheus Press, 1959.
Okakura, Kakuzo. *The Book of Tea*. New York: Dover Publications, 1964.
Patai, Raphael. *The Messiah Texts*. New York: Avon, 1979.
Petersen, Gwenn Boardman. *The Moon in the Water*. Honolulu: The University Press of Hawaii, 1979.
Pevsner, Nikolaus. *The Sources of Modern Architecture and Design*. New York: Oxford University Press, 1979.
Poncé, Charles. *The Nature of the I Ching*. New York: Award Books, 1970.
Reischauer, Edwin O. *Japan Past and Present*. New York: Alfred A. Knopf, 1946.

Scholem, G. G. *Kabbalah.* New York: New American Library, 1978.
————. *Major Trends in Jewish Mysticism.* New York: Schocken Books, 1965.
————. *The Messianic Idea in Judaism.* New York: Schocken Books, 1971.
————. *On the Kabbalah and Its Symbolism.* New York: Schocken Books, 1973.
Schuré, Edouard. *The Great Initiates.* New York: St. George Books, 1961.
Scott, A. C. *The Classical Theatre of China.* Nanking, China, 1947–55.
Séjourné, Laurette. *Burning Water.* Berkeley: Shambhala, 1976.
Sheppard, Richard. *On Kafka's "Castle": A Study.* New York: Barnes and Noble, 1973.
Singer, June. *Androgyny.* New York: Anchor Press/Doubleday, 1976.
Soustelle, Jacques. *Daily Life of the Aztecs.* Stanford: Stanford University Press, 1962.
Sperling, Murray, and Maurice Simon, trans. *Zohar.* I. London: The Soncino Press, 1933.
Stabb, Martin S. *Jorge Luis Borges.* Boston: Twayne Publishers, 1970.
Suzuki, Daisetz T. *Zen and Japanese Culture.* Princeton: Princeton University Press, 1973.
Trismegistus, Hermes. *The Kybalion.* Chicago: The Yogi Publication Society, 1936.
Tyng, Ann G. "Geometric Extensions of Consciousness." *Zodiac* 19 (1966): 131–52.
Wang Shih-fu. *The Romance of the Western Chamber.* Translated by S. I. Hsiung. New York: Columbia University Press, 1971.
Ware, James. *The Sayings of Confucius.* New York: New American Library, 1955.
Werblowsky, R. J. Zwi, and Geoffrey Wigoder. *The Encyclopedia of the Jewish Religion.* New York: Holt, Rinehart and Winston, 1966.
Wheeler, Mortimer. *Roman Art and Architecture.* New York: Oxford University Press, 1979.

Index

DATE DUE

DEMCO 38-297